WHICH YET SURVIVE

WHICH YET SURVIVE

IMPRESSIONS OF FRIENDS, FAMILY AND ENCOUNTERS

JOHN MILLS

QUARTET

First published in 2017 by Quartet Books Limited
A member of the Namara Group
27 Goodge Street, London W1T 2LD
Copyright © John Mills 2017

A catalogue record for this book
is available from the British Library

ISBN 978 0 7043 7 4355

Typeset by Josh Bryson
Printed and bound in Great Britain by
T J International Ltd, Padstow, Cornwall

'We have all been young.'
A plea in mitigation by
John Aubrey (1626-1697)
Brief Lives

CONTENTS

1
EARLY YEARS

MADGE

I was born at home, 3 Bury Street, Guildford, on my mother's 32nd birthday, 7 September 1928. My parents Harry Mills and Hilda Annie Stuart had married four years before and already had a daughter, my sister June. My mother gave me my middle name, Stuart, since she feared that it would die out on our branch of her family, women relatives being far more abundant than men.

Mother had around forty first cousins. This was a consequence of the Victorian tendency towards large families and the perceived need to take second, or even third, spouses to help manage them if one passed away. As most of these cousins were female and arriving at marriageable age just after the Great War, which had much reduced the supply of eligible young bachelors, many of them failed to secure husbands. They got by in various ways: staying at home to look after ageing parents; going out to work in the now acceptable female roles such as nursing; or by becoming 'companions' to older spinsters or widows with money to spare. They might even make do on the tiny income which a small legacy provided, living in the homes of married friends or relatives who were content to take them in as 'paying (or indeed non-paying) guests'. So it was with Madge who, having already lived with us at Bury Street, moved into the spare room in our new house in 1934.

She and my mother, besides being cousins, were old friends. For they had lived near one another just outside Guildford during the First War and had shared happy days of youth in what the old photograph albums seem to imply was an eternal summer of boating on the river, picnicking, tennis and playing with the animals about the farm. And always in the company of what were ever after fondly referred to as 'the Canadian boys' – soldiers from the camp at Witley to whom

1

even Madge's stern, old Victorian father (as he undoubtedly was) could not refuse hospitality in such times. Nor were they alone in all this, for Madge's was a large family of girls: Mildred, Evelyn, Madge, Vera and Ruby. These were the survivors for they had, in the Victorian way, been struck by multiple tragedies, above all by the death of their only brother. 'Little Phil', aged about ten, had cut himself 'on a rusty fag-hook', as was always said, and had died of tetanus. Quite unnecessarily for anti-tetanus injections were well into use even then. Two other children, twins and little more than babies for they were still in their prams, had been left outside in winter by the nursemaid 'to get fresh air' and both succumbed to pneumonia. Auntie Lucy never really recovered from this, my mother would always assert, and she too came to a tragic end, though whether in any way as a direct consequence of these misfortunes no one could know. One hesitates to say how her death occurred for it could seem like the invention of farce rather than a real life tragedy. She fell from an upstairs window (she was said to have been cleaning it) head first into a rainwater butt and was drowned.

When I was about fourteen I was trying to compile a family tree and after I had got down all the above my mother continued:

'There was another sister too.'

'And what became of her?'

'Put her head in the gas oven.'

'Why?'

'Had enough of it all, I suppose.'

Great-Uncle (by marriage) William Thorne died in 1922, aged only 51, at which time Madge was still only 24 and the younger girls were only children. I suppose the farm was given up and I believe the family moved not far away to Littleton, though how they supported themselves I do not know. It wasn't until the next decade that only the two youngest, Vera and Ruby, found husbands and had children. Did Madge ever have romantic attachments? None was ever spoken of and by the time she came to us she must have been in her mid-thirties and had evidently settled into spinsterhood. She had always suffered badly from asthma and tended to wheeze. This was a real trial for her as in consequence she had to avoid animals, especially horses, of which she was particularly fond.

Once moved in with us she soon seemed, to me at least, to be very much a part of the family, yet she was strong-minded and retained considerable independence, often going off for visits to her sisters in their various homes in villages around Guildford. One time we went with her to see her sister Evelyn who was living with a rather grand farming family at Shere. There was a large party for Sunday lunch – I had never sat at so huge a table with so many people around it and in retrospect it has always seemed like a scene from *Dear Octopus* – and I was very worried that gravy might be poured on my roast meat. I could not abide gravy as it might cover up the fat, which I always meticulously removed, but that passed off all right and I listened enthralled to the conversation. An unforgettable item concerned one of the family's daughters who was a member of the League of Health and Beauty, a band of girls who used to give PT displays around the country, especially at seaside towns in summer. Apparently she had allowed herself to get a tan, which was not approved of that year, and 'she had to have it all peeled off'. The story was greeted with horror but nobody seemed to question its veracity.

I was quite often left alone with Madge when my mother was out and we got on rather well. She would tell me stories of her home life as a child about the farm and the severe reprisals from her father when rules were violated: the horsewhip was often in requisition, it appeared. These confabulations usually took place in her room and would be accompanied sometimes by a glass of sherry (this was to be kept secret) and selections from a wonderful tin of cocktail biscuits bought at Holden's, a high-class grocery on High Street. Although I was only about eight at the time I was already forming a taste for exotic foodstuffs including olives, which my father bought sometimes, and passion fruit which I myself bought, though rather rarely (they cost sixpence which would have bought three bars of chocolate), from a fruiterer in Friary Street. These were eaten with a spoon like a boiled egg. In 1936 Madge's youngest sister Ruby was married from our house and at the reception at The Abbot's Kitchen restaurant I enjoyed my first glass of champagne. I was denied a second glass but there were no restrictions on sampling the fare. It was a second trifle, with pieces of green crystallised angelica, which was my undoing.

Those middle years of the thirties seemed to me fairly harmonious domestically and my parents were less likely to embark on rows at mealtimes; perhaps the presence of Madge made them more intent on keeping up appearances. Outings and long walks were often a feature of Sundays or bank holidays and we would go out by bus to well known 'beauty spots' around Guildford: St Martha's, the Silent Pool, the Punchbowl at Hindhead, Frensham Ponds and so forth, and perhaps have tea at one of the country tea rooms that abounded in those years or, more likely, enjoy a picnic. Madge would come too sometimes, yet often she would prefer to remain at home by herself. I cannot recall that she ever really 'let her hair down'; she was always correctly dressed and never seen in the rather skimpy, semi-beach clothing which my mother tended to adopt in hot weather and of which Madge, I suspect, rather disapproved. It may be that her manner was rather 'superior'. Certainly her family considered itself to be quite 'county', going to 'meets', gymkhanas, point-to-points and so forth, and her now reduced circumstances may have led her to emphasise this. But she had a sense of humour and she probably shared moments of amusement with my father which may have passed over my mother's head. However, one such shared by all the family occurred one summer when we were at dinner at our boarding house at Sandown. The food was slow in arriving and, an explanation being sought of the waitress, there came the response: 'Cook says there's no force in the gas'. This was repeated with appreciation for long afterwards.

Apropos of 'meets', these used to take place on Boxing Day and gathered initially at Tuns Gate on Guildford High Street, often turning up on the Hog's Back below which we lived. My mother, who loved animals and had taught me to do so, did not go but my father and Madge did and went up to join them there. Once I went too, aged about six or seven. In my innocence I asked 'What happens when the hounds catch up with the hare?' 'Oh, they tear it to pieces,' my father unthinkingly answered. I burst into tears, was inconsolable and had to be taken home.

One morning in 1937 Madge came downstairs all dressed up and announced to my mother: 'I'm going up to town today, Hilda.'

The effect was electric and devastating.

'Well! You might have told me. Perhaps I could have come with you.'

It was immediately understood that Madge, anticipating this possibility, had deliberately kept her plan secret: she wanted to go on her own. My mother was deeply offended and a complete break ensued. Madge left our house never, so far as I can recall, to return again.

How much this affected me I don't now remember; probably rather little though obviously it made a great impression. I was just going on nine and about to start in the first form at grammar school so I had plenty of new experiences to occupy my thoughts and feelings. What had been Madge's room remained vacant for the next two years but then came the War and it was taken successively by evacuees, billeted officers and others. Where Madge lived during this time I never learnt exactly, or I took no notice. Nor did I ever see her but she was talked about from time to time and friendly relations with her sisters were maintained. Alluding to the break my mother would sometimes say 'It's all so silly', but whether this meant that Madge was blamed for maintaining the feud or that neither could bring herself to take the first steps to reconciliation I do not know.

One day in 1945 or 1946 I ran into Madge on the high street and she invited me to meet her later for a drink in the lounge of the old Lion Hotel: it was sherry again. By now I was a seemingly assured, probably rather too talkative, schoolboy of sixteen or seventeen but she seemed to like me, no doubt fascinated by the changes brought about by eight or nine years. For me those years were an unbridgeable gulf – before the War; half my life ago – and in the flood of adolescence my nine-year-old self and its experiences was a long disregarded thing of no interest. No doubt I went on rather about myself but I was still too bashful, too conscious of being of a younger generation, to ask Madge about her own life, how she lived and how she had spent the war years. It was a wasted opportunity but I was not to know that I would never see her again. Still suffering from the effects of her asthma she died early in the 1950s.

Remembering the happy days of their youth, my mother must often have regretted the long estrangement. But great events and new habits and attachments had dimmed the memories, except for when the photograph album was got out. Perhaps it was a certain guilt at her own role in this (It's all so silly) that led her at the end of her life to formulate a completely new explanation for Madge's leaving us. When she was 90, and her mind rather prone to fanciful excursions, she confided to me one day: 'It was your father, you know, he wouldn't leave Madge alone. She had to get away.'

LENA

Old friends of one's parents, especially those who were still single, had a way of becoming, or at least being seen by the children as, a part of the family and as such might be accorded the courtesy title of Aunt or Uncle: Lena was one such. Auntie Lena was around from my very earliest years, since she had been among both my mother's and my father's circle of Guildford friends from well before their marriage in 1924. In fact she had gone with Mother on a holiday to Bognor in 1921 as well as down to East Dean to stay with the family. They are there together in photographs dressed in those strangely becoming clothes of that short interim period between the severities of the War and the extravagancies of the roaring twenties. After 1924 she was happily incorporated into the family group and often came to our house for tea or accompanied us on picnics. She also sometimes came with us on summer holidays; in my very early days the family was still faithful to Bognor (where the honeymoon had been) and then in the mid-thirties to Sandown.

Lena was good with children, or at any rate with me. What was so attractive about her was that she never set herself apart from us as an adult. Un-aloof and un-patronising she included one in the conversation equally with anyone else present, often looking to get one's reaction to her humorous, sometimes rather 'wicked' remarks.

Indeed she made one feel as if there was a rather special understanding between us, something to which parents and other grown-ups present were not privy. Perhaps it was that in her unmarried state – perhaps unmarriageable state, for she was now in her late thirties or even around forty – she found comfort in the absence of any trace of the possible censoriousness or condescension that she may have suspected in her contemporaries. Of course, we knew and cared nothing as to why she was still single, this was after all the condition of so many of my mother's relatives, but Lena was anything but dowdy. Always carefully and attractively turned out, in the flowered frocks and diaphanous accessories of the period and often with hat and gloves, she would arrive with happy smile and waves of scent. Concerning the latter I remember once asking her whether one called Californian Poppy, which I had seen in Woolworths, would be an acceptable present for someone. She thought perhaps not; it might be rather 'common'. This was for me an early introduction to this concept, later to be enlarged. It was attached, for example, to people who came down to the sea only for the day, rather than staying for a fortnight as we did, and who were described as 'trippers'. They were spoken of with much contempt, and much consideration was given as to how to avoid them.

During the War and for a while after Lena worked in a rather high-class stationers in the high street called Stent Clarke's. When I, still a schoolboy, went in there she would waft towards me with a welcoming smile and attend to my simple requirements as if I were an important customer. We saw rather less of her at home during these years: everyone seemed to be too busy with their enforced or voluntary activities for tea parties, and holidays, of course, were out of the question. The years of austerity afterwards also saw a changed pattern in relationships, and I was away doing National Service and then my degree course in London. But sometime in the late fifties my mother gave me the extraordinary news: Lena had a gentleman friend and was engaged to be married! 'She's just like a little girl,' Mother said, 'full of all the plans for the wedding, the honeymoon and their life afterwards.' How she had met her prospective groom never emerged, at least to me, but he turned out to be a man of fairly advanced years who held one of those strange positions in the House of Commons, Black Rod or a carrier of the mace or perhaps more likely simply an usher.

The wedding took place and they settled down to a happy and respectable married life. Only a year or two later he died and Lena was bereft. She lost interest in life, became depressed and neglected her appearance and, no doubt, her nutrition. She moved into a small flat not far from my parents' house and became increasingly reclusive. My mother would call and try to entice her out to some activity but rarely with any success. She would stand at the half-opened door, perhaps in her dressing gown: 'I'm afraid I can't ask you in, Hilda.' 'Can't ask me in because she is in her dressing gown, when I have known her for forty years!' Lena faded away and soon went to her grave.

Long after this, in the 1980s, during one of the long, reminiscent conversations I would have with my father, then in his nineties, the subject of Lena came up. 'Oh yes. She came to the dances that I used to organise at Brett's Restaurant in the high street just after the First War. She was a good dancer.' He leaned forward slightly and looked meaningfully at me. 'Yes, she was a popular girl, *and not ungenerous with her favours.*' This was the only time he ever referred, even obliquely, to sexual adventures in his bachelor days.

THE GREAT-UNCLES

Uncle Jim and Uncle Will were always spoken of as the successful, 'well-off' members of my maternal grandmother's side of the family (surname Bridger). They were her brother and half-brother respectively. They were of course my great-uncles and I never knew them but they featured largely in family mythology. Uncle Jim can, however, be dealt with fairly briefly. In speaking of him my mother would always say: 'He patented the inverted incandescent gas mantle. He didn't *invent* it, he *patented* it.' This sounded like sharp practice to me. Why didn't whoever invented it patent it? And how come he could patent it if he didn't invent it? I could get no answers to these questions and a rather desultory search on the Internet for the history of this invention has not yielded me any. At all events this was apparently the fount of his fairly comfortable wealth. His extended family looked forward to one day inheriting a share of his estate but they were doomed to disappointment. He married an actress named Jean (no more was known of her than this single appellation), died not long afterwards and left her all his money. She was heard of no more. Grandmother's half-brother Uncle Will turned out much better.

He became agent to J. Pierpont Morgan Jr. at Wall Hall, Aldenham and looking through Mother's old photograph albums again there he is: holding his baby daughter Grace and looking plump and prosperous enough, it must be said, and rather old to be the father of such a young daughter. How did he become agent to Morgan? It was said in the family that he was working as a lift boy in a large London hotel when he was spotted by Morgan who 'took a fancy to him' (that was how it was expressed) and took him into his employ. Nowadays this would be given some sort of sexual implication but I like to think of it as more like Scott Fitzgerald's account of Gatsby's early life when he is taken up by the rich yacht owner Dan Cody, employed in various capacities and helped on his way in life. There are no pictures of his wife Winnie but she may not have been all that happy since when Mother went up to visit, and Uncle was not about, Mother would sometimes be sent out to buy a bottle of gin.

This much I had learnt from my mother when I was about thirteen or fourteen and diligently questioning her while constructing the family trees. These were drawn out roughly on full-size sheets of paper – obtained from Father's printing establishment – which often had to be pinned together sideways to accommodate the accumulating aunts and uncles and cousins. By good luck I still have them, otherwise I would have been incapable of recalling the names and relationships. But of course I wanted to check up on these and so I started on an Internet search for any mention of Uncle Will, hardly expecting success. To my amazement I found a page devoted to him and his family. One could get carried away by all the ramifications but I will restrain myself, apart from clarifying the matter of his mother (my great-grandmother). Her maiden name was Elizabeth Thair Gill (*ca.*

1830-1893) and her brief second marriage, intermediate between those to Bridger and Biles, to one James Gosden, had never been mentioned by my mother and I am unsure that she even knew about it. It seems to have been childless and he died only two years later aged 24. But what on earth was she up to, a widow of 39 with four children, marrying a young man of 22? Then again, she was 42 when she married Joseph Biles (age 28) in 1872 and proceeded to have five children by him in six years. He then died aged 40 (worn out?). What a femme fatale! I did not know it was even possible for a woman to have five children in her forties but they were real and healthy enough (apart from one who died at only a few months) for in the photograph album there are Aunt Bel and Aunt Flo at Mother's wedding in 1924. Moreover they lived into their eighties and even nineties. I met some of them when I was a child but paid them little attention.

But back to Uncle Will. When he started work with Pierpont Morgan is unclear but by 1901, aged 27, he was his butler at 2 South Street, London. In the middle of the First World War, in March 1916, he sailed to New York with his employer and wife on the SS *Philadelphia*, returning a month later on the *Nieuw Amsterdam* and by this time he was house steward at 12 Grosvenor Square. He married on 25 November 1919 and by March 1921 was house steward at Wall Hall, remaining in Wall Hall Lodge until his death (of cancer of the jaw) at only 56 in 1929. Winnie, his wife, survived until 1955 in nearby St Albans but by this time she and my mother had long since lost touch.

Unlike Uncle Jim, Uncle Will did not disappoint in the matter of legacy, for he left my grandmother £500. This was enough for her to buy a small house near the station in Guildford and so live closer, during her brief widowhood, to my parents. And to me too, for I re-member her in that house and also on her frequent visits to us half a mile away in Bury Street. I was less than five and I never formed any great attachment to her but I was memorably struck by one incident. She was knitting a tea cosy – inevitably in the shape of a crinoline – and this had to be surmounted by a female form. A small celluloid doll had been bought and taking sharp pointed scissors Granny, to my horror, pierced it in the stomach and cut it round the middle, throwing away the severed lower torso and limbs. It was more shocking than anything I had ever encountered in my comics.

So what do I know of Uncle Tony, Granny's other true brother? It would seem that he and the other three children of the first marriage – my grandmother Ann, her sister Eliza, and James – did not have a very comfortable life once their father was dead and their mother remarried. Perhaps they seemed a burden to their stepfather Biles, for by the time of the 1881 census all four were living away from the family. Eliza and Ann were both in service in fairly menial capacities; Tony was working as a gardener in a London suburb (his wife and two young children were back living with her father); while James, who was only 15, had been decanted off to board with his mother's aunt, widowed Mary Capron who kept the Swan Inn in the market square in Midhurst. He was working as an ironmonger's assistant there; perhaps that was when he first got ideas about inverted incandescent gas mantles. From gardening Uncle Tony went on to have a curiously varied career but he only impinges on my story by virtue of his having begotten, like his parents, another large brood of children; a contribution of a further ten – eight girls and two boys – to Mother's tally of cousins. I got to know only one of them: Elizabeth, known to us as 'Auntie' Betsy or Bessie.

Bessie used to appear at our house from time to time, usually for Sunday lunch, during the late thirties. She had been born in 1883 and so was fully thirteen years older than my mother and even three years older than my father. She had been married to one Joseph Powell but whether she was widowed or divorced I do not know. Although I was still only nine or ten at this time I had long been an avid reader of anything I could lay my hands on, and this included newspapers. Consequently I had some inkling of world events (Italy and Abyssinia; China and Japan) and had of course read of Hitler and his doings in Europe. A remark which my mother made to a visitor caught my attention and lodged in my brain forever. 'My cousin Bessie agrees with what Hitler is doing to the Jews.' I must have known or realised that this was not the accepted view and I asked Bessie about it. She had lived in Berlin with her husband (said to have been in the film business); as had her sister Grace, who married a German (Kurt Hubert), also in films. Her answer now suggests to me that she had been largely influenced by the Nazi propaganda of the time. Or were her sister and brother-in-law Nazi adherents? So far as I can recall she went on about how the Jews were everywhere, in the theatre and restaurants, 'the women dripping with jewels'. This sounds much like images in the notorious anti-Semitic film *The Eternal Jew*, though this was not made until 1940.

Once the War started this sort of talk ceased, of course. She continued to visit us off and on for the duration, my mother sometimes asking whether there was any news of Grace and Kurt who had remained in Berlin but of course there was none. On the whole Bessie talked rather little. She could speak German and as I was trying to teach myself that language she would help me out with elementary sentences: '*Nun essen wir Mitagessen*'. Once Berlin had fallen to the Russians and the War was over Mother asked again for any news of Grace and Kurt. 'Both killed!' I got to know no more than that; nothing as to whether it was in the bombing or during the final assault by the Russians. I went off for National Service and afterwards university and so saw no more of Bessie and never heard, or have forgotten, when and where she died. The details she had given me of her siblings included all the names of their spouses but no indications of children. But surely there will have been some, so out there must be numerous second cousins and second cousins once removed who are unknown to me and to whom I am unknown. It is strange that I should think about them. Let it be.

2
ME AND MY PARENTS

HILDA

I have so far written all this about Mother's relatives but little about my mother herself. As one grows old one becomes more understanding of the characteristics of aged parents which had been irritating at the time. I often think now that I did not do my mother justice in her later years, though I did try to make up for this in her last. I see now that she had had a varied and selfless life, encompassing two world wars in which ideals of voluntary service were much to the fore and which she embraced, never to lose. The trouble was that she was not able to understand and sympathise with my own scientific interests as they developed during my boyhood and consequently our closeness during my infancy progressively gave way to a closer relationship with my father, who was invariably sympathetic and encouraging. Later, following my good school results, National Service and university, she was resigned to the course my life had taken even if she never fully understood what it was all about.

Hilda was born in September 1896, nine months (less one week) after her parents, William Stuart and Ann Bridger's marriage, by license, at All Saints Church, Fulham in December 1895. They were both 33. This makes me wonder whether there was perhaps some urgency in the marriage and indeed also how they had come to know each other, for Ann was living in Fulham (still in service?) while my grandfather William Stuart's address was still that of his father Henry, namely Artington Farm near Guildford (later the home of Madge and her family).

I have not been able to get back further than my great-grandfather, Henry Stuart. He looked like a formidable Victorian father figure judging from the large pencil drawing of him we used to have, by his son-in-law Harry Sage, the well-known Guildford watercolourist. The family presumably had Scottish predecessors but this must have been some way back for Henry Stuart actually came from Bassingham in Lincolnshire before moving to Ash in Surrey. My mother had only vague intimations of this and the only Scottish characteristic she herself retained was to have salt on her porridge rather than sugar.

The wedding was witnessed by Ann's siblings James and Eliza but no one from grandfather's family was present. At the time of my mother's birth they were living in Guildford but how grandfather employed his time there I am unsure. Like others I have described above he was to have a varied career but his early life on the farm obviously led him in an agricultural direction. After a few years in Guildford, the family (now with a young son, Mother's brother Billy) moved to Westcott, near Dorking, where William had secured a position as farm bailiff (whatever that entails). My mother remembered her life there, even though she was still only a child when they left, and one particular incident naturally made a great impression on her and was often recalled. There was a large pond, even a lake, on or near the premises with a path round it where she often walked with her little brother. One day, after rain, he slipped on the edge and slid down the two or three feet into the water! Somehow – she never could quite understand exactly how – she got him out. Some sixty years later she asked me to drive her out to revisit the lake where she thought she recognised the exact spot.

When Great-Grandfather Henry Stuart died at Artington the farm was not taken on by his son but by his son-in-law. Why was this? Had his marriage been disapproved of? Was he perhaps thought inadequate for the job? Mother never broached this subject but told me that life at Westcott was bad for his health. It was damp there and the doctor advised that the family should move away. How William secured the position of landlord at the Star and Garter Inn at East Dean in Sussex I can't imagine but he did and around 1906 the family moved there and stayed until shortly before Grandfather died in 1930. My mother looked back on her life at East Dean as idyllic, and she always wanted to remain in touch with it. The inn was the centre of village social life – at least for the men – and the position of landlord was an honourable and influential one making up a sort of triumvirate with the vicar and the schoolteacher. Of course all owed suzerainty to the Duke of Richmond, the local landowner, and such men in the village as were not farm labourers worked in his woods. Hilda went to the village school and once she had finished the top form she stayed on to help with teaching the infants. She learnt to play the piano and also the little portable organ for church services. This was carried up to the church from the vicar's house every Sunday as it could not be left there permanently on account of the damp. She always retained a tremendous respect for her father whom I, unfortunately, just missed knowing as I was not quite two when he died. 'Whatever would Father have said?' she would remark about some modern development. She followed him in planting the garden of our new house in 1934, putting in his favourite fruit trees: Czar and Victoria plums; a Blenheim Orange apple tree; Kentish Cob nut trees. These all yielded prolifically and were greatly appreciated by me as a boy. I was still having, in my fifties, to climb the Blenheim to pick the best apples which were always at the top. They would last until Christmas.

But her main joys were nature, animals and the countryside. By the time she was about eighteen she was already an enthusiast for taking 'snaps' and in the now sepia-coloured prints are to be seen the beloved dogs (cocker spaniels), happy teatimes out in the garden and visits from the 'rich uncles', in suits, stiff collars and spats, down from town for the races at Goodwood which, of course, was only walking distance away. Apparently on these occasions the villagers would let out their rooms and sleep in the barns. Somewhat earlier, when King Edward VII came down for the races and stayed at West Dean House, there would be scandalised but delicious gossip of his carryings-on with mistresses there.

I myself have memories of East Dean as it used to be before the War since even after my grandparents moved away in about 1929, and indeed died not very much later, Mother continued to visit old friends there and sometimes took me with her. We would stay with the Wests who lived in the end cottage of a row facing away from the Star and Garter. Mr West was a woodsman and had many injuries to his hands to show for it including half a thumb. Mrs West kept house and a fine, old Victorian interior which was unchanged, I should think, since first they were married. The village had no mains services of water or electricity which only came during and just after the War. Safe provision of water and light was governed by careful ritual. The well cover was removed, the galvanised iron bucket carefully clamped to the rope and wound down and back up full to be carried to the larder. There a glass of the excellent fresh water would be appreciatively drunk. When the shades of night were falling the big decorative oil lamp had to be lit and then placed centrally on the velour-covered table. More cottagey Victoriana decorated the mantelpiece: its edge was embellished with a Berlin woolwork tapestry pelmet while above was a clock flanked by Staffordshire dogs and, much envied by my mother, two fine glass lustres.

While we were there, usually in late spring, walks up into the woods were our main amusement, sometimes to look out for Mr West at his work. Charcoal burning was still practised at the time, the big turf-covered mounds giving off smoke from the slow combustion. We would look for morels though only rarely find them. However these delicious fungi were well known and appreciated by the villagers who put them into stews.

With the outbreak of World War II visits became problematic as a coastal exclusion zone was created with East Dean just inside it. Residents could leave and re-enter it freely but others could not. Undeterred, my mother consulted timetables and maps and resolved to get there by walking over the downs from a village to the north. It must have been in the summer of 1940 and I was to go with her. It was too far to be completed in one day and in fact we slept out under the sky somewhere on top of the downs, walking down to the village, and a much appreciated breakfast, early the following morning.

Returning to Hilda's early days, with the outbreak of the 1914-18 war there came changes in her life. One of her maternal aunts, Isabella (always known as Aunt Bel), kept the village shop and post office at St Catherine's, just on the edge of Guildford. By strange coincidence[1] this was only a few hundred yards from Grandfather's former family home of Artington Farm, now occupied by Madge and the rest of the Thorne family. With her husband gone off to war, and with two small children, Aunt Bel needed help to run the business; Mother was recruited for this and remained there for the duration. Her duties were manifold: serving in the shop; running the post office, including operating the little telephone exchange and receiving and dispatching telegrams; and driving the pony and cart to deliver bread, baked on the premises, around the extended neighbourhood. The pony knew the rounds, of course, and would sometimes impatiently go on ahead leaving her running after. But she enjoyed all this and anyway had the enormous compensation of almost continuous companionship with her cousins at the farm. Apart from the (agreeable) contiguity of the Canadian soldiers from Witley, and setting aside the growing food shortages, the War made relatively little impact on life in St Catherine's. There were however a few memorable incidents that she would recount.

The first of these was the zeppelin raid on 13 October 1915. Mother never mentioned any specific romantic attachment from these St Catherine's years but after all she was at the end of her teens and might have been expected to form some. She told me that on this evening she was with a young soldier friend walking along the river path which leads to Guildford when the zeppelin came over. They were under the tall beeches which overhang the path when a bomb fell, just on the bend before the river curves round to where the ferry was. I am sure she told me that the boy was injured though this does not accord with other accounts which say that nobody was. The bomb knocked down a flint wall, the boundary between the path and somebody's garden. This was afterwards closed off with chestnut palings, which were often pointed out to me as the bomb site, and remained in place at least until the 1960s or '70s!

---

[1]   Or perhaps not. Maybe this adjacency was how Grandfather and Grandmother (Aunt Bel's half-sister) had come to know each other.

More amusing was the establishment of a mini-brothel close to the shop, in a little house on the adjacent corner. Two entrepreneurial girls ('My, what a pair of beauties they were,' Mother would say), recognising in the local soldiery a niche market, took up residence there and word of mouth soon brought success. Of course such goings on could not remain a secret in a small village and the local policeman asked to be allowed access to Mother's bedroom window from where he could note down details of the frequent comings and goings. So it soon all ended in tears, and presumably worse.

Another incident, which was to have a lasting influence on her life, was when a local grande dame (was it Mrs More-Molyneux from Loseley or the lady from Braboeuf Manor? I forget) came into the shop and said to her 'I want you and Miss Thorne to come to the house to discuss an important matter'. This visit was for no less than to get their support for the formation of a branch of the recently founded Women's Institute. The branch was duly formed and Mother remained an active member throughout her life, more than once as chairman (no murmur of resentment was ever heard against that designation). Of course as children my sister and I had usually to go with her to attend the meetings during the 1930s. After our removal to our new house in Wodeland Avenue in 1934 it was a pleasant walk up over the hill, along the cemetery path by Booker's Tower and down to The Hut, a large ex-army barrack which had been bought and donated to the Institute in 1919. The meetings, of course, were rather boring for me and I became very familiar with the accounts of funds raised by jumble sales, whist drives and sales of work; plans for forthcoming fetes and the assignment of miscellaneous duties to names which also became familiar: Miss Butcher, Miss Maughling, Deaconess Hughes etc.; nearly all spinsters. The teas which followed the meetings were enjoyable though: the ultra-thin bread and butter rolled into little cylinders; the bridge rolls filled with paste and cress; the Battenburg cake. The summer fetes too, with their simple stalls and sideshows, were also an outing to look forward to.

A single incident somehow impressed itself upon me towards the end of one. I approached a very plain, sad-looking middle-aged lady who was standing by a large bowl of lemonade which she had made and was selling at 6d a glass. 'I've only sold two or three glasses', she confided to me, 'and it will all be left over.' I didn't have a 6d and went off and fetched my mother in the hope she would provide one. 'Oh that's much too dear. No wonder you haven't sold much,' said she to the vendor, 'put it down to 3d', and she started calling it out at that price. This struck me as rather unfeeling and imperious and I was sorry for the sad lady who had sought sympathy from me, a mere child. Of course I didn't know those words but that is what I *felt*.

Amateur theatricals also played a small role occasionally. When only about five or six I was roped in to take part in a nativity play with a line to speak. I found it terribly embarrassing. Miss Maughling (pronounced Moffling) was in charge and did not seem to think much of my performance. However, I much enjoyed hers for after the nativity play she gave a dramatic monologue. Transformed by heavy make-up and wearing a sort of bandana like a gypsy she looked through a window opening to the audience and delivered, with great verve, a story of a betting success at the racetrack. I was fascinated by this revelation of an unsuspected side to the hitherto sober and rather drab lady. Was this the start of a love for the theatre? Probably Mother's own love of theatre was more influential. There was theatre in Guildford, before the building of the current Yvonne Arnaud theatre, and it took place in a hall in North Street. I do not remember going there, except perhaps to an unmemorable pantomime, but certainly Mother took me to my first London theatre performance. This was Terence Rattigan's *While the Sun Shines* in about 1943. Today stage lighting comes from all directions but then it was still from footlights and I was astonished by the heavily made-up actors illuminated in this unnatural way. But I was hooked and it was only two or three years later, in 1945 and 1946, that I would go up to town by myself and get into now famous productions by the Old Vic company then playing at the New Theatre in St. Martin's Lane. With Laurence Olivier there was *King Lear*; *Oedipus* partnered with Sheridan's *The Critic*; *The School for Scandal* and many others in later years.

THE WAR

On 2 September 1939 we walked up the road from the station, returning from what would prove to have been our last family holiday; taken, for once, in Swanage rather than Sandown. It was already dark, for Mother would never relinquish the holiday until the last possible moment and moreover a blackout had already been imposed in anticipation of what might follow next day. In the house suitable curtaining had to be improvised but, exhausted by our morning on the beach and the tedious journey home, my sister and I soon went off to bed. The following morning we all listened to Mr Chamberlain's now famous broadcast after which I went out to impart the news that war had been declared to any small boys I might encounter. I did find some but my news was greeted with incredulity. 'Where's all the fighting then, and the soldiers?' In a few days I was back at school where of course the new situation was the dominating factor, with solemn talks from masters and, outside, the construction of new air-raid shelters (some dug in 1938 had been filled in after Munich). But soon school life continued as formerly and it was only in 1940 that we had often to respond to the sirens and troop out to the cold, dank shelters.

At home evacuees arrived. The first two, siblings Gordon and Sylvia, picked all the unripe apples, took a bite and threw them aside but fortunately did not stay long. Their mother, heartened by the period of the 'phony war', took them back to London. Another, seemingly better behaved boy, Ronny, stayed longer but he appropriated items from my train set and sold them off to other boys at school. But one who was to become all but a member of the family arrived in October 1939. My mother came home pushing a pram containing a ten-month-old baby girl who had somehow arrived in Guildford, unaccompanied by parents, with other evacuees! Of course her stay with us was not expected to be a long-term arrangement but it turned out to be. Her family status, as finally revealed (to me only later) was not simple. Her mother's husband, who was not actually her father, took nominal responsibility for her and visited us from time to time. Her mother came only once and I can just remember a black-eyed, black-haired, probably Irish girl in a tight-fitting black dress in conference with my mother.

For a while she kept in touch, with wishful plans for her daughter, but after a year or so wrote, without an address, saying that she had met someone whom she wanted to marry and was renouncing all further claim to her daughter. So Susan stayed with us throughout the War, a little sister to me of whom I was very fond. The family albums are full of photographs: Susan in her pram; Susan among the chickens; Susan with the Canadian boys (yes, another generation of them); Susan off to school (my old elementary school).

In 1945, with the end of the war in Europe, Susan's nominal father, who had been an occasional visitor all this time, announced that he was about to marry and would take Susan back to live with his new family. This was distressing to us all and although I suppose the legal situation was quite unclear I don't think that clarification of it was ever considered or sought. So one day Susan was taken away to go and live up north. There were tears on our side yet seemingly stolid resignation on six-year-old Susan's part. Even though so young I think she must always have been vaguely conscious of her slightly anomalous position.

My mother, of course, remained concerned and for the next forty years kept in touch by letter. At first it did not turn out well. The new wife did not care for Susan who was put into an orphanage where she remained until grown up. But she married and had two children who themselves turned out well. Mother would sometimes make the journey north and once the adult Susan came down to visit and I saw her for the first time in twenty years or more. But after so long no sort of rapport was possible and we met as strangers.

When Ronny finally departed it was time for billeted officers. One, Captain Payne, was good fun and good company both for me and for my father. He had a particular love for Gilbert and Sullivan and gave me a copy of the lyrics of the former – *Songs of a Savoyard* – which I still have. I puzzled over the title of one which was in Latin, *Eheu fugaces...*, so I asked our elderly English master at school, Mr Simpson, what it meant. '*Eheu fugaces anni labuntur*; alas, the fleeting years,' said he, smiling to himself. 'You don't have to worry about that yet, Mills.'

Throughout the war years my interest in chemistry developed apace. It had started when I was just 11 and had asked for, and been given for my birthday, a simple chemistry set. Soon I was pestering the father of one of my school colleagues, Mr Edward Jones, who had a well-established chemist's shop in the high street, for more exotic (and dangerous) chemicals. He asked my father about it but apparently got the go-ahead. Apparatus and other chemicals I ordered from a strange, small firm in Stoke Newington (which seemed to use this business as a cover for selling chloral hydrate. Was this a controlled substance then?) and later from Baird and Tatlock, major scientific equipment suppliers. As with any other small boy, a prime objective was to produce explosions and in this I succeeded in many ways, at some risk to myself. I need not go into detail here but I cannot resist mentioning that I found the way to make nitrogen triiodide in, of all places, one of my sister's Bessie Bunter fourpenny monthlies! I made a lot of it over the years and did the classic thing of scattering it (before it was quite dry) in the fourth form schoolroom. The mini explosions during Mr Thomas's geography lesson were most gratifying yet I came through unsuspected.

That had been when I was around twelve or so but more serious preparations followed and were a real trial to my mother as they had to be carried out in her kitchen where the only gas supply for my Bunsen burner was located. They were mostly standard organic chemistry preparations from a textbook. I particularly remember making amyl nitrite and the dramatic effect it had on my complexion and mood. Of course this was long before one had heard anything about its medical and recreational uses.

But my course was still not then absolutely set on a career in chemistry. I was fascinated by horticulture and natural products and I had a large collection of *materia medica*. One summer, I think it must have been 1943 or '4, I spent a month working for nothing at the Royal Horticultural Society's gardens at Wisley. I cycled over there each morning and back in the evening. Hard to imagine now, thinking of the present A3.

PARENTS' MARRIAGE

I have often wondered what induced my parents to marry each other. Throughout my childhood and later they seemed to be frequently at loggerheads and I have no recollection of their ever showing any signs of mutual affection; certainly I never saw them kiss. Despite this they made a practical go of it once committed and I don't imagine that divorce or separation ever so much as entered their heads. They were 37 and 27 when they married in June 1924 and it may be that both had reached the conclusion that it was about time for decision. It's impossible to enter into the long ago feelings and hopes which then motivated them but some degree of kindness and consideration, each for the other, did survive and sometimes showed indirectly in their comments to me and, no doubt, also to my sister. Essentially they were both kind people.

I have also wondered how much my parents' seemingly rather loveless relationship affected my own emotional development. It certainly impressed itself upon me in sometimes memorable ways which have never left me. In 1933 we were still living in the rented house in Bury Street while the house in Wodeland Avenue, designed by local architect Wingrave Clark to my mother's requirements, was being built. This was a considerable financial undertaking and burden for my father; as he much later told me, it was far more than he had felt he could afford (I would guess now that he was making between two and three hundred pounds a year. The house was £1,000 and the land £200). Early one morning I came downstairs to breakfast to find my mother, still in her nightdress and with her hair down, sitting in the kitchen and crying bitterly after a row with my father who had left for work. Still only just five I tried to comfort her: 'What's the matter? Don't cry mummy.' 'Oh, I've been such a fool. It's my fault. I shouldn't have talked about it.'

It was only much later that I was to understand what it was all about. It turned out that the lease we held was a repairing lease and probably my father had hoped to get away without this being enforced. Probably he never could have done so but nevertheless he blamed his wife for the ensuing expense. The house was filled with builders and decorators for the next few weeks. After his death I found the schedule and account still in my father's desk.

At around the same time there was another row, probably from the same cause. We were in the garden, Father had rushed upstairs and, seizing a small vase from Mother's dressing table, hurled it from the window. In its broken state it was returned to the dressing table (A reminder? A reproach?) remaining there throughout her life.

In addition to the transient romances (if such there were) of the war years, Mother had also had a previous engagement to a man named Harry Scott. She quite often spoke to me about this affair with thoughts, no doubt, of what might have been. She met him when he was posted to Guildford during the First World War but their contact must have been brief and largely conducted through letters. He came from Gainsborough, Lincolnshire and in 1919 she went up there to meet his mother. Scott was employed by Sir Hickman Bacon, the local grandee, who evidently wanted to assess her suitability. He picked her up at the station and they drove through the town in his open car, to the astonishment of the townspeople who all stared as 'he was said to be a "Woman Hater"' and had never been seen with one of the sex in his car. But apparently she passed muster, got on well with Mrs Scott, and the engagement was confirmed. But not consummated by marriage. Mother never told me why but revealed to my sister that it turned out that he had had a fling with a local girl resulting in a pregnancy and he had to marry her.

So mother was jilted, yet strangely remained friends with Scott's mother and kept up a correspondence with her up until my day. In the photograph album Harry Scott looks a horrid, dapper little man and I am so glad he was not my father. But would he have been? The mystery of whether 'I' would have existed baffles the mind.

So, some four years later my mother married another Harry. There are the pictures in the album: the visit down to East Dean to meet the prospective parents-in-law; the wedding at the little East Dean church; the honeymoon at Bognor. Still surviving is the browned and tattered cutting from a local paper minutely describing the 'pretty wedding' with every detail of the dresses and presents. With the end of the War and the return of Aunt Bel's husband my mother had no longer been needed at St Catherine's and she had taken a live-in job at Forest Stores in the village of Rusper. There she worked with another girl under the supervision of the manager, a Mr de Bow, who was in want of a wife. He chose the other girl (another lucky escape for me for he turned out a harsh father) and that family too became Mother's life-long friends. After the wedding and honeymoon her things were still there and were left to be taken by carrier to Guildford. It was an awkward, cross-country journey to make by train or bus and she told me that she cycled as far as Gomshall where she was met and taken on to the house in Bury Street that my father had rented for them.

My sister was born there in 1926 and I followed in 1928. We were there until February 1934 so I still remember the house and garden quite well and particular incidents too. Some concerned my two albino guinea pigs which were always hiding in their clump of bamboo and could hardly be got out. Their hutch was outside supported on two columns of loose bricks. I once got underneath and managed to displace one of the piles leaving me like a mini-Atlas bearing the hutch on my shoulders until my cries brought relief. Alas, one cold winter night killed the guinea pigs. Efforts to revive their stiff little corpses by warming them were to no avail.

HARRY

My father was born in 1886, the eldest child of James Mills and Maria Rose. James was a local man, the Millses having in fact been millers at the water mills of both Guildford and, I believe, Shalford. Maria came from Woodbridge in Suffolk. As with my other grandparents, how they came to meet remains a mystery.

Nor do I know how my grandfather got into printing but he did and founded the business in Castle Street, just opposite the entrance to the castle grounds, where the facade of the 'shop' survives. No doubt life was tough but did he really need to take my father from school, aged 12 (the same age at which Dickens was put into the blacking factory), to work there? Certainly Father did not think so and always resented being thus deprived of his education and his childhood. He didn't like his father who seems never to have shown him much love. He remembered one Christmas when, hoping for a present, one was produced – a pencil. He was not alone in not liking Grandfather. My mother hated him and thought him a miserable old bugger, though she didn't put it like that. Curiously he must have mellowed in his old age as he was quite generous to me as a child, once even giving me £2 for Christmas, a large sum in the 1930s. I would go down with my mother to 'Elmhurst' in Stoke Road to visit Gran. He would remain in another room while we had tea, Gran keeping her voice down as she was quite scared of him, I think. There I was introduced to tomatoes which I ate quartered and dipped in sugar! That was a common mode then, I believe, or perhaps it was something Gran remembered from her own childhood.

So my father started work in 1898 and continued until the business closed down in 1968. Seventy years! Grandfather died around 1942 and after that it was run by the rest of the family: Father, his three brothers and one of his sisters. Two of my cousins also started work there but later left for jobs with better prospects. My father never wanted me to join the firm and I had no intention of doing so. It was not a large enterprise, constrained by the size of the premises and I don't think expansion was ever considered. I always enjoyed visiting and seeing the compositors working away, the big belt-driven printers rolling back and forth and my father at his Linotype. He was always happy to produce a line with my name on it or perhaps headings for notepaper. Later, when I was working abroad, he would set up his letters to me on the machine, so much more natural to him now than handwriting, and then roll them off on the galley tray.

I believe that he consciously treated me, his son, as he would have wished to be treated by his own father, for he was invariably kind to me as a child. He got up early to go off to work at the shop, probably around 7 am, and brought my mother a cup of tea in bed and one to me also, together with a couple of particular cheese biscuits, buttered. This was during the thirties and he would also proffer any choice news item that he had heard on the wireless that morning. I particularly remember his telling me: 'The Crystal Palace burned down last night.' Apparently the blaze could be seen from the top of the hill which faced us and I was indignant that I had not been woken up and taken to witness this historic event.

Soon I started to get up with my father and cook myself some breakfast. I had often watched the vendor of a patent egg-beater in the market in North Street. He would whisk up the egg white to a froth, stir in the yolk, produce a soufflé-type omelette on a portable burner and then distribute it to his audience. I persuaded my mother to buy his egg-beater and thereafter (at least until wartime shortages prevented it) would make myself such an omelette each morning. This early interest in, and practise of cookery meant that in later life catering for myself and others came quite naturally.

I now greatly regret that I did not question him more intently about his early life and the effect on it of the great historical events of the last hundred years or so. I did once ask him about Queen Victoria's diamond jubilee and how it was celebrated in Guildford, but he had no remembrance of any great stir at the event. Other silly little questions: did he remember Hansom cabs and horse buses? Were there such in Guildford? When did he see the first motor car? He did once volunteer where he had first seen 'moving pictures'. It was at the so-called Constitutional Hall, premises at the top of High Street (long occupied by Thorpe's bookshop during my youth and later and where I spent many a half hour rummaging). He well remembered the Boer War as he had collected memorial buttons, at a penny each, of the various heroes and events at the time. Eighty years later he asked me, more out of curiosity than hope of gain, to put them into auction and was delighted when they fetched fifty pounds. But obviously the great life-changing event of his early years was the First World War, though he did not often talk about it to me. He had volunteered right at the start and was rejected on account of his poor eyesight but in 1916 he was conscripted and served at the front in the King's Royal Rifle Corp. I have said life-changing but was it? After the armistice on 11.11.18 the troops were very soon sent back to Britain and discharged with little ceremony. My father arrived back home in the morning, as must have been anticipated for Gran passed on to him the message: 'He [she always so referred to her husband] says they're very short-handed up at the shop and could you go in and help out this afternoon.' Well, my father did so but after two or three days decided that a short holiday was his due.

He must have retained some kind of nostalgia for his army days for as soon as the Local Defence Volunteers (as the Home Guard was originally called) were formed he joined immediately. He continued, as sergeant of his platoon, until they were stood down after D-Day.

Despite his lack of formal education, education came through the nature of his work. He was always concerned with correct grammar, and English generally; hated affectations such as the Frenchified pronunciation of words long Anglicised; and knew many of the familiar quotations from Shakespeare and other poets. In the post-war years he and my mother always took their holidays separately, he usually for a week in Brighton. He would go to the theatre there (he had in his earlier life been a devotee of music hall) and on one occasion, through a mix-up of booking dates, found, when the curtain went up, that he was at a performance of Hamlet! He had never before seen a Shakespeare play and was utterly thrilled by it. There he was, hearing all those famous phrases that he had so often set up on the page.

But there were many other quotations that had taken his fancy and which came out in his speech when they seemed apt. Fitzgerald's *Omar Kayyam* had been all the rage in his youth and he continued to love it and quote from it (the first version, of course):

The moving finger writes and, having writ
Moves on: nor all thy Piety nor Wit
Shall lure it back to cancel half a Line,
Nor all thy Tears wash out a Word of it.

He also had biblical quotations to hand. Should I mention some important or (as it seemed to me) useful new acquaintance he would say 'Ah, put not your trust in princes'.

Another remark he had come across which seemed simple to the point of being simple-minded, was, he alleged, from Robinson Crusoe, which he must have encountered in childhood: 'Relieved of its weight the raft floated again.' This naïve statement of cause and effect he found applicable in many situations, not least when the sound of the front door closing indicated my mother's departure for the theatre or Women's Institute.

When we were out walking he had other favourite remarks. He believed, or affected to believe, that the theatrical life invariably ended in destitution. On spotting a ragged and bearded tramp – and they were many in the 1930s – he would say 'Ah look, an Ancient Thespian'. When a raucous individual was heard he would quote Goldsmith: 'Ah, "the loud laugh that speaks the vacant mind".'

In his bachelor days and after, his social life and principal relaxation involved the river and the Rowing Club, just as my mother's great pleasure during the First War had centred on picnicking and punting with her cousins and the Canadians. Indeed the river was the great recreational resource of Guildford and remained so through the Second War and my boyhood. At St Catherine's ferry (there was no bridge until many decades later) there was a delightful tea-garden which also offered, until into the War, the most delicious home-made ice cream I have ever tasted. This part of the river was also the stretch used by the Rowing Club for its annual fete, involving not only races but also foolery with greasy poles and fights with bags of soot and flour. One year (1935 or 1936?) an enormous airship hovered above for a while. Was it the Graf Zeppelin or the Hindenburg? I forget.

Harry's other social activity was centred on the Freemasons. He belonged to two lodges and he was Master at both during the thirties. They had functions known as 'ladies' nights' which the Master and his spouse had to host. My parents did this twice, in 1933 and 1939, and happily retained the programme which contained a lavish multi-course menu. The ladies had to receive presents and Mother was contemptuous of the thirties tat (nowadays elevated to 'Art Deco') that they tended to get, so when she had to choose them she opted for pottery from the Watts Pottery at Compton. These were indeed very pretty but they were also hopelessly under-fired and tended to crumble to pieces, especially if they were used as flower vases. I doubt if a single one of these now survives.

Near the town there were two boathouses for the hire of boats of all the usual kinds and happily, through my father's influence and with so many young members away, I was allowed to join the Rowing Club at the age of 14 and made very good use of it. Then he bought me a strange, little flat-bottomed canoe, clearly home-made and quite often needing caulking and varnishing, but which was serviceable and in which I spent many of my summer leisure hours on the water. Inspired no doubt by some boy's story or other I took to taking it out at night and even going swimming in the dark. I must have let on about the latter for one night I descried the dim figure of my father downriver on the opposite bank, evidently concerned for my safety, but he did not reveal himself. Perhaps he was recalling a rare act of concern shown to him by his own father. As a very young boy – perhaps even earlier than aged 12 when he started full-time work – he acted as a delivery boy for a women's dressmaker and carried the completed dresses in their long baskets on his back to the customers. He remembered the rustling of the tissue paper as he walked along. One night he had a delivery to somewhere over Pewley Hill near St Martha's, several lonely miles away, and this time his father did accompany him.

I enjoyed fishing but also I would take books with me to read when tied up by the bank. I particularly remember wading through Macaulay's *History of England*, two fat volumes borrowed from the library of the Guildford Institute of which I had been made a member. The third chapter, 'The State of England in 1685', was a set text for 'matric' (the School Certificate examination) and I had thought it stupid to read only one chapter. I can't say that such solid reading was my principal fare during my mid-teens. More commonly it would have consisted of such as The Saint books of Leslie Charteris or novels by Dornford Yates. Of course I had also long been reading, as well as practising, chemistry. My older cousin Ted Mills had given me his copy of E.J. Holmyard's *Elementary Chemistry* by which I was utterly fascinated, not least because it was illustrated with portrait engravings of notable chemists such as Joseph Priestley and Lavoisier and also, apropos of the latter, a picture of the guillotine. I read it over and over and virtually knew it by heart.

From my earliest days of serious reading my great resource was the six fat volumes of *Harmsworth's Household Encyclopedia* which stood on top of the writing desk. I think these had been collected in parts by my mother, probably in the late 1920s, and had then been bound. They inspired me to all sorts of practical activity, especially electrical and electronic for there were complete instructions for winding coils and so forth for use in primitive wireless sets. The cookery sections also grabbed my attention with their lurid colour pictures of (completely out of reach) pies and puddings.

3
SCHOOL AND SCHOOL FRIENDS

I made many good friends at school, some for life though, alas, nearly all gone now. One, David Sibbald, I had met on my first day at Guildford Park Elementary School in September 1933. I still remember that day: I was given something called a sand tray and told I could draw in it with my finger. I was utterly disgusted, indeed I felt insulted, as I had been told by my mother of the exciting things I should learn at school and I had already been taught by her to read to some degree. Nonetheless it turned out to be a good school with very good women teachers. I remember little more of schoolwork during the first two years, apart from enthusiastic participation in the percussion band, but great events did not pass unnoticed: the death of King George V (we all wore black armbands); the abdication crisis ('Mrs Simpson stole our king'); and the coronation of George VI in 1937 which was a happy occasion of fairs and festivities. In the third and fourth years I was taken up by Miss Downs who had discovered that I had a very good boyish treble and was also quick to answer questions in class. Coleridge-Taylor's *Hiawatha* was all the rage in those years and she took me to London to hear one of the then annual performances in the Albert Hall. She also took me to see my first ever cinema film: Reinhardt's *A Midsummer Night's Dream*. I retain only one memory from that film, an image of Oberon merging into a tree trunk. I have never seen the film again and wonder how true my memory is.

My teachers nurtured me well enough to get me (and David) into the Royal Grammar School in 1937 when I was just nine. I have touched on one or two aspects of my nine years spent at the school, most of which can be glossed over as the normal schoolboy experience of a day school. Ever since, after reading many an account of tormented years at boarding schools, I have been grateful that it was a day school. I remember nearly all of the boys with whom I was in contact and I was always interested in how their lives developed insofar as I got to hear about them.

The best times started in 1945 when the War finally ended. It had seemed interminable; thoughts of it ever present with the news on the wireless, in the much depleted newspapers and on the cinema newsreels. The horrors of the concentration camps had been revealed; the wild eruption of joy on VE day came and went and we settled into a forgetful summer until the two atomic bombs brought the end of the war with Japan. The lights were now on again – a great lifter of gloom in both senses – and going out at night was a rediscovered pleasure. We knew we would be called up for National Service at 18, something we all wanted to avoid if we could (faint hope!) but at least we were unlikely to be killed. Senior boys we had known by sight had been killed but there had not been the wholesale slaughter of the First War that our fathers had known and spoken of. But we had missed much of boyhood's pleasures. There had been no family holidays for six years and it was now too late for those, but at last there was the prospect of travel. We could go to London on day visits while in Guildford there were the daily forgatherings in a favourite teashop for endless conversation. What an age that is, the late teens! How one loves one's friends; how infinitely fascinating and important they seem, so varied and brilliant; how one can't bear to be apart from them for more than a few hours at a time.

I was now in the first year science sixth, yet that did not mean that I was entirely cut off from the arts. There was a play reading group in which I loved to participate, especially if I could be given a tragic role such as that of Louis Dubedat in *The Doctor's Dilemma* or, better still, Dr Faustus in Marlowe's play. Shakespeare plays were too long for a single session and until a few years later the only one I knew remained *Henry IV, Part 1* which we had done for the School Certificate examination. I knew many passages by heart but I didn't at the time appreciate its excellence and thought it would be the play I would never want to see again. How wrong I was! One play selected by our

33

supervisor Mr Malleson was Kyd's *The Spanish Tragedy*. He told us that there was much in it that was ridiculous and that we could guy it as much as we pleased, which we duly did. Yet there is also in it much to fascinate, as our greatest twentieth-century poet discovered.

There is a photograph of the Science VI from summer 1945 which shows me and several of my school friends at that time. There too is David Sibbald, from my elementary school days. We were still quite close and indeed that summer we went off together for a cycle tour of Wales, staying in youth hostels. But thereafter we tended to drift apart as David did not share my increasing interest in music and literature. Nonetheless we remained in rather intermittent touch until his death in 2010, though by then it was mainly a question of shared memories on the telephone. Also in the photograph are Peter Hamshere and Gordon Hibbert, the two cleverest boys in the form, at least in maths and physics (I was top in chemistry). They were good but not intimate friends and we largely lost touch in later years after National Service and university. Both eventually went into teaching and in the early 2000s I managed to resume contact with Gordon but not then with Peter who later responded kindly after he learned from me of Gordon's death in 2014. He and Gordon had been close friends at school and university but had lost touch.

Other, and in fact more lasting, friends were in separate forms. The dashing and amiable David Lloyd Jones became a much loved friend and, if not exactly a role model, an immediate influence on my lifestyle. He had a motorcycle on which he came to school, often with his brother Bryan in a sidecar, and this seemed to me the height of manly stylishness. I managed to persuade my father that I should have one too (not too difficult as he himself had had one in his youth) and he inquired among garage owners and retailers he knew in the town eventually finding a 1933 Levis for £25. Bikes were, of course, cheap at the time on account of the very small petrol ration (I think four gallons a month). Whenever I mentioned the name Levis to anyone interested in motorcycles they invariably responded 'Ah, a two-stroke' but it wasn't. It was a 350cc four-stroke. In the two or three years that I had the bike I had the good luck never to come off it for helmets were still scarcely thought of and I certainly did not have one. The roads were, of course, much emptier and safer in those immediate post-war days.

In the fifties, with his marriage to June and removal north to York, David and I lost touch for some years until his growing success as a potter with exhibitions brought us together again. Alas, heart problems resulted in his death at only 66 in 1994. He had partly anticipated this, saying to me that the men in his family, including his father, had often died young. In 1996 June organised a big exhibition of his work at York City Art Gallery which was a huge success as he was very popular locally.

But my closest friend during the last two years at school – and until the end of his life – was Victor Willing. I do not remember exactly when it was that this started but the main mechanism was probably that we lived not far apart and so tended to fall in together as we walked to or from school. Listening to music was becoming an important part of our lives and was initially our main shared interest. But how did we get to hear any? Well, there was a concert every evening on the BBC Home Service and from 1946 on the new Third Programme, though I remember that reception of this on the original AM channel was excruciatingly poor. There were also concerts, held at the Technical College in Stoke Park, often given by distinguished artistes including Elisabeth Schumann. We could even afford to buy a few gramophone records (78s of course) though at first these would be largely restricted to short pieces such as overtures or old recordings of operatic arias by Caruso or Gigli. Soon I got to be more adventurous and startled my friends by buying a newly issued recording of Bartok's fifth quartet; the first to come out I think.

There were also sometimes gramophone 'recitals' at school of records brought along by masters from their collections. Mr Bowey, an English and history master, was our principal music authority. He impressed us (or me at least) by telling us that he had seen Wagner's 'Ring' cycle four times and that this was enough. I think I must have borne that in mind later on. Less enthusiastic about Wagner was our chemistry master Mr Wiseman, who seemed to have had a bad experience before the War. 'On no account go to *Siegfried*,' he would say when we were talking about music, 'It goes on for five hours and there isn't a tune in it.'

As Vic's main talent was drawing he soon involved me with art also. Curiously, though himself a good essayist, he was not much interested in literature apart from poetry and he never joined in on our play reading. But perhaps I misremember for by autumn 1945 he had already left regular school and started down at the art school, also located within the technical college, to fill in time before the dreaded call-up to National Service on reaching 18. One evening I went down to visit him and see what he was up to. We were free to wander about the building and at one point we were in the entrance hall when the pianist Benno Moiseiwitsch turned up with his wife outside the glass door seeking admission as he was to give a recital that evening. We could not let him in but vaguely indicated he should continue on round the building. Attendance at the recital was half a crown which we could not or did not want to pay so we ensconced ourselves under the platform and heard the performance very well there.

We also still saw much of each other in our homes or in the town in our favoured tea rooms where we would all meet for long hours over a single coffee or pot of tea. By this time a good few girls were of our company, some from the County School and some from the art school. Most relevant to my narrative was Hazel Whittington. Hazel, always stylishly dressed, had many admirers among the boys and went out with them, including me, but it was with Vic that she most closely associated. We were all more reserved in those days and did not flaunt or boast about emotional or sexual affairs and it was only many years later that I learned, from Hazel herself, that these two had been lovers since they were sixteen.

Art teaching at school had concentrated exclusively on drawing, and indeed that was how the lessons were designated. Vic excelled in this and thus endeared himself to old Mr Collins – Edward Collins – who, I later discovered, had been sole art master since 1911. Two of Vic's meticulous drawings survive from this time: a portrait of me and another of Peter Hamshere. I shall have much more to say of Vic later but now it is time to move on to the next phase of all our lives.

4
CALL-UP

During 1946 individuals of our group were successively called up for National Service, most going into the army. David Jones went first, got his commission, and was soon sending back letters from India. I was myself a good correspondent and encouraged replies with long, newsy letters. Vic was the next to go, off to Maidstone for the six weeks' basic training. He did not take well to it and sent me lamentations and warnings of the horrors I was to expect when I followed him there in a few months' time. Before that occurred I was able to feel some satisfaction at my good results in the Higher School Certificate examination and enjoy the summer holiday. After Wales the year before I felt I ought to see something of Scotland and my ever-generous father found me £20 so that I could go. I could find no one to go with me so I set off by train to Glasgow on the first of what would prove to be a lifetime of solo journeys. This memoir is not primarily meant for travellers' tales, though it may tend that way, but one episode of my trip I must tell.

On the train from Tyndrum to Fort William I decided, on a whim, to get off at Rannoch station, supposing I could find accommodation in the small hotel there. I entered the reception lounge where two or three tweedy sporting gentlemen were cosily sitting by the fire (although only the middle of August it was already quite cool). There was no room available, I was told, the hotel was full. No kindly suggestion was made that I could be put up in some way, perhaps be allowed to sleep on a chair, nor was any other advice offered. I went back to the station where a porter told me that there was a youth hostel on the moor a mile or so from Corrour *eight miles along the railway line*. There were to be no more trains that day and I set off, carrying my suitcase, over bleak Rannoch Moor. I found that the sleepers were just too far apart for convenient stepping from one to another; one had almost to jump, so for much of the way I walked along the rough edge of the track. Strangely at first I felt quite light hearted, certainly not afraid, though it would have been impossible to be in a more lonely situation. I did not notice anybody about at Corrour Halt and I set off along the dirt track to the hostel. When I got there I found it closed up, dark and deserted. My spirits did sink a bit then and I even felt a bit delirious (I noted in my diary). I sat down in a relatively sheltered spot and ate some biscuits and cheese that I had with me. Fortified I trudged back to the station where I found the waiting room open. It was cold by now so I put on all available clothing from my bag and tried to sleep on a bench though with little success. About 4 am a man came in to get some food from supplies which were stacked up in the room. Surprised to find me there he invited me into his warm stationary carriage on a siding where track workers were accommodated. He then went to wake up the cook to prepare their breakfast. He too was very amiable and took me into his little galley while he got on with the job. He gave me welcome hot tea and breakfast (reconstituted dried egg, that great staple of the time) and eventually, about ten o'clock, took me outside to hail and catch the morning train, which did not routinely stop at Corrour, on to Fort William. There I had a comfortable hotel and, of course, after a solid twelve hours' sleep, walked up Ben Nevis the following day.

Once back home I enjoyed a final six weeks of freedom. I was mad about music now and anxious to hear as much as I could before being, as I expected, cut off from it. I went up to London at least seven times to go to Promenade Concerts, mostly on my bike I believe. Programmes were much fuller then before the BBC squeezed them into their regular schedules, quite commonly with different soloists in the two halves. Conducting rotated through Basil Cameron, Adrian Boult, Sir Malcolm Sargent and a few others even including Constant Lambert. I will give one typical programme.

1 September 1946. Conductor Sir Adrian Boult

Overture Leonore No. 3	Beethoven
Violin Concerto (Soloist Max Rostal)	Bartok
Symphony No. 5 in E Flat	Sibelius

Interval

Introduction and Allegro for piano	Schumann
(Soloist Maurice Cole)	
Symphonic Poem Till Eulenspiegel	Strauss

DEPARTURE

My call-up papers and travel voucher arrived and in early October I went off to Maidstone.

As Vic had foretold I did find conditions rough initially; the coarse, tickly woollen shirts and trousers and having to sleep between blankets without sheets and in one's shirt (nobody wore pyjamas, they would have been the object of mockery) was upsetting at first. But one gets used to anything and we were all in the same boat. It was a true cross section of society: middle-class boys like me; working class lads who seemed to miss mother and home more than most and were most prone to go AWOL; real wide boys and 'spivs' from London who boasted about their black market activities. The training and drill seemed nothing special, much like what we had done in the JTC (Junior Training Corps) at school, but there was early rising and constant activity so one was always hungry. The food was fairly dreadful, as one might expect, and the mid-morning break and visit to the NAAFI to consume Russian Slices and Eccles cakes was eagerly looked forward to. Fortunately I had another food resource. I was very fond of Camembert cheese, which had reappeared (of course new to me) not long after the liberation of France, and my mother would send them to me. They cost two shillings (10p) each, I recall. For the first time in my life I was receiving pay; very small of course but more than I was used to. 'Four shillings a day, blooming good pay,' to misquote Kipling.

I had already made up my mind that I was not going for a commission as this would have been in the infantry and accompanied, by all accounts, with endless square bashing and 'bull'. I hoped to acquire some useful knowledge or training not wholly remote from my scientific interests. Towards the end of the six weeks we were allowed to put forward our preferences and I opted for the Education Corps (a bit impudent, that) or the Signals Corps. I was assigned to the latter and so in early December I and others made the journey, which took the whole day, by special train to Richmond, Yorkshire, for Catterick Camp. We arrived at 4.30 pm and it was already dark when lorries took us to our allotted 'lines'. These were all named after First World War battlegrounds: Kemmel, Vimy, Loos etc. It was late at night when I and a few fellow signallers-to-be were finally assigned a barrack hut and issued with palliasses, pillows and blankets.

When I got up at half six the following morning and stepped outside the hut I was astonished – appalled even – by the vision as far as the eye could see of the rows and rows of barrack huts, the 'lines' of old military parlance. 'My God', I thought, 'it must be much like this in a Siberian prison camp.' It became even more like Siberia later as I shall explain.

We had our introductory talk that morning and were told that the wireless mechanics course would last for thirty weeks, so Catterick would be my base until well into next summer. We would get leaves from time to time – I was home for that Christmas – and sometimes these coincided with friends' leaves and we were able to get together. Otherwise contact was entirely by letter and I must give the army credit for a remarkably efficient postal service. Despite one's being moved around from barracks or lines the letters were re-addressed and got through. I even heard from David Sibbald who turned up in adjacent lines and was overjoyed when I found him. After that we were able to see a good deal of each other. But mostly one had to make new friends and this was not difficult as many of those taking technical courses had enjoyed a similar education to mine and we all found we had a good deal in common. This included a love of music and we could sometimes commandeer a radio to listen to a concert, defending it against all would-be marauders. One such occasion I remember vividly. It was a performance of Bartok's *Concerto for Orchestra* – the first UK broadcast performance I believe – and we were truly thrilled by it.

I got leave that Christmas and happily made the long journey home to Guildford and back again. In early January heavy snow fell and stayed for a few days but on 26 January more snow came and the famous winter of 1947 set in and stayed for many weeks. There was, of course, a great fuel shortage and heating our barrack rooms became a major problem. The only heat source was a simple iron solid fuel stove in the centre of the hut with a pipe going up through the roof. Coal was non-existent for us so scavenging parties went out to find wood and were not expected to be scrupulous about where it came from or of what it consisted. Many a piece of old furniture went up in smoke.

Evenings, Saturday afternoons and Sundays were free and, so long as one could escape prowling NCOs looking for victims for guard duties or kitchen fatigues (mostly peeling potatoes – 'spud bashing'), one could get out of camp. The nearest approach to urban life was to be found at Camp Centre, about two miles away at a crossroads. This boasted a cinema and some shops but more important to me and like-minded friends was Hipswell Lodge, a large house which functioned as the education centre. I would trudge down there through the snow most evenings to enjoy its warmth, small library and collection of records which one was free to play. It was a haven in the wilderness. There were lectures on many different subjects, often quite gripping, and I even went in for a maths course.

Our radio mechanics course continued as normal; there were more heavy falls of snow and if one lingered too long around the barracks one was in danger of being drafted for snow clearing or, rarely, coal hauling. On 21 March I noticed that it was thawing and that patches of green, not seen for so long, were appearing in the fields: it was over.

Easter was in early April that year. I did not get leave and instead planned an outing with one of my new friends, Quenet (pronounced

Kenny. I never knew his forename) who had a special interest in geology. On the Saturday we took the bus from Richmond to Keld, right at the end of Swaledale and indeed of the road which did not then continue to Kirkby Steven. We stayed in a youth hostel and the next day we walked over Great Shunner Fell. I found this quite challenging as there was still some snow, the terrain was very rough and there was a headwind against us! Then down to Askrigg where, after one or two unsuccessful applications to hotels which were full, we reluctantly applied to the Sykes Temperance Hotel (still in existence today as Sykes's House). The proprietress in her turn seemed very reluctant to have us (as soldiers in uniform she possibly feared we would come back drunk from the pub) but finally relented and gave us a room. This had the appearance of being intended for honeymoon couples with a vast double bed, a most elaborate dressing table with multiple mirrors and wonderful pictures covering the walls including a large illuminated address in a big black frame. We had, of course, to share the bed; nothing particularly unusual in those days. I have never been back to Askrigg but it gained fame as the location of the BBC TV series *All Creatures Great and Small*.

The following day we paid our bills (9/- each which included supper the night before and an excellent breakfast) and walked to Aysgarth to see the falls. Later we took a bus to Leyburn and from there walked back to camp. Not satisfied with this, after cleaning up we went into Richmond to dine at the Kings Head where we had booked a table. I already had a taste for wine and had a half bottle of Chablis which abstemious Quenet declined to share.

But often on Sundays I went for long walks by myself. One in May was to Jervaulx Abbey, the fields and banks now covered with wild flowers.

In mid-May I got leave and went home. On the Saturday I went to a recital by Clifford Curzon at the technical college while most of the following day was spent with Vic (home from Deepcut) and Hazel. We played my records and drank a bottle of South African 'hock'. I volunteered to take Vic back to his camp that night if petrol could be found. Hazel's father managed to scrounge a gallon or so and late at night we set off on my bike. Peter Hamshere was known to be at Aldershot and we deviated to find him and succeeded after lengthy searches through darkened barrack huts. He was asleep and seemed strangely unsurprised by our appearance. The sight of his kit rigidly laid out above his bed, the items stiffened with cardboard, made me grateful that I was not engaged on an officers' training course. We went on to Deepcut and there located Gordon Hibbert; equally unsurprised to see us. I left Vic there and got back home around one o'clock, to the relief of my rather worried parents.

Quite daringly I decided there was no reason why I should not take my bike with me back up to Catterick. I put it on the train to Waterloo, rode across town to Kings Cross and loaded it on to a night train to Darlington which cost about 10/-. I rode back to camp, arriving around 4 am which gave me time for some two hours' sleep before parade. I put my machine in a corner of an open shed used as a lorry park and it remained there unquestioned and not interfered with throughout the summer. Having it was wonderfully liberating for me and selected friends. We rode all about North Yorkshire, over hills and up the dales. I remember one trip, on my own, to Tan Hill Inn. I was the only visitor and the owner cooked me up a good (though rather dear, I thought) late breakfast. Another memorable outing was with a friend named Godlee who was a great botany enthusiast. He had somehow heard of a finding of a lady's slipper orchid by two nuns near Rievaulx. We went there and located them and these two stout ladies took us on a lengthy trudge to the site. Alas, we did not find it in bloom; at least getting to see the abbey was some compensation.

So the summer, and our course, went by. My group became qualified wireless mechanics and we were ready to be dispatched to outposts of empire where supposedly we were needed. Before we were moved to a transit camp at Thirsk I took the bike back to Guildford by the same route. As I expected to be away for nearly a year I asked my father to try and sell it for me which he successfully did for £10 more than had been paid for it originally. An increased petrol ration had helped to raise values.

At Thirsk in very hot August weather they seemed hardly to know what to do with us and in early September we were given nearly two weeks' embarkation leave. By now I knew that I was destined for Singapore and on 20 September we were up at 3.15 am to be taken by lorry to York, there to catch the train to Liverpool. There we embarked on the *Georgic* and set sail that night on the three weeks' voyage.

THE VOYAGE

How many tens (hundreds?) of thousands must still have memories of travel in that old ship? Only now have I thought to look up her history and I find that she was built in 1931 and served until the War on the transatlantic route. Bombed and severely damaged early in the War, she was refurbished to function as a troopship until about a year after I sailed in her when she was returned to passenger service, only to be requisitioned yet again during the Korean War. This was followed by a few years carrying emigrants to Australia and New Zealand until the final return to be broken up at Faslane on the Clyde in 1956.

How did I find life on board? Effectively it amounted to getting three weeks' leave from army routine. We were more or less left to ourselves to while away the long hours as we chose. The ship was terribly crowded and it was a challenge even to find a comfortable space on deck; but once found, one could sit or lie and read endlessly, or watch the flying fish at the bow, or 'the furrow that widens behind you' at the stern for occasional distraction. For the first few days we seemed to be always rounding capes or keeping close to coasts so I had my first sights of foreign lands: the Portuguese coast; Cape St Vincent; the rugged Tunisian and Algerian coastline.

Below deck I was at first dismayed by the crowded sleeping and washing arrangements. There were three-tier bunks and fortunately I grabbed a top one so ensuring adequate headroom. All ablutions were with seawater and we were given a special soap which was supposed to work with this (it didn't). Of course there was no air conditioning: ventilation was effected using metal scoops which were thrust through the portholes in calm weather. The food seemed very good by contrast with what everyone was getting in the UK at that time.

Our arrival at Port Said was absolutely thrilling. The sun had just set and there was a full moon in the east as we passed the de Lesseps statue and docked on the right bank by the city. We were immediately surrounded by dozens of boats of all sizes and descriptions, most of them with goods to sell. These might be passed up for approval but many young vendors got aboard and slunk about flashing wristwatches or other items which we had been warned to resist buying. The scene was so fascinating that it was well after midnight before I could drag myself away to my bunk.

So then it was down the canal and the Bitter Lakes and into the formidable heat of the Red Sea. Now we were allowed to take to our lighter cotton tropical gear to our great relief. Even so, on one or two nights it was so intolerable below that I slept on deck without any covering. We journeyed on past Perrin Island and into the Indian Ocean bound for Colombo. India had become independent only a couple of months earlier which is perhaps why we did not head for Bombay first. Some were granted shore leave at Colombo but I was not. I partly consoled myself with eating bananas, not enjoyed since before the War.

SINGAPORE

The approach to Singapore by sea is through the straight between the then Malaya and Sumatra, finally passing between numerous beautiful small islands, a mass of emerald green vegetation. In these still colonial times the arrival there of any large vessel, carrying family members as well as troops, was a big event and we were greeted by a military band and a crowd on the quayside. Our now quite small group disembarked in the afternoon and was taken to a temporary camp to await final postings. This turned out to be delightful and consisted of permanent tents with wood floors, three beds and electric lighting in a coconut grove. It was by the sea at the eastern end of the island. The following day I was handed a letter from Hazel (perhaps it came with me on the ship) telling me that Vic had at last got his commission. We were more or less at liberty and spent time on the beach or, in the evenings, walking the six miles or so to Changi village. This consisted of a dirt street lined with shops and cafés while down a side street were booths with girls displaying their enticing charms, their 'bullies' not far away to collect fees. The adjacent airstrip was freely accessible and in fact we walked across it dodging planes taking off or landing. All this, of course, has been long buried beneath the vast modern airport.

After about five very pleasant days doing little, I and the two other radio mechanics were moved to Selarang Barracks nearer Changi and then again to the rather dreary Tanglin Barracks in town. This at least gave us an even better opportunity to explore the fascinating streets and markets which we were completely at liberty to do as there was no hint of animosity against the British at the time. Moreover we now could wear our own civilian clothes when off duty. At last we three were taken to the receiver station for interview to decide which two should stay there and which one should go to the transmitter station. I was chosen for the latter and once there congratulated myself on a 'cushy posting'. It had a wonderfully relaxed atmosphere, there being only around twenty men in the comfortable little camp and virtually no distinction was made between the ranks and the two or three officers. Nobody got up before 8 am and the food was excellent.

I was put to learn about the handling of the large transmitters, how to tune them up and so forth. Each was dedicated to communicating with a particular centre – Hong Kong, Colombo, Rangoon etc. I was settling in very nicely when after only five days or so the O.C. told me that he had heard that I was to be sent to Rangoon! I went back yet again to Selarang Barracks for three days in a sort of limbo, there to be joined by another radio mechanic whom I already knew and who was going with me. On 5 November, after just over three busy weeks in Singapore, we were taken down to the Raffles Hotel to board, by launch, the Qantas Empire Airways flying boat bound for Rangoon.

RANGOON

The flight was my first and the most comfortable I was ever to take. As I recall there were only sixteen passengers seated on both sides

47

of four tables with a central aisle. A splendid lunch was served by a steward and one was free to get up and walk about on a 'promenade deck' towards the rear of the plane. The other passengers seemed to be mainly officers returning to the UK to be demobbed and their first question was 'How long will the journey take?' The answer was four days before they touched down in Poole Harbour and they would spend the nights in hotels en route. They were warned however that there were no hotels in Rangoon and they would be put up in the company's own building.

We flew at a low altitude over the sea nearly all the way, at one stage passing over myriad small islands. Forty years later I learnt from reading Maurice Collis's *Trials in Burma* that these comprised the Mergui Archipelago.

After eight hours or so we passed over the dreary salt marshes and the drab city itself of Rangoon, coming down with a swish of water past the windows on to the Rangoon River. We were taken by lorry to the former Strand Hotel, given tea and then to a camp on the banks of the Royal Lakes to the north of the city. For the next few days it hardly seemed that we were needed and most of my time was spent reading (*War and Peace* in five days) interspersed with miscellaneous 'fatigues'. Eventually I was sent up to the small transmitter station at Mingaladon, not far away, from where I could readily get back down to the unit by the lake which was far more agreeable. With the approach of independence I moved back down there permanently.

Although some of my diary entries appear to contradict it, life there seems in retrospect to have been almost idyllic. Despite the camp being very run-down (there was no running water in the showers or for the washbasins and we had to wash in the lake) the surroundings were beautiful, the birds, butterflies and dragonflies very fascinating and the long swims in the evening refreshing and delightful. As the sun went down there was a stupendous view across the lake to the distant Shwedagon Pagoda gleaming brightly and flocks of white birds would head across the water. The temperature was cooler than Singapore and very agreeable but I think one still slept with a light blanket and, of course, under a mosquito net. There was very little to be done in the way of useful work and much time was spent throwing away (i.e. into the lake) radio equipment which could not be left to the Burmese. We also had to empty several, presumably requisitioned, villas so that they could be handed back to their owners. I sometimes wonder whether this is where the now so famous Aung San Suu Kyi lived during her long house arrest. Her father Aung San had, of course, been assassinated along with fellow members of his provisional government only a month or two before my arrival which meant that we were told to take care when walking the streets of the city. In fact neither I nor others to my knowledge encountered any hostility. The people were very picturesque as everyone still wore longyis and other typical clothing. They also went about smoking huge cheroots and carrying baskets on their heads.

In spite of my trips into town I spent extended periods lying on my bunk, reading and awaiting the longed-for cry of the char-wallah. Other vendors also circulated: the cake man, the dhobi-wallah and a wonderful great bearded barber who would shave us almost beardless boys with his cut-throat razor. For once I was completely deprived of music but made up for it with endless reading from the breaking-up camp library. Shakespeare, Meredith, Dickens, Trollope and the Russians were but a small part of it. A book came into my hands that had a great effect on me: Aldous Huxley's *The Perennial Philosophy*. It was the right book for the time and the place. I wrote in my diary 'I think this is the book I have been awaiting for some time'.

After Christmas came some drill practice in anticipation of the Independence Parade. It was some time since any of us had done any of this and there was a good deal of merriment even among the NCOs and officers. But on Sunday, 4 January we rose at 4 am, paraded at 5 am and were driven down to Government House while it was still dark. Other contingents of the army, navy and air force also arrived and we were stood at ease and able to watch the very colourful array of guests assembling. Finally at 7 am the governor and the new president came out of the house and the ceremonies commenced: presenting arms, inspection by the two of them, a march past, the lowering of the flag etc. Then it was all over and we raced back to camp in our open Studebaker lorries.

Soon after this we were moved out to a rather dreadful transit camp (like all such) where there was absolutely nothing to do, no new books to read and uneatable food. It was amusing, sitting outside the canteen, to observe innocent newcomers to the camp emerging with their plate of meat and potatoes to be greeted with a swish of wings and the theft of their meat in the talons of the so-called shite-hawks. I took to throwing mine into the air to be expertly grabbed by them. In the end I could only stomach bread and jam but fortunately I was able to get out to a Chinese restaurant from time to time and eat the usual Cantonese dishes. I already knew that I was destined for Ceylon and on 11 February 1948 departed thence on the *Dunera*, the gleaming Shwedagon Pagoda receding into the distance.

Colombo

The four day voyage was unremarkable. We were supplied with hammocks but I could not take to these and instead slept on the deck. We arrived in the harbour in the morning, were taken to the Echelon Barracks in the town and were free for the rest of the day. Ceylon had also gained its independence a few days before and in celebration an elaborate *perehera* (festival procession) was planned for that very evening. Naturally, despite wandering round the town all day, I stayed up to watch though it did not start until 11 pm. It proved well worth it and as novel, I believe, to the good-humoured crowd as it was to me. Musicians, dancers, jugglers and acrobats mingled with numerous elephants. In fact I counted 120 of them.

The following day I was moved to what was to remain my base for the next six months: a pleasant semi-permanent camp at a village called Narahenpita just on the outskirts of town (now probably engulfed by it). The primary function of the camp was as a listening-in and intelligence station with quite a large and miscellaneous company. Although I never did learn any details of the activities, I was, the following day, severely enjoined by my commanding officer never to talk about them to outsiders *on pain of life imprisonment.*

Accommodation was in small yet spacious barrack rooms with single beds and rotating fans. Of course there was no air-conditioning and the temperature was uniformly high day and night. There were no mosquitoes (the geckos on the walls no doubt helped with that) and everyone slept naked under single sheets. It was also very humid so daily, often even twice-daily, showers were necessary to avoid prickly heat and the two varieties of tinea: pedis and pubis. Even so one couldn't always avoid these discomforts, especially on first arrival. Another occasional infestation, which drove some chaps almost mad, was with bed bugs. Their presence was revealed by spots of blood on the sheet where one had crushed their gorged bodies. The solution then was to inspect the mattress minutely where they were wont to lurk along the seams. One might then dowse them with some insecticide but it was not unknown for the enraged mattress-owner to take it outside, pour paraffin on to it and set it on fire.

I had a couple of fellow radio mechanics and we had a pleasant little workshop on the edge of the site looking out on an adjacent dusty road along which the locals (I am afraid we still referred to them as 'the natives') would endlessly pass, covering themselves with large banana leaves when there were monsoon rains. On the other side, as I recall, there was a wall on which would poise or dance large chameleons. My efforts to catch one never succeeded.

At weekends a lorry would usually be provided to take any who wanted to go to the beach at Mount Lavinia. I always went; the swimming there was so marvellous and I had enjoyed nothing comparable since family holidays before the War. A charming Singalese girl, Maggie, was always there with her basket of pineapples and one of these after the swim was a truly delicious pleasure. She had a clever way of removing the nobbly skin with spiral cuts, presenting one with the quartered fruit on its stem handle. This cost the equivalent of 4d.

During the monsoon the sea was too rough for swimming and one had to find other amusements. I often went into town as I was fascinated by the Chinese shops and longed to own a silk dressing gown decorated with dragons and pagodas. I never could afford one however. At home in the UK they were still in the depths of austerity, worse even

51

than during the War, and I managed to send a few parcels of luxuries and other presents. These included some for my sister whose marriage I had missed a few months before. I don't recall that Colombo offered any other entertainments yet it was often quite late evening before I would make my way back to camp. There was never a hint of danger and I would walk back by myself through the scented night to the sound of myriad insects and the occasional sleepy murmur of rickshaw-wallahs offering their services. I only rarely made use of them.

There was very little useful work for us and in my diary I find myself complaining of boredom. However I was now concerned for my forthcoming university life. Application forms for the Royal College of Science had been obtained and sent out to me by my father and these were filled in and sent off along with a certificate of good conduct which I had had to obtain from the CO! I studied previous entrance examination papers and was depressed by finding them so difficult. I was due to take mine in May, invigilated by our education officer who was most helpful. It did take place and eventually I received notification of my success. The special chemistry degree course was then still only two years but it was suggested to me that like other ex-service men it would probably be better if I preceded this with a year of revision. This was agreed so now the only thing to be concerned about was whether I would get home and be demobbed in time to start in October. There were several international developments which could interfere with this. The Malayan guerrilla insurgency was already a worry but even more threatening by midsummer was the Berlin blockade and airlift. Heroic though this was, I'm afraid the only concern for me and others in my release group was whether these events would delay our getting back to the UK.

I continued a vigorous correspondence even with former friends at Catterick, now scattered here and there. I had news of my Guildford friends: David Jones was attending a pre-release course in Wiltshire; Hamshere was recently commissioned but already expecting release; Gordon Hibbert was in Aden; Vic wrote from Dover Castle and was looking forward to his release. It was winding down for us and none too soon.

The final days came. The officers gave a party for those leaving and got us all horribly drunk, me in particular. An agonised day of packing followed but on 16 August we finally boarded the *Lancashire* for our voyage home. This seemed a very small ship but the below-the-waterline troop deck was in fact not too bad – fairly spacious and airy. There were numerous people on board whom one had met before, at Catterick, on the outward journey or even in Singapore. There was even the chap with whom I had flown to Rangoon. After a brief stay he had been sent back to Singapore by ship. Such are the unfathomable ways of the army.

As soon as we left harbour the ship began to roll and plunge and so it continued across the Indian Ocean. I was very seasick and remained on my bunk eating almost nothing for several days. As well as being small the ship was very slow and it was only after a week that we got into the Gulf of Aden and calmer water. We were allowed off at Aden; a horrible, oppressive place.

So we went on and in the Mediterranean I started to find it very cool but it was again quite rough. I had completely regained my sea legs and even enjoyed standing near the prow as the ship heaved up and down. We were now allowed to resume serge dress if we wanted to. We passed Gibraltar on my twentieth birthday and arrived at Liverpool after twenty-six days, on 11 September. We were speedily put on a special overnight train down to North Camp, Aldershot, where the formal demobilisation took place. Then to Woking to collect our hideous 'demob suits' and then I was on the train to Guildford and home where I found my mother and sister in the kitchen getting the Sunday dinner.

5
COLLEGE DAYS

After a few happy weeks resuming life with family and friends in Guildford it was time for college life in London. My mother had arranged with friends of friends that I should stay with them in their flat in Latymer Court in Hammersmith. Curiously my hostess had been in Singapore when it fell to the Japanese and had been interned there, in horrible conditions, throughout the War. I was supposed to stay only for the five weeknights and go home for the weekends which for a while I did as there was a convenient Green Line coach service from Hammersmith. However this did not really suit me as I wanted to enjoy the city at weekends and after one term I parted amicably from these new friends and started on a series of bedsitting rooms and flats to be partly detailed later. The first, so far as I can recall, was in Redcliffe Square, Earls Court and typical of the type: 30/- a week; a shilling-in-the-slot gas meter with gas fire and cooking ring; lumpy bed and broken-down armchair. But I enjoyed the independence and managed very well. In fact, in comparison with today's students we ex-servicemen were really very comfortably provided for. The college fees were paid and I had a grant of £213 a year which my father made up to £250. One could easily manage on this, especially as one lived at home during holidays.

The Royal College of Science was the 'pure science' college of the three that made up Imperial College, the other two being the Royal School of Mines and the City and Guilds College. Like all of South Kensington – indeed most of London – it was a fairly dingy and seemingly run-down place and even now I do not look back on it with any great feelings of loyalty or affection. During my first days there I recognised two or three men from the army years but, apparently by common agreement, we all ignored one another: that was another world now left behind us. Almost immediately I made two friends and we three more or less stuck together during the next three years. One, Philip Gundry, was of British parents living in South Africa. He came straight from school and so was only eighteen. As will be seen he remained one of my friends for the rest of his life. The other, MacPherson, was older than us and of a realist, not to say cynical, disposition and counterbalanced our 'liberal', arts and culture-oriented attitudes. He went back into the world of gas technology on graduating and I never saw him again. During the lunch hours we would make our way through the empty halls of the old Imperial Institute (now long since demolished leaving only the tower) with its old-fashioned dioramas clicking away and displaying scenes of native life in the colonies, to the student union building just behind the Albert Hall. If this proved too dismal, as it usually did, we would continue to Kensington Gardens to sit on the steps of the Albert Memorial to talk and eat sandwiches. I particularly remember the long-running great Groundnuts Scandal in Tanganyika (now Tanzania) as a source of much innocent merriment.

Some of my school friends were also at college in London but continued to live in Guildford and commute, as indeed did I for one or two terms. Gordon Hibbert and Peter Hamshere were both at King's College in the Strand taking general science degree courses while David Sibbald was at Battersea Polytechnic doing the same. I saw them only occasionally at weekends as was also the case with Vic who was back at Guildford Art School until he could start at the Slade School in autumn 1949.

But what of the course itself? I have never found myself able to learn much from lectures and I am poor (lazy?) at taking notes; I take in and remember better from reading or seeing. However I believe that the lecturers were in fact uninspiring and unfortunately there were no good and up-to-date textbooks. Laboratory work was devoted almost entirely to analysis of the kind that had probably been standard since the beginning of the century: qualitative (involving the use of much hydrogen sulphide); volumetric with endless meticulous titrations; and gravimetric requiring a platinum crucible which had to be signed for in and out. Essentially it was training for a laboratory technician which, perhaps, is what most of us were expected to become. With my years of home experimenting I was good at all this and apparently it proved the key to my future in research as I will relate. I hated physical chemistry and I disliked Professor Tomkins who taught it though Philip later went on to work with him. I do not remember being much inspired by the lectures on organic chemistry either even though that was what principally interested me. They were given by a young lecturer named Braude who was said to be very brilliant but a bit unstable mentally. In fact he did later commit suicide.

The whole of that first year has left little impression on me. I had no London friends outside college and it was only Philip whom I saw occasionally on evenings and weekends. He had adopted me as a cultural mentor so we went together to concerts and the theatre, activities which became increasingly dominant in my life to the detriment of my studies. I started going to Covent Garden, both the opera and ballet, which unlike today was still affordable. The gallery cost half a crown (2/6 or 12.5p) but 6/- (30p) for Wagner. The pre-war production of the *Ring* cycle was revived in 1949 and of course I went to it and again the following year. It was an absolutely traditional production with all Wagner's specified effects which I found quite magical, especially the opening of *Das Rheingold* with the Rhine Maidens suspended on wires and going round and round and up and down. In *Götterdämmerung* there was even a real live horse for Brünnhilde to ride on into the flames of Siegried's funeral pyre. Brünnhilde was Kirsten Flagstad! She also sang Sieglinde in *Die Walküre*. Hans Hotter was Wotan while Siegmund and Siegfried were sung by Set Svanholm, a Swedish tenor. He seemed entirely adequate to the inexperienced me. He was quite short and wore platform-soled shoes so that Flagstad did not tower too high over him.

I have seen other productions of the *Ring* since those days, including the excellent Coliseum production with designs by Ralph Koltai in the early seventies. Also, of course, I have heard it broadcast countless times and followed the libretto. Now I have reached the point where I cannot take it really seriously. Certainly I would not want ever to sit through it again in the theatre, especially in these days when primacy is given to directors and their 'new concepts'. The only Wagner I still really love is *Parsifal* which I also first saw in those early years.

Of course I did not neglect other opera composers and I love all Verdi to this day. Puccini I snobbishly looked down upon in my early years as 'popular' but again I love him now. Benjamin Britten's wonderful operas were appearing then and in the early fifties, and I saw them all in their first productions. *Peter Grimes* was the first opera I ever saw, in its first production at Sadler's Wells in 1946. Wonderful though that was for me it is not my favourite; the ambiguousness of the 'hero' and the ambivalence of Britten's attitude towards him has always rather disturbed me. I have never read Crabbe's poem and ought to do so. For me *Billy Budd* is probably the best: Britten's music, not least the stupendous choral writing and the heart-wrenchingly beautiful setting of Melville's poem 'Billy in the Darbies', is surely some of the finest he ever wrote.

FIRST STAY IN EUROPE

During the summer term in 1949 we were offered work experience on the continent during the long vacation and I chose to do mine in Spain. It was to be with the mining company Real Campania Asturiana de Minas in the little industrial town of Torrelavega, south of Santander. It was only ten years after the end of the Civil War, people were suspicious of the fascist regime of General Franco and generally did not go to Spain. A visa was needed and friends gave one all sorts of dire warnings. I booked my train travel through Thomas Cook, as well as a hotel for three nights in San Sebastian which was on the way.

But before that I had my first visit to Paris! I was amazed by the city; it seemed like a sort of Babylon. In contrast to austerity Britain there appeared to be no shortages of anything. People lounged outside at café tables eating and drinking and stared at one as one passed by, yet I soon felt acclimatised. I had found a little hotel, I forget how, called the Hotel d'Athènes, in the rue Gay-Lussac, near the Luxembourg Gardens, and not far away down the Boulevard Saint-Michel, near the Pantheon, a much-patronised cheap restaurant. The menus were cyclostyled in violet ink and at the end of the meal the *garçon* added up one's bill on the paper tablecloth. It was wonderful. But one day I went, of course, to the Eiffel Tower and after the ascent noticed the restaurant on the *premier étage*. It seemed like a nice place for lunch and I went in. I was startled when I saw the prices on the menu but it was too late to back out. I still remember what I ate: *champignon à la grèque* followed by tournedos Rossini. On the principle of in for a penny in for a pound I accompanied the latter with a half bottle of burgundy; Clos Vougeot I believe. That was not quite the extravagance that it might now seem. Classic French wines did not then cost the astronomical sums that, with worldwide demand, they now do.

There were no high speed rail routes then and the journey south was a long one. The first stage was overnight and in the morning, I think at Dax, there was to be a delay of an hour or two. I wandered out into the town where the open air market was going on. I was impressed by the snail sellers offering not only escargots but also *petits gris* – ordinary garden snails. These were constantly trying to make their escape and had to be plucked back. At the border, Hendaye-Irun, there was a long delay with much checking of passports and luggage but eventually I arrived at San Sebastian. It was the very fashionable summer season and a far cry from how things would be today. On the beach – La Concha – there were separate sections for women and men and the latter had to wear full body swimsuits. The Civil Guard, with their distinctive hats, were in evidence everywhere and ready to repress any offence against church or state. More than fifty years after this, on my way back from a tour, I thought to re-visit the town. I drove around for about an hour and a half amid a forest of apartment blocks unable to find anywhere even to stop. I left disillusioned and went on to St. Jean de Luz in France.

In 1949 there was a narrow gauge railway linking San Sebastian and Santander via Bilbao. It has now gone though I believe a similar line still operates further west. On the train I happily made the acquaintance of a Canadian professor of Romance languages from McGill University who was spending his summer in Santander. Somehow (how?) we kept in touch and met up once or twice during my stay. We also made friends with fellow travellers in the carriage and at Bilbao, where there was to be a wait for the onward train, we all went off to a restaurant for lunch. Once arrived at Santander I continued, I forget how, to Torrelavega where accommodation had been arranged for my whole stay at the Hotel Moderno, the main yet unpretentious hostelry of the town. I was to become all too familiar with its routine and cuisine during eight long weeks but I really had absolutely no justification for complaint. Spain was a ruined and impoverished country. Compared with many I was living a life of luxury, and for what now must seem an unbelievably cheap 35 pesetas (35p) a day for full board and lodging.

At the company (as at the hotel) nobody spoke English apart from the director. He was a kindly but sad man given to lamenting the state of the nation consequent to the Civil War. The laboratory was set up principally for the assaying of the ore for its content of the three metals: zinc, copper and I forget the third. I soon learnt the procedure and thereafter there was little for me to do. To make myself useful I corrected the English of the firm's publicity leaflets which had been almost unintelligible. Every lunchtime it was back to the hotel for the four course lunch. Typically (almost invariably) this consisted of:

Sopa de Pasta
Merluza a la Plancha
Filete de Ternera
Queso o Dulce

It seems a lot but the portions were small and I often supplemented it afterwards with a bunch of grapes for 5 pesetas.

The town offered little in the way of evening entertainment apart from the routine of the *paseo* in the central square. A local wind band played the shrill Asturian music while the younger populace walked round and round to view or greet one another. The older people sat on the benches looking on as did others such as the wet nurses, their charges in perambulators, identifiable by their nurses' uniforms and the three bobble earrings they wore.

Naturally I was not alone in the hotel. Guests came and went and I made friends with some of them and went on outings at weekends. One such was the inevitable visit to the bullfight in Santander. I never wanted to go again. I remember that we got back late and dinner was unhesitatingly served to us at midnight. Another outing was to the caves at Altamira, then still open to the public. The roof of the cave with the paintings was very low and one had more or less to lie on the damp floor to see the animals properly; a great privilege nonetheless.

The following year, 1950, I went back to Spain to try and traverse the whole country. I must not attempt a narrative of my journey though I remember it well and my parents kept all the postcards I sent. Essentially it was made possible financially, not only by the 35-peseta *pensiones* but also by the existence of a wonderful facility called a kilometric ticket, bought at the frontier. This was a booklet of small coupons for travel of over 3,000 kilometres. It cost £2! At the station one named one's destination and the appropriate number of coupons was torn out in exchange for an ordinary ticket. Of course this was third class: real hard class with slatted wooden seating.

I was away for six weeks or so but will only here give the most general impression of what I saw. The towns were full of street life including a tolerated black market with young men selling *tobacco rubio*, imported cigarettes less harsh than the official *nacionales*; also white bread rolls for those who could not take the standard brown bread. Numerous *mutilados de guerra* sold lottery tickets. Of course there were beggars too. Poverty was obvious and as the train proceeded over burnt up landscapes one could see dusty hamlets of one-storey hovels. A single experience of my own has stayed with me ever since. I was sitting on a café terrace in Algeciras waiting for the ferry to Gibraltar where an old school friend, Dick Pendry, now in the regular army, was stationed. I was eating a bunch of grapes (they still seemed a luxury) and I was hardly aware of a little girl hiding in the shadows of a wall. I threw away the grape stem which still had a few bruised fruits on it and she darted out, grabbed and ate them and fled. Sixty years later I still regret not having been able to relieve this starving child.

On the Rock, Dick was clearly taken aback by my travel-worn state and uncertain whether I would be allowed in to the mess for refreshment but that was got round somehow.

EXPANDING HORIZONS

To go back to autumn 1949, Vic was now due to start his time at the Slade and we discussed the possibility of getting a flat together rather than having to rely on dreary bedsitting rooms. I diligently scoured the newsagents' noticeboards and found one in Chepstow Villas in Notting Hill Gate. It comprised the top floor of one of the (still existing and very desirable) large houses there. I now forget the rent but it cannot have been more than £4 a week. The house was owned by the editor of *The Star*, the third evening newspaper, but it was his wife, Mrs Cranfield, who was doing the letting and agreed to let us in. Vic's own grant was as much as mine but I don't think it was supplemented by his father. Money was therefore tight and we often ran out of it. Food was still rationed and Vic specified that we should each not spend more than £1 a week on it 'in house'; just about manageable. In the event he was so taken up with his new life at the Slade that often he did not come back to the flat until quite late. I kept more regular hours, there being little to keep me at Imperial College.

We did not see much of Mr Cranfield but he turned out to be rather generous to us, handing over some records sent in for review to the paper and also, on a couple of occasions, tickets for the theatre. One such was a production of *Love's Labour's Lost*, I think with John Gielgud. The *coup de théâtre* in the last scene (the messenger arriving wearing high purple plumes) made a great impression on me as I did not know the play. The donated records included a set of four ten-inch 78s of Vaughan Williams's *On Wenlock Edge* performed by Pears and Britten which I got to love.

Vic's start at the Slade coincided with William Coldstream's inauguration as director and professor so the principles, and even some of the staff, were still essentially those of the old Euston Road School of the 1930s. Vic's fellow male students were mainly ex-National Service men like himself but there was also a sizeable number of older men who had done service during the War. The large contingent of women students was generally rather younger. This was all very exciting and Vic plunged into the life with enthusiasm. I meanwhile continued my daily life in South Kensington and frequent evening visits to the theatre and the opera. I never could persuade Vic to come with me to either of these. He preferred the cinema and his love of opera only developed much later during his life in Portugal.

I soon got to know several of Vic's fellow students, some remaining friends for life of whom I shall have more to say later on. One was Michael Andrews, Vic's particular intellectual disputant; the other Keith Sutton. Keith was a year ahead and about four years older than us having served in the navy during the War. He became attached to Vic, seeming to think he needed help and guidance, but although they always remained friends Vic never took this seriously, indeed often quite the reverse. I still have an unfinished portrait head of Vic that Keith started that first year.

So the autumn term progressed but in late November or early December domestic disaster struck at Chepstow Villas. I have described the debacle elsewhere but must give the outline here. We were having a very cold winter and sometimes the mains water was cut off in the street for some operation on the pipes. We would turn on the taps in the morning to find no supply. One evening I got back from college to find the Spanish caretakers, who lived in the basement, hauling out their soaking wet carpets into the frozen garden. Inside the house a horrible suspicion grew on me as I went upstairs. Indeed, in the kitchen, the copper pipe from the hot water geyser (which evidently we had left on) had shifted from over the sink to be delivering water at full force on to the floor. It had then gone through the bedroom and living rooms below to the basement – presumably throughout the day – causing catastrophic damage. Neither Mr nor Mrs Cranfield had been at home during the day to notice. When they came in shortly after my own arrival I was almost on my knees with mea culpas. She was distraught; he was stoical. Perhaps he had had his doubts all along. An agent was called in to inspect the damage and take a few immediate steps but of course the house was unliveable in except, ironically, for our flat. They went off to find lodgings elsewhere and I was left alone.

Vic came in only around 10 pm and I took him around the house. As he saw the collapsed ceilings, the ruined beds and wardrobes, the plaster-covered dining table and chairs, his initial silent wonder turned into helpless laughter. It was as if he was recognising what he had always suspected: life was like that.

We were able to stay on in residence in the empty house. Showing extraordinary forbearance, Mr Cranfield never reproached us further nor was there ever any suggestion of our paying compensation. I assume he had insurance but it must have been many weeks before they could resume occupation. We never went back again after that. The following term Vic got a room in the Slade's semi-official hostel, a house in Cartwright Gardens, while I resumed life in bedsitting rooms.

The great event to take our minds off such disasters and lighten the winter gloom was the Slade Ball. I had no right to go to it but already I felt myself to be a sort of associate member of the Slade community and Vic persuaded me I would be welcome. There was fancy dress, a cabaret put on by the students (including Vic), a band and, of course, dancing. Traditional jazz was the style then, much encouraged by the existence of the famous club, 100 Oxford Street, to which we sometimes daringly went, wondering into what depths of depravity we might fall. At the ball I was not a dancer but I much enjoyed the company. I don't remember that there was much, if anything, alcoholic to drink. If there was we had little money to buy it but the joyous mood did very well without it. Old bohemians were present, including Augustus John, no doubt remembering the Slade days of their youth. Outside Dylan Thomas and his cronies tried to gain entrance but were repelled as being hopelessly drunk. Vic was incredulous that he should be denied entry in any condition.

The experience was repeated the following year though I retain no particular memories of it. Hazel would now come often to London and was well known to Vic's friends. About this time he announced that he and Hazel were to be married: he wanted to do the honourable thing. They did in fact marry at Guildford Registry Office in January 1951 and went to live in an attractive flat in a large old house in Shalford, near Guildford. Though inconvenient for Vic's access to the Slade it was a charming place where we practised archery on the lawn and walked over the fields to the River Wey.

By this time I was becoming increasingly conscious that I was neglecting my chemistry studies in favour of theatre, literature and music but I cannot now recall that I reformed dramatically. That summer (1951) came the examinations and after the usual anxious wait for the results I was dismayed that I had only secured a pass degree. Philip, who had been receiving private coaching, got a first. It was humiliating and I went into penitential mode, cutting my hair short and disposing of all my gramophone records. What was I to do now? Of course all sorts of wild ideas went through my head but in the end it came back to looking for offers of work posted on college noticeboards (we had no career counselling at all) and weighing up the possibilities. Philip was immediately offered a Ph.D. course with Professor Tomkins. His work looked to be extremely boring but it was research and there seemed to be no chance of anything like that for me. I tried one interview with an oil company working in Trinidad: it was a disaster. The main trend of the interview appeared to be an assessment of how I would fit into colonial life. Eliciting that I was not much into games and sports I was finally desperately asked 'But don't you at least play water polo?' The interview was not followed up by either party.

At school more than one of the masters had quoted to us that most poignant of Shakespeare's *pensées*; Brutus's lines in Julius Caesar:

There is a tide in the affairs of men
which taken at the flood leads on to fortune.
Omitted, all the voyage of their days
is bound in shallows and in miseries.

I assume they were pondering the course of their own, essentially rather humdrum, schoolmasters' lives. Had they really wanted to spend their lives in this way? I thought now more of the corollary: start as you want to go on for almost certainly you *will* go on as you start. Though feeling desperate myself, I was clear that I should not take anything out of pure desperation. But chance – even luck – can also determine the course of one's life. I had been drifting for much of the summer, spending days at the South Bank exhibition for it was the wonderful year of the Festival of Britain. I went back to the deserted college to look once again at the noticeboard and found a small – I think handwritten – notice offering two three-year Nuffield Foundation scholarships to carry out research at the National Gallery. One was for a physicist to study the effects of solvents on paint and varnish films, the other for a chemist to determine the chemical composition of a natural resin called dammar, still used as a varnish for paintings. It sounded almost too good to be true but I wrote applying for the chemist's position, was called for interview and accepted! The course of my future life was set.

6
FIRST YEARS AT
THE NATIONAL GALLERY

In 1951 the small Scientific Department at the National Gallery comprised only three people: F.I.G. Rawlins (Ian Rawlins), the scientific adviser; A.E.A. Werner (Tony Werner), the research chemist; and Joyce Plesters, a scientific officer only fairly recently appointed. Ian Rawlins had joined the staff in the 1930s and had set up the X-ray facilities. These had become routine and had been taken over by the Photographic Department but Rawlins was still researching the use of 'soft' X-rays. His great achievement, however, had been to organise the evacuation of the paintings, at the outbreak of war, to be stored in the caves at Manod in North Wales. He had realised that although the relative humidity (RH) in the caves was near 100%, it was only necessary to house the paintings in huts within the caves and provide heating to be able to lower the RH to a suitable, stable, easily controllable level. The benefits to the paintings kept in such conditions became very evident and led to the creation of the first air-conditioned room in the Gallery where the most vulnerable, early Italian paintings on wood panel, were displayed. This had just opened when I first arrived there.

Joyce assisted Rawlins with his X-ray work but her main focus was developing the microscopy and analysis of paint cross-sections on which eventually she became a world authority.

Tony Werner, my nominal supervisor, was an organic chemist who had joined the department in 1948. Despite his Germanic name (pronounced with a W not a V) he was in fact of Irish birth and upbringing, his grandfather having migrated there from Alsace after the Franco-Prussian War of 1870-1. Werner had been a reader of organic chemistry at Trinity College, Dublin, where his father before him had been professor.

Rawlins and Werner had both attended a *conversazione* at the Royal Society at which they had seen a demonstration of paper chromatography by Dr A.J.P. Martin from the National Institute for Medical Research at Mill Hill. This is an analytical method which Martin had invented and they thought it might provide an entry to the study of the composition of dammar. Consequently they had arranged with Mill Hill that I should spend an initial month there to learn something of this technique. I started on my daily trips (I was living in a bedsit in Kemble Street, near Marble Arch) to what seemed like the outer reaches of north London.

I must briefly explain what is meant by chromatography which, despite its name, is not necessarily connected with colour. The name stems from its first use – the separation of coloured compounds on a column of solid adsorbent by the passage of a solvent through it. That was as long ago as 1905 and Martin's big contribution was to recognise that that was only a specific application of a more general possibility – the partition of the components of a mixture between two phases, a stationary one and a moving one. He had been working on the amino acid composition of wool protein and he demonstrated that by spotting his sample at one end of a strip of filter paper and then allowing a solvent to move down it by capillary action, the components were all carried along to different extents and separated out as discrete spots which, if colourless, could then be revealed by spraying with a suitable reagent. This allowed the analysis of complex mixtures, impossible before.

When I turned up in his laboratory that achievement was already several years in the past and Martin was now working, with A.T. James, on a new development – gas chromatography. Already set up and working was their very first apparatus, a crude gas-solid device which was able to separate a mixture of the lower fatty acids.

Martin himself was very kind and agreeable to me and gave me hints as to how I might proceed when I set to work. He himself was trying to make a gas density balance which would detect compounds as they emerged in the gas stream from a chromatograph column. I believe one was developed but was quickly superseded by much more sensitive devices. But the first thing that had to be completed each morning before work could start was *The Times* crossword puzzle, at which I was no help at all.

One morning there came the news that Martin had been awarded the Berzelius gold medal by the Swedish Chemical Society. Everyone crowded in to congratulate him. 'It will be the Nobel next,' they affirmed. It was, in 1952. He went on to work elsewhere including the USA but tragically, in his late sixties, his powers failed him: he developed Alzheimer's disease yet lived on until he was 92.

After a month it was back to the National Gallery where I was a bit dismayed by the small laboratory and the basic nature of its equipment. The apparatus needed for paper chromatography that I had seen was not available commercially but we managed to get it made 'in house'. I knew that it was essential first to clarify whether dammar was mostly a natural polymer or if it contained discrete chemical compounds. Paper chromatography should tell me this but as it had only been applied until then to polar, water-soluble amino acids I knew that a completely different solvent system would be needed for water-insoluble resin components. I devised a novel reversed-phase system, impregnating the paper with a high-boiling petroleum solvent and using aqueous isopropanol as the moving phase. After some tweaking of various parameters, and experimenting with reagents that would show up any separated spots on the paper strips, lo and behold it worked! Six discrete spots were revealed, perhaps with others overlapping.

This was very satisfying so of course I looked at what my system showed with a range of natural resins including mastic, the other one commonly used as a varnish. They proved to be easily distinguishable in this way. My very first publication, a 'Letter to *Nature*' with Tony Werner, appeared in print in 1952.

I had been joined in late 1951 by the physicist appointee, Ian Graham, and we shared a little office/study over Joyce Plesters's microscope room. Ian had been a student of Werner's in Dublin and he was significantly older than me having been born in 1925. To Joyce and me he seemed very sophisticated and socially aware for he was a real 'debs' delight', attending countless evening functions and talking of all the people he met. Yet apparently this was not how he saw himself, for in his autobiography he says that in fact he felt very insecure. He was the son of Lord Alastair Graham, himself a younger son of the Duke of Montrose, and this apparently entitled Ian to be addressed on letters as The Hon. Ian Graham. Is this usage still maintained?

Ian sometimes brought his evening clothes in with him so that he might change into them before going on to some party or reception. Included in this *tenue* was a wonderful waistcoat fabricated of woven platinum thread which, he declared, was very economical as it never needed cleaning. Apparently it was made from an altar frontal which some predecessor had long before brought back from Russia.

Ian was very skilled at making things and he fabricated some delicate apparatus for his studies of solvent penetration and the swelling of films. His was probably a more difficult task than mine and less likely to end with definitive results though in the event he did publish a paper and then decided he had had enough after three years and left for other ventures. He eventually became a dedicated and highly successful Mayan archaeologist with many discoveries and excellent research to his name. We met occasionally over the years as I mean to record later on.

I should perhaps say a little more about the permanent staff of the Gallery at that time. The director was Sir Philip Hendy, who was always very amiable though I saw little of him, and the keeper was Mr Gibson, a remote figure. The division of duties was that the director, who would not necessarily be a career-long civil servant, was in charge of the collection while the keeper managed the staff and all formal business. There were only two or three art historians researching the paintings, including Martin Davies and Cecil Gould. Just after I arrived I well remember the latter bringing round a newly joined staff member to introduce him to Rawlins and Werner. This was Michael Levey, later to overtake Cecil Gould in promotion, eventually to become director. There were three conservators of whom one, Helmut Ruhemann, was there on a freelance basis. The other two were Arthur Lucas and Norman Brommelle. I think there was something of a feud between these two and Werner. I knew nothing of this and on almost my first day they invited me out for a lunchtime drink (something I was totally unaccustomed to) at one of those long Irish saloons that used to exist on The Strand. Of course I don't remember the details of what they were after, apart from trying to enlist me to their side, for they plied me with schooner glasses of sherry. Rawlins saw me return in their company and later said, 'Don't get involved with Gallery politics, Mills.' I didn't want to and didn't.

Our working hours were probably unchanged from the nineteenth century. We started at 10 am and finished nominally at around five though I always stayed much later. Lunch hours were 'flexible' and most of the senior staff went off to their clubs in Pall Mall. I would walk up to Soho, usually taking a light lunch at the Café Torino (I describe my café life in a later chapter) but sometimes I treated myself to something more substantial at Madame Maurer's little restaurant in Greek Street. This was a small place – only three or four tables – which this elderly lady (possibly of Viennese extraction) ran by herself. She served an excellent veal *escalope chasseur* which one might follow with a slice of one of her delicious cakes. On one or two occasions there I bumped into a former school fellow, Tom Lingwood, with whom I had otherwise completely lost touch. He had had a strong reputation at school for artistic skills and had left early in 1943 to continue his studies at Guildford Art School. He was now a stage designer and working with Sadler's Wells. I later heard from David Sibbald that he had gone to Australia but I had no idea of the immense success that he enjoyed there. He worked as a designer of sets and costumes for opera and ballet in Sydney including the first production at the new Sydney Opera House, Prokofiev's *War and Peace*. In fact he became Artistic Director of Australian Opera. On retirement he moved to the Netherlands with his long-term partner and died there in 2001. This was little Tommy Lingwood, as we knew him when he was at the same Guildford Park Elementary School as David and me.

To revert to my life at the Gallery, we actually worked on Saturday mornings when a certain latitude in matters of dress was acceptable. Even Rawlins, who was very formal, might come in wearing a sports jacket, and the inference was that you were going off to the country that afternoon. Ian Graham had acquired an old Rolls Royce (he still proudly retained it sixty years later) and he could, on Saturdays, leave it parked on the north side of Trafalgar Square outside the staff entrance. This is now almost unimaginable.

While my work was going well my emotional life was passing through a rather turbulent phase. In 1951 I had started to hear from Vic of a new student at the Slade named Andrew Vaccari who had entered in autumn the previous year. He, together with a couple of his first-year cronies, were attracting a good deal of attention by flamboyant behaviour not untypical of boys just liberated from parental restraints but alien to more serious fellow male students who had mostly just come from two years' National Service. One of these boys had only one arm so they were easily recognisable and I would see them about in Soho. Not immune to the absurd infatuations of youth, I managed to envelope Andrew in a romantic, somewhat Byronic aura. This was wholly the product of my imagination, perhaps stimulated by reading Gothic novels or such plays as Maturin's *Bertram*.

By the time that I actually got to meet him I had come more down to earth and eventually the idea arose, urged on by Vic and others, of our getting a flat to share. Once again I scoured the newsagents' boards in Notting Hill Gate and in February 1952 we took a flat on the top floor of 1 Colville Square, just off Portobello Road, at £4 17s 6d (£4.87) a week which, with an interruption, was to be my home for the next two and a half years. Of course the first use to be made of it was to give a party. Many from the Slade came as well as a few Soho-ites. I *think* that Francis Bacon looked in but didn't stay long as there wasn't all that much to drink. Anyway it would have been no big deal in 1952. Also present were Henrietta (Moraes) and her then husband Michael Law. I don't know that anybody invited them but in those days if you heard of a party you went along to it with someone who was. Law, a famous womaniser, was a handsome man of about thirty-five and I remember him leaning elegantly on our mantelpiece in conversation with someone unknown to me. Henrietta was only 20 and no doubt in the midst of the dancing. Her fame as hellraiser and model to Freud and Bacon was then still in the future. Ian and Joyce from the Gallery were my particular invitees. When dancing was at its height poor Miss Lampson in the flat below came up white-faced and asked me down to look at her ceiling which was visibly flexing up and down. I had to go up and plead for moderation.

The party was reckoned a great success and Andrew and I went on fairly well for about three months. He went back to his family once and came back with a long recipe for *spaghetti al sugo* which his mother had written out for him and which he followed. The quantities were family-oriented so we lived on it for days. At the Slade he was getting involved with a film project of fellow student Lorenza Mazzetti and our flat, it appeared, would be the ideal place to shoot some of it. One evening, I suppose it was at a weekend, several people crowded in and shooting commenced of a scene from Kafka's *Metamorphosis*. Andrew was initially intended to play Gregor Samsa but he had neither the physiology nor the acting ability to be able to suggest an insect so Michael Andrews, who had both, took over.

As the evening wore on I was getting pretty fed up with this invasion of my living space and in the small hours, with everyone staying over, a violent altercation ensued between Andrew and me about sleeping arrangements. We were parted and somehow the night was got through. The following morning I fled to Shalford and threw myself on the hospitality of Vic and Hazel. I continued to pay my share of the rent but Andrew was unable, or unwilling, to do the same and the upshot was that eventually I moved back in and my old college friend Philip Gundry was happy to join me as co-tenant.

Lorenza later (1956) went on to make a rather successful short film called *Together* which had Michael Andrews and Eduardo Paolozzi as two deaf and dumb men in the docks. Until very recently (2016) I had supposed that nothing more came of the Kafka film but I was wrong. Lorenza has published a little book (*Diario Londinese*, Palermo, 2014) in which, although entirely ignoring the above episode, she describes how she went on to find other premises and needed co-stars for it in the Portobello Road and shot more scenes. These she carefully preserved and they have been assembled and digitised by a young Italian enthusiast. Entitled *K* they were put on a DVD which was given away with an Italian film magazine. I have not been able to see it.

The following two and a half years were an enjoyable and fairly fruitful period. My research grant amounted to about £30 a month, relative affluence compared with my friends at the Slade, and Philip too had a comfortable grant for his post-grad work. He also had some small private means bequeathed him by his father. We were thus able to offer modest hospitality and so often had visitors at weekends for coffee or light meals, generally brought along by Vic. The critic Andrew Forge, for whom Vic then had a high regard, was one while Mike Andrews was also a regular. Girls were not lacking and one day in 1953 I was introduced to a beautiful, very young Paula Rego. That was more than sixty years ago as I write. She remains one of my closest and dearest friends.

Music and the theatre continued as my main relaxations. A year or two earlier the plays of Christopher Fry (*The Lady's Not for Burning; Venus Observed*) had been much in fashion on Shaftsbury Avenue, as also were works by Anouilh such as *Ring Round the Moon* which made a star of the young Paul Scofield. The Lyric, Hammersmith, put on excellent productions which were cheaper to visit. Here I saw Scofield again along with John Gielgud and Pamela Brown in a striking performance of Otway's *Venice Preserved*. I have only once seen it again (at the Almeida) though I have read it and heard radio productions. Other absorbing shows there were Anouilh's *Point of Departure* and Noel Coward's *The Vortex*, both with Dirk Bogarde. He was already known from his performance as a petty criminal (with the wrong sort of glamour) in *The Blue Lamp* and other such films and this meant that too many young fans came to the plays and spoilt the performance. I think these were the only ones he did on the stage. Incidentally *The Blue Lamp* is a fascinating film to watch now. It was very largely shot in the vicinity of the Harrow Road in areas subsequently demolished for redevelopment. It shows a vanished world in other ways too.

It was about this time that I first met David Sylvester. Then known as A.D.B. Sylvester he had been invited to the Slade to lecture, probably about Bacon, and Vic had got to know him well. On the strength of that, Vic invited Bacon himself to talk to them there, which he did, fortifying himself from time to time from a hipflask. I cannot remember exactly under what circumstances I met David but we did meet and became friends. I would sometimes bump into him in Soho when both of us were shopping for food in the lunch hour. He favoured the wonderful grocers Randall and Aubin in Brewer Street. Rationing was still in force for some items and I remember his saying that he was particularly looking forward to when butter came off the ration. David was still quite slim then but this was not to last. I shall have more to say of our friendship when we get to the sixties.

TRAVELS 1952 AND 1953

I shall keep this as brief as I can but something needs to be said of my summer travels. I always aimed to go as far as my money would take me and in 1952, not having enough to get to Istanbul, I opted to make for Athens. I bought train tickets through Italy in advance and also my passage from Brindisi to Patras. In Naples a station disaster struck me as follows.

The train to Brindisi was scheduled for midnight but unfortunately a strike had been called and was due to start at exactly that hour. The train was standing at the platform and potential passengers had boarded it in the hope that it would go. Naturally everyone was talking with one another discussing this and I had some Italian so joined in. In the carriage I had chosen were two nuns and we were joined by an Italian who had spoken to me on the platform and who had said he too was going to Brindisi. The two nuns somehow got the idea that we were travelling together. Just before midnight I realised that it would be a long night without any refreshment available and I briefly got out of the carriage to fill a bottle with water from a tap, unthinkingly leaving all my things in the carriage. On returning, the nuns spoke to me from the window: 'Your friend has taken your things to the other train.'

Of course I realised at once they had been stolen and my dismay was plain to see. It was midnight; whistles blew and the train started

74

to pull out. Like a scene from a Hitchcock film the two nuns stood at the window, their faces a picture of open-mouthed horror as I stood on the platform. I was left with nothing but the jeans and shirt I had on.

It is strangely disturbing, even after this length of time, to recall this incident. It was, after all, a novel revelation to me of deception and treachery, though it was not to be the last. I rushed about the station and an official, to whom I had spoken earlier, took me to the office of the station police. I made my *denunzio* and spent much of the night looking through file indexes with photographs of Neapolitan villains but without success. When it grew light I went out to hang about outside the British Consulate until it should open. A very sympathetic consul denounced Naples and advised me never to return to it. For a temporary passport I needed photographs and I found a street photographer – one of those with a tripod and a black cloth over his head and the camera – to make some. Armed with my new passport and a loan of money I then had to go to the French Consulate to get a visa to travel across France! All this took much of the day but eventually I was back at the station to catch the train north. I now forget but I think I must have at least retained my pre-bought tickets in the pocket of my jeans. Trains were very crowded in those days and I stood in the corridor up to Rome and then on to Florence. I remember that I experienced a strange lightening of my mood as I was on the train; a sense of freedom at being without luggage or other possessions. Perhaps I was a bit light-headed as I don't remember having had any food.

I knew that another good Slade friend, Hermione, was in Florence working with an old American art historian as a general amanuensis and I must have had her address for I found her and she was able to find me a place to sleep. The French visa was valid for one week so I was able to remain for a few days and recoup some of my lost holiday, most agreeably taken round by Hermione.

Andrew Vicari (I allow him his new name in what follows) was himself in Florence, provided with accommodation by the extended Mazzetti family. He had left the Slade at the end of the summer term after only two years, announcing that thereafter his surname would be spelt in the new way: Vicari. We did not contact each other but he was to be seen in Piazza della Signoria on the periphery of the café circle of the already popular painter Pietro Annigoni. Later, back in the UK, I heard from Hermione that he had gone on to Rome and that his parents had come out to Italy to see what he was up to. By his own account (*The Observer* Supplement, 5 June 1983) he spent two years in Italy before returning 'penniless' to the UK. He gave no reason for this prolonged exile or explanation for how he managed to support himself.

After these relaxing few days it was time for me to resume my train journey home. This was easier then than now as there were through trains from Milan to Calais.

The following year, undaunted by my misadventures, I determined on travelling to Yugoslavia. Under Tito this country had largely detached itself from the Soviet block and visitors were welcomed. However, my mother, who had never been abroad, asked that I should take her for part of the way so we resolved on a short stay in Innsbruck and Venice. At Cologne station we had a wait of a few hours for the connecting train and so we walked out into the town. Now eight years after the War, a single row of new buildings stood along a main street; behind them remained total devastation.

The great experience of Venice was on stepping into St. Mark's Square at its western end. It seemed to explode into my sight like the sounding of a great bell.

After a few days I had to pack my mother off on the train to travel by herself back to the UK. In fact she managed well and was daring enough, in Switzerland, to leave the train, travel by boat along a lake, and pick up a train again at the other end. She became an enthusiastic holiday traveller, usually going with friends, and once even went overland as far as the Black Sea in Bulgaria on a package trip organised by the washing machine magnate John Bloom.

I went on via Trieste to Belgrade. There were still many people displaced by the change in the frontier between Italy and Yugoslavia at the end of the War and the train was full of them carrying suitcases and bundles of possessions. The frontier guards were ruthless in having these all opened for inspection and I helped those in my carriage repack and put back on racks their utterly disordered things. One woman wanted to thank me and handed over the only thing she had to give – a lemon.

Arriving in Belgrade, just as it was getting light, was a bleak experience. I stayed only a day or two and then took the night boat (which went only twice a week) down the Danube to the last available stop, a small place named Prahovo. Thankfully I had paid the small extra fare to go 'first class' which meant I was able to sleep after a fashion on the saloon bench rather than in the foetid hellhole in the bowels of the boat. At dawn waiters came in with trays of glasses of slivovitz (plum brandy) to 'revive' the passengers (I did not partake) and we went on downriver, now with the sentried watchtowers of Romania on the left bank. At Prahovo a huge hissing locomotive was waiting to pull the train to Niš. In the fields were peasants in national dress engaged in rural activities: this was still the true unchanged Balkans.

I remember rather little about Niš and Skopje but from the latter I made a trip to Ohrid, on the lake, where I found a room for two nights and made friends with some young restorers who were treating wall paintings. Ohrid was rather inaccessible and in fact I had flown there on a very small plane though I went back by bus. Then it was on to Peć by train via Kosovo Polje. I vividly remember the crowd of hacks with their poor skeletal horses outside the station at Peć, in one of which I was rattled along the rutted dirt road into town. I should mention that all the towns had an office of the state tourist organisation which would recommend somewhere to stay. The main point of visiting Peć was to visit the Patriarchate, now a World Heritage Site. I was the only visitor and I was hospitably received by a young priest whose name I still remember: Svetomir Spasić. He brought a tray for me carrying slivovitz, coffee and honeycomb. He had learnt English by himself and I was the first person he had been able to try it out on. It was in fact remarkably good. We had a long talk and he told me that the religious life was very much oppressed. He asked me to get in touch with a fellow priest or relative in England and I have to confess, to my shame, that I never did. It has weighed on my conscience ever since.

The next step was a long bus ride over the North Albanian Alps to Titograd (now Podgorica, Montenegro). I put up in a largely empty new hotel where all the bathroom fittings were either missing or broken. Then it was on by smoky old steam train to wonderful Dubrovnik for two or three days followed by the coastal ferry up to Rijeka, the formerly Italian Fiume. By this time I was pretty well out of money and subsisting on bread and some dried up old goat's cheese I had bought in a market. I made it to Ljubljana where once again I had to appeal to the consul who found me a bed in some student hostel and then sent me on my way to Trieste, from where, as usual, I prudently had my return ticket.

RESEARCH AT THE NG CONTINUED

By this time my work was going quite well and I had isolated some pure, crystalline components of dammar resin. This is the dream and aim of all organic chemists working on natural products. The isolation procedure was a lengthy one and I quite often stayed on in the department until late at night. I would not want to compare myself to Madame Curie, in the old film, stirring away at her vats of pitchblende, but I did feel dedicated to my quest: it was to some degree inspirational. It was not without danger either, for large volumes of flammable solvents were involved. Looking back I think that perhaps I should not have been there alone.

Once a new compound is discovered it has to be characterised by measuring various properties: its melting point is one which was simple. Another was something called its optical rotation and we did not possess the instrument (a polarimeter) for that. I had already been in touch with D.H.R. Barton (Derek Barton) who was then reader in organic chemistry (later professor) at Birkbeck College, London University. Ten years older than me he was already the most notable among the few academics working on natural products in the UK and especially triterpenoids, the class of compounds to which my new findings belonged. Eventually he was to become one of the world's leading organic chemists and, indeed, was to be awarded the Nobel Prize. He was very amiable and immediately took a great interest in my work and allowed me to use some of the instruments in his laboratory. When I arrived there smoking a Turkish cigarette (as I must confess I did) with its characteristic smell, he would emerge from his glass cubicle in the corner of the lab saying 'Ah, I detect the presence of Mills'. Some of his Ph.D. students however were quite snooty when I first went in with my little phial of crystalline material. 'Oh it's probably β-amyrin [a common triterpenoid],' said one. It wasn't. It was a member of a new series which I named (of course) the dammarane series. Barton, however, took me seriously and became enthusiastic as my studies of the structures confirmed the theory of the biogenesis of triterpenes which had been proposed by Professor Leopold Ružička in Zurich.

I also isolated a minor constituent of the resin which was not a member of this series but which had a pentacyclic structure rather than a tetracyclic one. This too was new and I had to give it a different skeletal name. One source of dammar is trees of the *Hopea* genus, itself named after John Hope, a noted botanist, so I called my new compound hydroxyhopanone as the first member of the hopane series of triterpenes. Little did I imagine that, years later, hopanoid compounds would be found to exist in huge amounts as components of bacteria and blue-green algae and as relics of these in shale oils and other petroleum-type deposits. Equally little would the authors of the hundreds of publications on these compounds be in any way aware of the young scientist who thought up a name for his newly discovered compound. But that's science for you: as someone remarked, we all bring our few crumbs to add to the pile.

A PARTY AT THE MOYNIHANS'

Despite my hard work at the Gallery my life was not devoid of social engagements, though they were rather sparse. One was a party of which I made a written record. It gives a flavour of bohemian life at the time and so I will insert it here slightly abbreviated.

31 July 1953. Michael Andrews rang me at the National Gallery and asked me to a party at the Moynihans' at 155 Old Church Street, Chelsea, with whom he is staying for a month before going to Italy in September to take up his Rome scholarship. I happily accepted, for I go to so few parties and seem to see so few people in London. I was pleased with the hope of meeting again the few celebrities with whom I have become acquainted during the past year or two, and also my closer friends.

I arrived about nine o'clock to find about twenty or so people present and already very merry as there was plenty to drink, including champagne, and excellent food. The occasion of the party was, I think, the twenty-first birthday of Rodrigo's son John, whom I had met, together with his father, once before back in the winter at a party given by Susan Benson. I was introduced to Mrs Moynihan, Elinor Bellingham Smith, who is also a painter and a very kind and charming woman. I talked with her and Michael for some time and for a while with such of the Slade people as were there: Vic, John Beadle, Joe Hope; also Andrew Forge, whom I had met only the day before when Vic brought him round to tea at the flat. He is a painter and also writes art reviews in *The Listener*. In a most recent number he devoted some space to Vic's painting in the present ICA exhibition, so they have been spending the past week painting each other. Francis Bacon arrived and I talked a while with him and two others whose names I have forgotten, college people I think, but the conversation was mainly about personalities, and since I did not know the people involved I took little part; except that I was able to confirm the general impression as to the falling off in looks of Henrietta, whom I had last seen a day or two before in the Torino.

I found Vic and John Beadle talking to a girl whom I just recognised as Elisabeth Frink, as I knew her slightly three or four years ago when she was at Guildford Art School. She is a sculptor, and I was very impressed back then when I saw some of the great grotesque heads which she used to produce. She has had considerable success recently, at least insofar as reviews are concerned, has had work in various exhibitions and was selected for the final British entries to the Unknown Political Prisoner competition. She remembered me and we spoke of two girls who were her particular friends and with whom she has now completely lost touch. She did not even know that one of them had married about a year ago. This seems very strange; they were quite inseparable once.

Vic left us, and John Beadle made some remarks about Vic's work to Liz, who had not seen any of it. We had been talking about Vic when we walked in Regent's Park together last Sunday. He, that is John Beadle, thought it highly intellectual painting and very eclectic (this has been generally observed), but that nevertheless he usually produced completely coherent, unified painting, often of great beauty. He thought, however, that it was a hit-and-miss business, and that when he didn't succeed he fell badly, citing the last summer picture of *Musicians*, which he considered hideous and vulgar. I couldn't agree with him in this as I had liked *Musicians* very much, though I had not seen it in the finished state, and I don't suppose I now shall as I believe Vic, in disgust, sold it for some insignificant amount to someone at the Slade.

I talked again with Bacon, David Sylvester and others. All of us were a little drunk and swaying rather on our feet, so the conversation did not pursue a very coherent course. I remarked to Bacon that I had heard he had some pictures going to America for exhibition in New York. He looked slightly curious that I should know, but said that it was so but that he didn't know if they would like them and he was afraid they weren't very good. (Vic had told me yesterday that he had seen them, that they were dreadful and would lose him his reputation if shown there.) There was talk about making money and Sylvester said gambling was the only way. Bacon told me he once kept a gambling house in London for two years and finished up with £7000 which, he said, he soon got rid of. He said it was too much trouble and he wouldn't do it again. I asked him if he had read any Jean Genet, as I had read some extracts from his *Journal du Voleur* in a magazine called *Merlin* only that morning. He said he had read a little, but that David would know more about him and he turned and asked him his opinion. David said that he didn't like his flat, dull style, a characteristic upon which we all agreed, and then burst into a panegyric of authors whom he preferred above him, but the only name I recall is Camus. I compared Genet with Defoe, particularly *Moll Flanders*, with which they concurred.

Holidays were discussed, and everyone seemed to think the South of France still the most desirable place to go. Much consideration was given to the problems of one Eve, apparently the ex-wife of Robert Buhler, the painter, with whom earlier I had had a long and formal conversation on the subject of how she was to obtain a husband and what should be his qualifications. Was she to go to the South of France with an old man, who had said he was too old for sex and with whom she was sure she had no soul in common, or to Sardinia with Alan Lomax, the folk song collector, who would require nothing more of her than to carry his tape recorder? All advised the South of France; after all, once there she was sure to meet someone agreeable but in Sardinia ...! Bacon announced that he was going to Japan. He thought it terribly interesting. Yes, Japan now rather than Japan intrinsically, he said in answer to my question. He is going on a Dutch cargo boat, which takes some months, 'with Peter'.

During most of the rest of the evening I sat downstairs in the kitchen with various people, not talking much myself. Nothing of great substance was talked about that I recall. Sylvester made a long confession of his mediocrity and was consoled and encouraged by various people. I left about 2:30, walked as far as Gloucester Road, and then succumbed to a taxi.

Another brief diary entry which I made gives a glimpse of Vic's situation at the time. He had just left the Slade after completing his fourth year.

12 August 1953. I was talking with Vic and discussing the problem, which he has now had with him for some time, of how he is to live. Ideally, of course, some rich connoisseur should provide him with a small competence, and the two most suitable and able to do so are Sir Kenneth Clark and Sir Colin Anderson; the difficulty is, how they should be approached. Coldstream at one time, hinted that he might say something to Clark, but did nothing. But more recently, Sir Colin has been the more favoured candidate, mainly by virtue of his having just bought one of Vic's pictures, a life painting which he saw at the Slade when they gave an exhibition there last term for the Contemporary Art Society [this painting is now owned by the Tate Gallery]. Vic has been to lunch with the Andersons a couple of times at their house in Hampstead. Vic was talking of this problem with Sylvester and Bacon, and Bacon said that David should write and ask Sir Colin to provide Vic with enough to live on. David said Bacon should write, but he said he couldn't because he hadn't given Sir Colin any pictures. Apparently he himself received £600 from him about a year ago, which he promptly lost at Monte Carlo and then wrote asking for more, receiving another £400 and promising pictures in return, which he has never provided.

Sylvester said he would write and told Coldstream so; Coldstream said no, he would write, which he has not done. And so the matter rests.

REMOVAL

By summer 1954 Philip had finished his research at Imperial College and been awarded his Ph.D. Now he had obtained a post-doctoral position at Princeton and in September departed for America. I could not afford to keep on Colville Square by myself and it was agreed with Vic and Hazel that we should share a new flat, perhaps with others also. Hazel, no slouch in such matters, went straight to Harrods property department and found a grand maisonette at Lancaster Gate at six guineas a week. It had two large rooms, one on each of the ground and first floors, and several smaller rooms and it was partially furnished with beds and odds and ends. It is still there and now looks out on the triangle of land on which the Royal Lancaster Hotel stands but which then was encircled by terraced houses like ours. I moved in at once and took the big room on the ground floor. Vic also moved in upstairs but Hazel initially declined to give up the Shalford flat permanently. Michael Andrews, long since returned from his period in Rome, lived there from time to time, and Keith Sutton was very much a presence though he never moved in.

An old friend of ours from the Guildford days, Dick Wilson, did move in and I must here say something about him. He died in 2011 and, shamefully, never received any obituary recognition. He was briefly at school with us in Guildford until his parents sent him off to Cranleigh School. We were always in touch, however, as the family lived in Guildford. Now, after National Service and university, Dick was working for the *Financial Times*. Later he went to Hong Kong as editor of the *Far Eastern Economic Review*. Back in London from 1964 he became a prolific author of books (at least seventeen) on China and the Far East, the best known of which was probably *Mao: The People's Emperor* (1979). In the mid-1970s he also took on the editorship of *The China Quarterly*. From about 1965 he and his wife Sally lived in a fine detached Georgian house in Grove Lane, Camberwell, later with their two adopted children Ben and Emma. I learnt of his death too late to call for obituaries, while Sally herself was also ill in hospital and died a few months later.

So, back to Lancaster Gate. Eventually Hazel did move in permanently and we all lived fairly harmoniously in our communal life together. Things though were not going too well with Vic and Hazel's personal relationship. Not only was money very tight (when indeed they had any) but Vic's affections were now largely directed elsewhere: to Paula Rego. Hazel was not naturally adapted to a bohemian, make-do lifestyle. She aspired to a comfortable and elegant way of life as exemplified in *Vogue* and *House and Garden* magazines. Alas, she was given to taking on accounts both at the big stores and local grocers. This sometimes led to heated disputes when a bill was presented at the door. One got to be nervous about answering the bell.

Things were looking up though in Vic's career. He had already in 1952 and 1953 shown some of his work in exhibitions at the ICA (Institute of Contemporary Arts), then in Dover Street, and in 1955 he was offered his first one-man show by Erica Brausen at her prestigious Hanover Gallery. He painted both in the flat and in a small studio that he rented in Chelsea, which I never got to see. As the time for the show approached he realised he had too few paintings and filled in the gap with one of me sitting elegantly in a rather skeletal (Giacometti-esque?) armchair smoking a cigarette. I remember that one reviewer said that the sitter 'had been taken too much at his own estimation'! This caused much amusement at Lancaster Gate and I still laugh aloud when I think of it but really it missed the point. Vic's paintings of people and heads were not intended as portraits but as *presences*. Sadly, although the painting was said to have been bought by Sir Colin Anderson, its whereabouts are now unknown.[1] Two paintings met with general approval: a splendid reclining nude (Paula on a camp bed) which was sold to 'someone in Belgium' and

---

[1]   It is just possible that it is on the back of one of Bacon's 'destroyed' paintings which Bacon had given to Vic to use. Two of these somehow got back into the market after Vic left the country and are mentioned in Ronald Alley's *Catalogue Raisonné*. One is said there to have a painting by 'a young artist' on the back. I do not know who owns this painting.

has been lost to view, and a standing nude (Hazel) acquired by The Arts Council. As was common in those less lavish days there was no catalogue and it is uncertain whether the paintings were photographed. The Gallery's record book of exhibitions is now in the Tate Gallery's Archive Department but sadly it does not even include a list of the paintings exhibited. The show was taken seriously by the critics, even if they were puzzled by the more daring works such as *Man Playing with a Kitten* and the racing car on a kitchen table; both now lost but which clearly foreshadowed his later work.

It is not clear whether the show included some of the portrait heads of his friends which still survive. He painted Andrew Forge and also Rodrigo Moynihan (this remains with the Royal College of Art). Rodrigo painted a beautiful portrait of Vic but years later this was stolen by a disgruntled student and, it is thought, destroyed. A black and white photograph survives. Vic also painted Lawrence Alloway, then big in the ICA and later a senior curator at the Gulbenkian Museum in New York. As I recall the image was rather striking, the sitter with a mop of hair rather like Andy Warhol later, but it is now lost. Another lost portrait is that of Stephen Spender's wife, Natasha Litvin the pianist. Coldstream had recommended Vic to Spender for this and the latter paid a visit to Lancaster Gate to meet Vic and discuss the project. For some reason he was kept waiting in our big living room and when Vic came in he found him leafing through a copy of the Olympia Press first English edition of Genet's *The Thief's Journal* which I had bought in Paris (it was banned in the UK). He hastily, almost guiltily, put it down. When the portrait (which I never saw; it was done at the Spenders' house in Loudoun Road) was finished it was not liked and it is uncertain whether it was ever paid for or what became of it. It does not survive in the family now.

ANOTHER PARTY

In autumn 1954 I went to the first production of Britten's *The Turn of the Screw* at Sadler's Wells Theatre. Unusually Vic had come with me and by chance we encountered there Johnny Minton and his train. Though I had sometimes seen him in Soho, this was the first time I had actually met him. He was amiable and very lively but naturally time for conversation was brief. The opera was terrific. It must have been not long after this – in late 1954 or early 1955 – that Minton gave a notable and eventful party at his studio in Apollo Place in Chelsea and I was invited along. The party followed a private view of an exhibition by Dennis Wirth-Miller to which I had not been. The first area of the long studio, into which you entered from the stairs, was the quieter part and had a large table serving as the bar and kept by one of Johnny's sailor friends. Beyond that was given over to dancing to loud recorded music. The place was soon crowded with Slade and college people together with the usual Soho party-goers and denizens of the York Minster and the Colony Room. I, of course, stayed at the quiet end and talked mostly with Slade friends. Notable among the dancers were Henrietta (now famous as a model to Bacon and Freud) and Minton's much-loved companion, the handsome Norman Bowler. Norman was admired even by the most heterosexual of the Slade men for his fine figure, used as they were to the weedy, even under-nourished male models provided for the life classes.

At my end I listened as Colin MacInnes and Jeffrey Bernard compared the modes of corporal punishment they had experienced at their schools: the thwack of the cane; the swish of the birch. As the evening drew to a close Norman and Henrietta passed us and went down the stairs together, pausing at the bottom to turn and look back up. As Frances Spalding has said in her biography of John Minton (*Dance till the Stars Come Down*), this was probably the tipping point for Minton, initiating his disastrous decline. It was some two years later, reading the airmail edition of *The Observer* that was sent to me in Detroit, that I was shocked to read of his suicide. I learn from Spalding's book that with amazing magnanimity Johnny bequeathed his studio to Henrietta. She soon sold it and spent the money.

7
A New World

By late 1955 my paper with Werner on the chemistry of dammar had been published in the *Journal of the Chemical Society* and my own on the structures of the new compounds was in press. My work financed by the Nuffield Foundation grant was therefore done and I had to think of the future. Things had changed in the Scientific Department. Werner had gone off to the British Museum to work under the keeper of conservation, Harold Plenderleith, eventually to be keeper himself. His job as research chemist was advertised and I, perhaps rather presumptuously, applied for it. At the Civil Service Commission interview one member of the board was Harry Hoff, better known to the public as William Cooper the novelist. Although I met him often and knew him quite well in later life I never reminded him of this first encounter. Mercifully I did not get the job: I would have missed out on wonderful experiences if I had. The new man appointed was Garry Thomson who came from the world of scientific publishing. He had been chosen largely because Rawlins wanted someone who would shoulder the burden of editing *Studies in Conservation*, the journal of the International Institute for Conservation of Historic and Artistic Works (IIC). The institute had been set up in 1950 and it had its office within the Gallery. Rawlins had been the main editor of *Studies* but now wanted relief. Garry and I overlapped for a few months *en poste* and we got on well enough.

I had dreams of continuing with research in America and consulted Derek Barton. He suggested that I apply to Professor Carl Djerassi at Wayne (now Wayne State) University, Detroit, and agreed to recommend me to him. Carl Djerassi was one of the very few people in the US working on triterpenoids; those to be found in cacti. I wrote and was accepted, to start in February 1956.

I suppose that when I said farewell to my friends at Lancaster Gate I thought that this was to be a parting for a year or so after which we might all be together again. In fact everything was to change for all of us; it was a farewell to the youthful mode of life.

I crossed the Atlantic on the *United States*, an almost new liner. Of course I travelled third class (£60) which was still luxury in comparison with what I had known from troopships. Alas, I scarcely enjoyed any of the wonderful food offered as I was seasick nearly all the way. It was, after all, February and stormy. When I stepped ashore in New York all the symptoms vanished almost immediately.

Philip Gundry had come up from Princeton to meet me and we walked off from the dock to where he had parked his car. I was struck by how old everything looked when I had naively expected New York to be all shiny and new. Philip had managed to lock his keys inside the car (a 1953 Chevrolet convertible) but by dint of its having a soft top we managed to get it open. We spent two or three days in the city, though I cannot remember where we stayed, and did some of the usual new visitor things: tea at the Plaza Hotel, a cocktail in the Rainbow Room on top of the Empire State Building and so forth. More memorably we went to see the Brecht/Weil *The Threepenny Opera* with Lotte Lenya still in her original role.

After a few days down in Princeton, where Philip introduced me to dry martinis, of which he was already fond, I came back to New York to fly to Detroit. There was snow everywhere and a delay while the plane (one of those reliable old DC-3s) was sprayed with de-icing fluid. Detroit also was snowbound and remained so for the next several weeks. Someone had organised a room for me in a rooming house on Hancock, not too far from Wayne to which I trudged daily through the snow. One or two others of Carl's students also lived in this house but I formed a particular friendship with someone with whom I remained in touch for life. His name was Louis Sucheston (he later told me this was Gallicised from the Polish Suchestov) and he was a mathematician with a position at Wayne. I do not recall when his family had left Poland but he had spent many years in Paris at the Sorbonne and was essentially

French in behaviour and attitudes. He was a great womaniser and, indeed, eventually got himself expelled from the house for some misdemeanour. He confessed to me that he had already got a wife in the Polish community of the city from whom he was now separated. In his later life in the US he had three more; the third of these, Genevieve, survived him.

I cannot now recall my first impressions on meeting Carl (first names were immediately the order of the day, a great contrast to life at the Gallery). He was in fact only five years older than me but had this large laboratory of doctoral and post-doctoral research students, including two or three others of my countrymen. I soon settled into the problems I was set and got on well and was even able to introduce the team to the chromatographic methods I had developed. At first the bench facing mine was occupied by an American, John Zderic (a friend until his death in August 2016). His family was of Serbian origin but the pronunciation of his name had been Anglicised to Zedric. He was five years older than I was and soon went off to join the firm of Syntex in Mexico, of which I have more to say later. He was replaced by a young Itallian, Riccardo Villotti, who also was to remain a friend for all his life.

I am not sure what Riccardo was set to work on but for some reason he was in part supervised by Franz Sondheimer, an old colleague of Carl's from years before in Mexico. I have never been able to forget how Riccardo, whose English was still very rudimentary, was harried and bullied by Sondheimer's questioning on one occasion shortly after his arrival. I rather took against him then and never really liked him though we got on adequately in later years. He had a distinguished career, of which details may be found elsewhere, and somehow made a lot of money. In the 1970s he made newspaper headlines in London by paying three quarters of a million pounds – then an absolutely unprecedented sum – for a flat in 'Millionaire's Row' in Kensington and he lived there, apparently not very happily, with his wife Betty. While at Stanford in 1981 as a visiting professor he killed himself by taking cyanide in his laboratory. Carl told me that it was he who found the body. Mark Whiting, a professor at Bristol who had known

Sondheimer from student days, told me that even then he was always talking about suicide and how best to carry it out.

Life settled into a comfortable routine but it was, of course, absolutely essential that I should learn to drive and buy a car. A fellow Englishman took me to Jefferson Avenue, where all the used car lots were sited, and helped me to choose a 1950 Ford for $200. He drove it back for me and in a few lessons in the university car park taught me to drive. I took my test, passed and received my Michigan driving license. This was very liberating and once spring came allowed me to make trips out of town.

It's hard for me now to remember how I fared for cultural activities during my eighteen months in Detroit. I did go to an occasional concert and sometimes there were functions within the university. I remember a Ravi Shankar recital and there was even a poetry reading by Edith Sitwell who was doing an American tour. There was, of course, the cinema, for the city had around fifty or sixty houses each showing a programme of three films. They reeked of popcorn and in many cases were simply warm places where lonely people went to doze off in company but they did provide an opportunity to see films still unavailable or even banned in the UK. One of the latter was Brando's *The Wild One*, daring at the time but no doubt tame enough now. Another curiosity that I saw was an early film with Burt Lancaster, obviously made in England just after the War, called *Kiss the Blood Off My Hands*. The story was by James Hadley Chase, notorious in my schooldays for a supposedly erotic novel *No Orchids for Miss Blandish*. I have read that he was good friends with and admired by Graham Greene, a favourite author of mine. In the first-run cinemas I remember seeing Elvis Presley's first film, *Love me Tender*. His fame had preceded it and I recall how his appearance on screen in the distance was greeted with ironic cheers from the audience.

As for nightlife, I was soon acquainted with the gay part of town though I forget how I learned about it. Probably from Louis as he liked to take his lady friends there; he said it excited them. American town life had activities neatly categorised, and indeed segregated, so there was a specific street for drunks known as Skid Row ('shot and chaser

50¢') and Farmer Street for the three gay bars. Only one of these, the Rio Grande, was popular and lively, the others usually empty. Clearly it paid protection money to the police who never interfered. Once a year (I think at Halloween) there was a sort of licensed Saturnalia with drag and much camping about in the street which the good people of Detroit would come out to watch.

In the 1950s America was still a very violent place (as indeed it still is) and arguments would often be settled with fist fights or worse. I saw such fights, one in the car park outside a non-gay bar, the girl standing by awaiting the outcome to find out who would claim her. It was like a story in Arthur Morrison's *Tales of Mean Streets*.

A TOUR WITH MY FATHER

My father had always spoken of his dream of one day visiting America, which had been inspired by his teacher at school talking about the foundation of Yellowstone as a national park. We arranged that he should come over that summer and we would go on a short tour from New York. It's hard to imagine now how we settled all this in those days before mobile phones and credit cards. Moreover the foreign currency allowance was then almost unimaginably small – I think £50 – and I had to fund our trip largely myself. I drove to New York, found a hotel and met him after his long ten-day crossing on a small Dutch liner. We spent a few days in the city and did things which pleased him such as a visit to Radio City Music Hall and a trip to Coney Island. Here he was delighted by the performances of the barkers outside the sideshows and for some years afterwards he would perform their spiels. 'Put away those tickets at $5; put away those tickets at $2. For only $1 and for this one performance only, you may enjoy this amazing show…'

We had decided to go up through New England and make a brief foray into Canada. I remember little of the journey (except where it went wrong) but I recall staying in Provincetown, Portland and somewhere else in Maine where we enjoyed the seafood. When we got up to Quebec our money was running short. It was a weekend and moreover the Monday was some sort of public holiday. I had a checking account with a good bank into which my pay was credited at the end of each month. Overdrafts were illegal and desperate phone calls to my bank revealed that the money would only be available on the Tuesday, so we had a very lean weekend spending much of the time on the boardwalk outside the Chateau Frontenac! When it finally came through we joyously ate a large breakfast and set off on our long drive back to Detroit.

After a few days there my father went off on the train to Montreal for his voyage home via the St Lawrence Seaway. I believe he had greatly enjoyed his adventure despite the setbacks and it must have given him considerable cachet among his Rowing Club and Lodge friends. Visits to America were a rarity then.

NEWS FROM LONDON

I had been in regular correspondence with my friends since my arrival. Vic did not write much but Hazel did and she had stories to tell of parties and other socialisings. Since his exhibition the year before Vic had continued to be in favour with Erica Brausen who had bought three more of his nudes. But at the beginning of January 1957 came very different news: Vic had left the flat a day or two before Christmas and had not come back. Did I know anything of his whereabouts and plans? Of course I did not but it was obvious that he had made a momentous and probably definitive decision. Hazel persuaded herself that he would reappear after a few days and I wrote to her to say that I did not think he would and that it would be better for both of them if she did not expect or hope that he would. Eventually it emerged that he had gone to Paris to meet up with Paula, later going on to Portugal to be welcomed into the Rego household. Paula's father, Jose, was particularly considerate and understanding to Vic and in fact became a second father to him. They settled down at the family *quinta* in Ericeira painting and leading a quiet domestic life. I was not to know anything about this until later – and after much had happened to me – as I did not hear from Vic until February 1958 when for some reason he was spending a lonely time in Madrid.

At Lancaster Gate friends had rallied round to give Hazel support. Michael Andrews and Keith Sutton were in regular attendance and the latter kept me informed with quite a flood of letters. Vic had made a small financial provision for immediate expenses but this was no long-term solution to the question of whether the flat could be kept on or must be given up. After a few weeks Keith conveyed to me the surprising news that Hazel had found a degree of consolation with a twenty-five-year-old young man named Robin Cook. I will have more to say about Cook, now better known by his pen name Derek Raymond, later. Suffice it to say here that he was already involved with other ex-public school Chelsea-ites, who thought the world owed them a living, in a dubious property and rental business. I am unsure how Hazel had met him but clearly she saw in him someone on the make and a possible solution to her life of penury. She had always wanted a smart lifestyle and perhaps thought that this was the way to it. Lancaster Gate was given up and the household removed across the park and upmarket to a house in Trevor Place, Kensington! Mike Andrews was still around and Dick Wilson, who disliked and was very suspicious of Cook, also moved in. Keith did not leave Blackheath, where he was living with his parents, though he continued monitoring the situation. I never knew the house for when I returned from Detroit in the summer it had already been given up.

My year in Detroit was now up but the work was still going well and Carl told me I could stay on for as long as I wished and he even put up my stipend a bit. The second winter was as harsh as the previous one and I moved to another location closer to Wayne on West Warren; less of a battle through the snow. As the months went on I was perhaps beginning to feel a bit homesick. Philip Gundry had already returned to London and had got a lectureship at the Royal College of Science. Other friends were dispersed but I was anxious to follow them up and also, perhaps, to look to my future. Carl was now spending much of his time in Mexico City as director of research at Syntex. This was the company where he had done his early steroid research, notably the synthesis of 19-norprogesterone, the first orally active progestogen and precursor of 'the Pill'. Several of his doctoral and post-doctoral students had already moved down there to join the firm's very active research programme and I was told I could do the same if I wished but I wanted to go back to the UK first to see how I felt about this.

I was reluctant to leave my new friends but in late June it was time to go. One of them, the ever-considerate Louis, saw me off, as it were, and I took the train to Montreal having booked a passage from there like my father the year before. It was a slow crossing but at least a calm one in contrast to my journey out sixteen months before. I remember almost nothing about it. I went straight to Guildford and had a happy reunion with my parents but few, if any, old friends were to be found in the town.

A PERIOD OF INTERMISSION

I was soon back up in London. I had brought back little money with me and I asked my father for a loan (£200) to tide me over, which he freely granted. It was to last me for nearly five months. Philip Gundry had rented a small furnished basement flat in Kensington Gardens Square and he had brought back his Chevrolet convertible which, in those days, it was still possible to park outside your front door. I stayed with him, though he only had a sofa for me to sleep on, and also in similar conditions at his cousin Anne's house near Parson's Green. Eventually I had better accommodation in a large flat which Dick Wilson (who was still working at the *Financial Times*) had rented on Elgin Avenue. This was a time when the famous 'wind of change' was starting its sweep across Africa and Dick was much involved with African affairs. He often accommodated visiting African nationalists and during my stay there Kenneth Kaunda, later to be president of Zambia, was in permanent residence. We often shared the kitchen when getting our breakfasts.

I did not do much in the way of exploring job opportunities. I believe I had already made up my mind that I would take the Mexico option which, if I remember correctly, was not available immediately. I must confess that I spent a rather dissipated time (insofar as my limited means allowed) exploring the sleazier domains of West End nightlife including those small transient Soho drinking clubs which Angus Wilson has so well depicted. No harm came of it; quite the reverse.

One outing of note during this interlude came as the result of a letter I received, I think forwarded on from Guildford, from one of my young acquaintances of the Chiquito's espresso bar days (to be described later). He had been called up for National Service and had initially kept in touch with me but finally could not stand the life and had gone AWOL. 'On the run', as it were, he had turned to minor crime to survive, had eventually been caught and received a short prison sentence. He wanted to 'straighten everything out'; would I visit him in Durham prison? Visiting hours were at ten in the morning and to be there at that time I needed to take a night train. I arrived there at 5 am. It was still dark and in the deserted streets a few coal miners, wearing helmets with lamps attached, were going to or coming from their shifts. I walked up the long hill to the cathedral and went in (churches and cathedrals did not lock their doors in those days). I am not religious but I do have a sense of the numinous, strongly experienced there alone in that vast cavernous enclosure.

At the prison I waited with others in a cramped waiting room, handed over to a warder the few things prisoners were allowed to receive and was then faced with Pat (as I shall call him) behind a grill. He would be released only when I was already abroad but I promised to leave some modest postal orders with Philip that he could collect as needed. Years later, on my return from Mexico, I met up with him again when he seemed to be leading a reasonable life. Later still some indicators suggested that he was addicted to drugs (I assume heroin) and he robbed me by breaking into a gas meter, presumably to pay for them. We never met again.

I sometimes wonder what my parents made of this, my long period out of work and seemingly uncertain prospects at age 29. It must have made them anxious; did they discuss it together? Indeed, more generally, what was the nature and extent of their intercourse when we, my sister and I, were not there? I can never now know.

I was not entirely idle during these five months. My position in Carl's laboratory had been anomalous as a simple graduate, neither with, nor working for, a Ph.D. He had urged me to pursue one but to do so externally I had to take an M.Sc. first and I now successfully wrote up my National Gallery dammar work as a thesis for one. To anticipate: three years later, I wrote another thesis for my Ph.D. on my Syntex work, again successfully.

Eventually a date for my starting at Syntex was fixed and I arranged my journey there. I wanted to stop off in Detroit to meet up again with friends so I flew there first. It was bad weather and all passengers for the flight were taken up by train to Prestwick followed by the long, noisy flight. It was still propeller planes then. After a day or two it was down to Mexico City with a refuelling stop in Dallas.

8
MEXICO

It is hard for me to reduce my time in Mexico to a single chapter for it deserves a book. It can be no more than a taste.

A small flat had been found for me in Avenida Leibnitz, my landlord being a long Mexicanised Englishman of slightly dubious character with a passion for the novels of Dornford Yates.

I had no car so each morning I was given a lift to the Syntex facilities, which were a few kilometres out of town on the road to Toluca, by a fellow researcher, the Canadian John Edwards. I was to share a laboratory with him for much of my time there. We started work at 8 am, quite a shock for me, and went on until 1 pm with only a brief break for coffee which was brought round to us at the bench. It was a long morning and lunchtime came as a big relief. A free lunch was available in the staff canteen but one soon got sick of that and John, who was married and went home to lunch, would often drop me off at a good Argentine restaurant where commonly I ate a tender steak. Then it was back to work until 6 pm.

I was new to steroid chemistry, moreover this was synthesis rather than structure determination which I had been doing before. My first project was a new synthetic route to 19-norprogesterone. This was soon accomplished and I was put to synthesising new modified corticosteroids. There was a great race in progress between the big pharmaceutical companies to produce such compounds which would be even more pharmacologically effective than hydrocortisone or prednisolone. These had been known and synthesised in the 1940s and they remained a white hope for the treatment of arthritis and a number of skin conditions. I will summarise my work now so as to get on to more readable matters. I completed a synthesis of the sought-for compound, now known as fluocinolone acetonide. Its anti-inflammatory properties were indeed found to be many times those of hydrocortisone; much more than I had at first succeeded in making was needed for toxicity tests and other trials. I started again on an improved route and made eleven grammes of the compound which then passed to the development stage. By the time it was ready for marketing, after I had left, the use of corticosteroids systemically was in decline because of their severe side effects but Synalar, as it was now called, became important for topical application in skin allergies and other conditions such as psoriasis. I believe it remains so today.

During this work, which must have lasted for the best part of eighteen months or two years, I was not entirely unassisted. I was provided with intelligent graduates who could do some of the more routine chemistry and also a simple uneducated girl (Lupe, diminutive of Guadalupe) who watched over column chromatography separations. All conversation with them was in Spanish and as I had started off with an existing basic knowledge I soon became fluent. Mexican Spanish is easier than Castilian; it is spoken more slowly and the Zs and Cs are not lisped.

My starting pay (and I don't remember if it changed) was equivalent to about £200 a month, four or five times what I had ever had before, so I felt very well-off. I was soon able to repay my father his £200. He was delighted with the sterling draft covered with stamps, seals and signatures, and the reaction of his bank clerk who declared he had never seen such a thing before. He got the money but how on earth were such things negotiated in those days? By mysterious processes in the City, I suppose.

ACAPULCO

I had arrived only a short time before Christmas when there was to be a significant break. I longed to see the coast so flew down to Acapulco for the first of many stays there. I say down advisedly for Mexico City is at over seven thousand feet and I had felt the effects of this altitude. On arrival at sea level one is suddenly filled with energy.

There were two airline companies, Aeronaves de Mexico and Mexico de Aviacion, the latter operating the domestic flights which criss-crossed the country with old DC-3s (Dakotas). Taking these was remarkably informal, more or less like catching a bus, and one could buy a ticket and get on almost as the plane was about to take off. Flights were also very cheap; I think the fare to Acapulco was about £10.

I took a cab into town and asked the driver for suggestions as to where I might put up. He clearly sized me up accurately and took me to the Hotel Sans Souci, a small establishment in a raised position with a wonderful view which was owned by a Frenchwoman named Suzie. If I ever knew her last name I have long forgotten it. She ran a very relaxed establishment with no detectable rules or prohibitions which meant that all her guests behaved with kindness and consideration to her and to one another. It has always seemed to me to have been a very 'Tennessee Williams' sort of place. There were usually one or two Americans who appeared to have washed up there and might receive a remittance once a month or so. A good deal of rum and Coca-Cola was drunk (rum and other spirits cost only 30p a bottle) but, perhaps strangely, I do not remember that cannabis was smoked or even mentioned. This came to the fore in the next decade.

Acapulco was still a small place in the late 1950s. The long stretch along the bay, as one came in from the airport, was completely undeveloped and unused. Only Caleta Beach was built up as a resort and very delightful it was. I had not known such balmy air and seas since Colombo and I revelled in them. Delicious tropical drinks were available including coconut milk in the shell, supplemented with gin if desired. The large Pacific oysters were for sale as was also freshly prepared *ceviche* – raw fish pickled with lime juice. I soon developed a taste for this.

I was to return many times over my stay with Syntex, especially on weekends in the last year when I was sick of Mexico City. But I was also fond of Vera Cruz in the opposite direction on the Gulf. This had not developed into a resort, partly because the beach was not so attractive and had blackish sand. There were few tourists and one had the feeling of having it to oneself. It was very quiet; completely somnolent during the siesta hours. There was also a separate beach where delicious meals of excellent oysters, prawns and fish were to be had very cheaply.

DOMESTIC LIFE

Life on Avenida Leibnitz was rather dull at first and cultural experiences in short supply. There was no TV as far as I remember and little classical music on the radio. One went quite often to the cinema where British comedies were particularly popular, especially those with Alec Guinness. They were all dubbed into Spanish which helped one with the idiomatic language. There was also the nightlife, of course, mainly comprising the bars and mariachis off San Juan de Letran. On weekdays however, after a long day's work, I mostly stayed at home and cooked my dinner. The safety of food and drink much exercised everyone, though most particularly the Americans, especially the supposed danger of 'the amoebas' from water and uncooked vegetables. The tap water was deemed unsafe and drinking water, AquaPura, was bought in large carboys. Salad vegetables were sterilised in dilute hypochlorite solution. At home one drank very little alcohol. There was no wine and one had beer with meals, usually a Mexican brand named Dos Equis.

One evening in early 1958 I arrived home and nearly fell down the stairs when I found my old colleague Ian Graham sitting on the banisters outside the door to the flat. He had been in the USA and had come down almost on a whim to Mexico. In fact this was his first visit to the country and was to prove the start of his long adventures and career in Mayan archaeology, mostly in Guatemala.

Not long after this I had more companionship in my life as Riccardo Villotti came down from Detroit to join the team at Syntex. It was suggested that he stay with me pro tem but this settled into a permanency. Eventually he wanted to live in a larger flat and we secured one in Avenida Polanco, altogether a better district. I was to remain there for the rest of my stay. We took on an engaging daily maid, Margarita. She relieved us of all housework and sometimes had amusing stories to tell. She was of uncertain age and had a daughter. One day she told us she now had a grandson by her. '*Se compro un hijo*' ('She bought herself a baby') was how she put it.

TRAVELS

Saints days and other holidays are frequent in Mexico and I made good use of them for exploring the country. It's impractical to describe these trips in detail but I cannot resist mentioning some high points. On the Pacific coast there was delightful, isolated Zihuatanejo with its single hotel and deserted beach. Then there was Puerto Vallarta, still undeveloped and with no road connection, where I stayed in an old hotel which later I recognised in the Tennessee Williams film *The Night of the Iguana*. While there I went on a quite long boat trip to the otherwise inaccessible beach at Yelapa. On the way back there was a wonderful experience. A pod of cetaceans, a species unknown to me, started to swim alongside our small open boat; huge, twelve or fourteen foot speckled things breaking the surface as they lolloped along, sometimes within a couple of yards of us. It was not at all scary, rather quite joyous. The boatman was evidently familiar with this experience and he banged on the side of the boat which he said encouraged them.

On the Gulf side too there were interesting places, though of quite different character and with a longer history. Just down from Veracruz was a fishing village, Alvaro, and just inland from there the charming town of Tlacotalpan. Apparently it had once been an important port but the river had silted up and left it isolated. In its silent grass-grown streets children played or cantered merrily along on donkeys. In one of the single-storey houses I secured a memorable meal: crab with chilli and other spices put under the grill. One of the most delicious dishes I have enjoyed, I have never managed to recreate it.

Further down were the still small towns of Coatzocoalcos and Villahermosa, now, I believe, busy industrialised places on account of the petroleum industry. From there one took the train to Merida in Yucatan. This was an old colonial town still of markedly Spanish character where one got around by horse-drawn carriage. I went to the major Mayan sites such as Chichen Itza and rented a jeep and driver to take me to the other more inaccessible ones.

By far my biggest adventure came just a few months before leaving Mexico in 1960. I went to Palenque, the marvellous site then still only accessible by small plane from Villahermosa. There I encountered a young German archaeologist who, like me, was anxious if possible to visit the even more remote site at Yaxchilan on the Usumacinta River. Ian Graham, who had stayed with me once or twice during the past two years, had told me about it and how to get there. It was necessary to hire a small plane and pilot to fly to a river station named Agua Azul and go from there by boat. We arranged this in Villahermosa and set off in our four-seater Cessna. This was all done very impromptu and so we went without taking useful supplies with us which would have helped at Agua Azul. This was simply a clearing in the jungle by the river with a rough airstrip and a single large shed, and here we encountered two Conradian desperadoes who agreed to take us downriver in a large dugout canoe. An outboard motor existed but was unfortunately locked up in the big shed and its owner was away so the canoe had to be propelled manually. A fee was negotiated which was in fact quite modest.

Canoes are not comfortable and I chose to lie down flat looking up at the jungle, the macaws flying overhead and monkeys screaming in the trees. Of course I went to sleep and on waking could not immediately recall where, or even who, I was! I told myself not to panic, it would all come back, which indeed it did after less than a minute.

Having arrived at a small landing stage our boatmen made off, we knew not where, with the promise to return three days later. We introduced ourselves to the guardian of the site who lived there with his wife and small boy of about ten. Naturally he had had no notice of our advent but welcomed us with seeming interest (company was rare) and offered us the use of two hammocks strung outside near the river. We had not brought mosquito nets though I had brought anti-mosquito cream which was only partially effective. The following two nights however he took pity on us and produced two nets. Our hammocks were strung very close to the river and once I was awoken by flopping sounds. Big toads or frogs were making their way down over the mud. By day this mud was a wonderful sight. Myriad butter-flies, in colour groupings, settled on it, presumably for the moisture.

At one moment I was seized by a perverse desire somehow to possess this beauty and grabbed a handful which turned to dust and broken wings.

We were kindly offered food by our hosts in the form of river turtle stew – very acceptable. They lived a lonely life, this little family. The boy had never been anywhere else and so had had no schooling and never seen cars or trains. The guardian was slowly clearing an airstrip but it was still far from usable. They had some young macaws, taken from the nest, which they were feeding and bringing up on maize porridge.

The next day the boy escorted us through the ruins. These were still largely covered in jungle through which he hacked a way with his machete. Nothing had been removed; the wonderful lintels over the doorways were still in place. Later all of these were removed and placed, I believe, in the new museum in Chapultepec Park in Mexico City. I took many photographs which tragically never came out. The advance mechanism in my camera seemed to have stuck and my three 36-exposure films came back blank. One of the biggest disappointments of my life and I still cannot understand it.

After three nights we were pleased when our boatmen reappeared and took us back upriver, naturally a slower journey than the downward trip. To our great surprise, when we arrived there was our friend the site guardian! He had made a calculation: there would be a spare seat in the plane and perhaps we would give him a lift to Villahermosa, so he had followed us on foot. Of course we agreed to take him once our little plane reappeared that afternoon.

I had plans for further travels and so got set down at Tenosique to continue to Merida. There I said goodbye to my German friend whose name, sad to say, I have long since forgotten.

From Merida I made a side trip to Cozumel. Ian had told me of a single hotel there run, so he said, by a grandson of Neville Chamberlain, our one-time prime minister. I did stay there but never had the courage to ask my English host whether he was indeed that. I was, in fact, the only guest; fine by me. The deserted beach was littered with huge conch shells and there was a marvellous lagoon, connected to the sea by underwater channels, full of brilliantly coloured fish which one could swim among. One evening we were visited by two sailors from a small ship engaged in some coastal trading. They were Hondurans from the Mosquito Coast and they spoke preferentially a very strange English which I found hard to understand. I asked them to speak Spanish but they were not very comfortable with that.

I went back to Merida so as to fly on to Belize in British Honduras, now the name for the country itself. This seemed the strangest little place, far more backward than Mexico, and I put up in a small hotel which faced a river or inlet crossed by a bridge. I stood on this to take in the view but doing so was evidently against the rules for small schoolchildren as they passed me all said 'Not to stand on the bridge. Not to stand on the bridge!'

I was aiming for Tikal in the Petén, Guatemala and I took a bus to Benque Viejo on the border, from where there was supposed to be a flight. I stayed there overnight in a primitive 'hotel' and did indeed get this plane for the short flight the following day.

Staying in Tikal was relative luxury as there was a team of Americans working on the buildings there and they were, of course, well provided with comforts.

Tikal is one of the best preserved of the Mayan sites and has the much photographed 'Temple of Ah Cacao' with its formidable height and very steep steps. Yet many other buildings were still half concealed in jungle and it was fun to seek these out. I think I stayed a couple of nights and then took a plane to Guatemala City.

I had still further plans and took a flight to Copan in Honduras, changing planes in San Salvador. In Copan there was actually a small village and a hotel immediately adjacent to the marvellously preserved site with its superb stelas and almost complete structures such as the ball court.

I stayed for two nights and then flew back to Guatemala City from where I took a bus to Chichicastenango. This was already the most visited town in the country yet there were only a few foreigners besides myself. The town is marvellously picturesque on account of the market and the brilliant costumes and jewellery of the native women. Here I took many photographs which *did* come out. Then it was to Quetzaltenango where I bought two splendid locally woven blankets (I still have them), afterwards returning to the capital to fly back to Mexico City.

TRAVELS WITH PARENTS

The year before the above adventures I had a long tour with my parents. I was able now to better meet all expenses than three years before with my father and I was anxious that my mother should also be a participant. We arranged that we would meet in New York but there were many arrangements that had first to be considered and dealt with. Although I had no car in Mexico I had secured my Mexican driving license. In order to work in that country I had been required to enter with the status of *inmigrante* – an immigrant – and as such I was not allowed to bring in a car bought in the United States, at least not without paying some enormous tax. Obviously we had to have a car and as my only experience of buying one had been in Detroit I decided I should go there to buy one, which I did. On Jefferson Avenue I spotted a wonderful 1957 Chrysler New Yorker convertible and immediately fell in love with it. In short I bought it and registered it somehow in my father's name for the purpose of entering Mexico.

I drove to New York, found a hotel and met my parents who had come over on the *Queen Elizabeth*. It was more than eighteen months since I had seen them so it was quite a joyous reunion. No doubt it was especially so for them since they must have been anxious to see me waiting for them on the quayside. We forget now that we had no telephones or email, all arrangements had to be made days, even weeks beforehand by letter so unanticipated slip-ups were always possible. But all was well.

Nowadays a visit to America is no big deal but it was then and we were about to set off on a very long journey. When I look back on it I cannot but see myself as daring, if not rash, in putting my parents, who were now 72 and 62, through it. What insurance did I have? Did I have any? I just don't remember. Much could have gone wrong but for the most part didn't and they stood up well to the long drives.

We spent a few days in New York for my mother's benefit, activities including a memorable visit to the theatre to see Tennessee Williams's *Sweet Bird of Youth* with Paul Newman and also the original production of *West Side Story*.

So we set off west, back in fact along the Pennsylvania Turnpike I had traversed from Detroit, and spent a night in Cleveland. Then it was Chicago for two nights and on to Omaha. The car was a joy to drive and as there were no speed limits we sometimes touched a hundred on the open roads. The landscape of the Great Plains is monotonous and one is content not to linger. It was all new to my mother and she kept notes of all the novelties she spotted: drive-ins, burger bars and fried chicken vendors, motels and gas stations. She also noted all our stays and hotels which (when I can read her handwritten notes) fills me in with these forgotten details. After Omaha we got into more interesting scenery in Colorado and made three stops there: a motel in Yuma, another in Boulder, and a third in Grand Junction to view the impressive canyons of Colorado National Monument. Then it was over the still snow-capped Rockies into Utah for a night in Salt Lake City at the Hotel Congress. Counties in Utah have differing drink laws and getting a glass of beer for my father was tricky, I recall. So on we went for a night in Reno, that mini-Las Vegas, for a taste of US gambling culture. Then it was another mountain range to cross, the Sierra Nevada, passing Donner Lake and Donner Pass, where again there was snow despite it being now the end of May. Finally we were into San Francisco where we found a nice hotel, the Beresford, near Union Square. We needed a bit of a rest from the long drives and stayed for three nights enjoying the sights of the city but also crossing the Golden Gate Bridge to Marin County to visit Muir Woods and the giant redwoods. Nine years later I was to visit them again.

I was determined that we should see the Grand Canyon despite its being rather a diversion from our direct route south to Mexico. We set off across the Mojave Desert and stopped for a night at a motel in Ludlow. At Grand Canyon we got rooms at Bright Angel Lodge, on the rim. I see that this historic hotel (built 1933), with its stupendous views over and down into the Canyon, is still in operation today. My mother put a luncheon menu into her scrapbook and it is interesting now to note the prices. Main courses and varied salads were around $1.35; desserts 35¢; tea and coffee 15¢. And this was at a time when the pound was still at the fixed rate of $2.80. My parents had adjusted to the prices yet they probably didn't seem cheap to them. Ten shillings for a main course! Why, you could get a complete meal for less than that in Guildford.

Had I been on my own I would have taken a trip into the Canyon but that was obviously impossible with my parents. Anyway, we could not linger as there was much ahead of us. We went on to Nogales, crossed the frontier (no problem with my father-registered car), stayed a night and continued to Guaymas on the coast. We were glad to get there for it had been unbelievably hot inland. My mother had always loved the beach and the sea so we stayed there two nights as did we also further down at Mazatlan and San Blas. Alas, 'Montezuma's revenge' hit my father and made him really ill so we had to stay four nights at Guadalajara (in a very nice hotel) while he recovered.

Back in Mexico City Riccardo had kindly moved out temporarily from our flat so that they could be accommodated. I, of course, had to show up at Syntex after what was considered to be rather a long holiday. At the weekend, however, I drove them down to Acapulco where I left them at the Caleta Beach Hotel for a couple of nights. They came back on the plane for a few more days and then it was needful to get them, and the car, back into the US.

We made the long drive up to Nuevo Laredo with an overnight stop in San Luis Potosi. We settled into a motel over the border in Laredo, Texas. I had arranged flights (how I can't now imagine) for my parents to Houston; a night's stay there and a flight to New York. This they managed without incident and then, after a further two nights in that city, they were safely back on board the *Queen Elizabeth* for the voyage home. In Laredo I found a small garage which agreed to house the car for as long as need be and I flew back to Mexico City.

It had been a wonderful tour and it gave my parents much to talk about back with their different circles of friends. I know that my mother gave a presentation about it to her Women's Institute and it should have given my father yet more cachet among his Masonic friends.

DECISIONS FOR THE FUTURE

Sometime in early 1960 news got to me of a possible opening in the conservation world in New York. Although my work at Syntex was still going well and was very interesting, I had mixed feelings about where I wanted to settle down. I was, after all, now 31 and I could not continue in temporary positions indefinitely. It was open to me to stay on with Syntex but I was tired of my life in Mexico City, where I never felt perfectly well. I was quite homesick for England and my friends there but a well-paid job ($15,000) in New York also had its attractions. It was to head a newly formed Conservation Center attached to the Institute of Fine Arts in New York. I wrote applying for the position and was called to New York for interview.

The Center was to be established in the former Doris Duke house on East 78th Street (now it is in a purpose-built facility nearby) and this was still completely unconverted. My board of interviewers included old stalwarts of the American conservation scene: George Stout, Rutherford Gettens and Sheldon Keck. The interview seemed to go well and there was also a pleasant lunch. Afterwards I crossed 5th Avenue and sat on a bench in Central Park to think it over. Before me a motley crowd of pigeons, starlings, squirrels and rats picked at bread and scraps left there by well-meaning New Yorkers. There was no squabbling; they all seemed to get on well together and I wondered if this was a paradigm of life in this city. Would I blend in? I had my doubts about this but also about the job itself. I wanted to continue with at least some research but it looked as though organisation and administration would be my lot for some time before this would be possible, if ever it would. On the whole I thought I would write and decline the job once I got back to Mexico City and this is what I did. Of course I never did know whether I would have been offered it. Eventually the position was filled by Larry Majewski, whom I got to know well later.

I never regretted that decision but I wonder now whether it was a consequence of an innate conservatism in my nature or, indeed, a fear of taking on unfamiliar responsibilities. I have to confess that twice in my later career I turned down important positions, one professional, the other honorary. At the same time I did seek, and accept, others and I continued on a path that I thought best suited me. Once again I bethought me of Brutus's speech: 'There is a tide in the affairs of men…'

Did I make the right decision? What opportunities did I lose? But it *can* be the right thing to continue on the same old road.

FAREWELL TO MEXICO

During the first few months of 1960 it became clearer to me that my future – at least my immediate future – lay in England. Nobody wanted me to leave Syntex but I knew I could not commit myself to working in Mexico City forever. I made preparations for departure and the trip back to the UK with my car and somehow organised the paperwork needed to import the latter.

After parties and fond farewells with my by then long-term colleagues I left, with such baggage as I could carry, one night in June on the *Aguila Azteca*, a sleeper train, up to Nuevo Laredo. I picked up my car, which seemed to be in fair condition, if rather dusty, and set off.

I have largely forgotten the details of that journey back to New York but I was determined to see New Orleans and made my way there first. It was terribly hot and humid there (still ninety degrees Fahrenheit at midnight) but my modest hotel fortunately had air conditioning. Of course I spent time in Bourbon Street. I saw the streetcar named Desire and lingered in the cocktail bars where one's icy drink was surrounded by further ice in another vessel to prevent melting and 'that dilution which is such anathema to the true cocktail lover', as the bar menu explained.

The drive from there up to New York must have involved at least one night on the road but I have no memories of it. In NY I went back to the old Knickerbocker Hotel near Times Square, where we had stayed the previous year, now pretty run-down. I was there for a couple of nights and took the opportunity of seeing *Fidelio* at the old Metropolitan Opera House. Why did they knock it down? So much nicer than its replacement.

Finally it was down to the docks where I and the car went aboard the *Mauretania* for the voyage to Southampton, from where I drove up to Guildford for a happy reunion.

9
INTO THE SIXTIES

So once again I was jobless in the UK. I needed somewhere to live in London while I looked out for one and Philip Gundry put me up in his newly converted flat in Loudoun Road Mews (now long since 're-developed'). He and Keith Sutton had become friends since their first meeting during my stay with Dick Wilson in Elgin Avenue in 1957 and Keith had designed and undertaken the refurbishment of this charming mews flat.

I made applications here and there. Glaxo offered me a job at a pitiful £1000 a year which I declined. An opening with the Mars company, down near Havant, which was trying to develop an oral contraceptive for pets, did not appeal, mainly because of its out-of-town location. I was offered a three-year contract at The National Institute for Medical Research at Mill Hill but Derek Barton advised me against further short-term positions: at my age I should be looking for a permanency.

Indeed I had spent nine years in un-pensionable research and that could not continue indefinitely. Yet nothing seemed to appeal. I was, in fact, experiencing a powerful feeling of rootlessness and uncertainty as to where I belonged. Had it been a mistake to leave Syntex? No one had asked me to and I was free to go back. Should I have pursued that opening in New York? Philip was a lecturer at Imperial College; shouldn't I be seeking an academic position or was it too late for that? With some misgivings I finally accepted a job with the pharmaceutical division of British Drug Houses (BDH), whose laboratories were located on Wharf Road in Islington. The salary was £1,300.

The man in charge of research was one Vladimir Petrow. He had formerly been an academic and I had known his work on triterpenes when I was working on dammar. Now, as with most pharmaceutical companies, he was doing steroid work with his sights on an oral contraceptive. The buildings and facilities seemed horribly old and even squalid and the company had an ossified hierarchical structure so different to Syntex. Most of the chemists in the lab simply did what they were told; they did not pursue, or did not have, ideas of their own. I was allowed to follow one of mine for a new reaction (successfully) in addition to making routine derivatives for patent purposes. On the whole though working there was a depressing experience. The only thing I enjoyed about it was my drive there and back every day in my Chrysler. I still remember the drumming of the tyres as I drove over the cobblestones in Agar Grove – since covered with tarmac.

I had been in touch with former friends and colleagues at the National Gallery. Ian Rawlins had now retired and Garry Thomson had moved up into his position of Scientific Adviser and Head of Department. That meant that his position as chemist was now vacant and, always preferring the familiar to the unknown, he suggested that I should apply for it. In short I did and after due process I moved back there in the summer of 1961 as a senior scientific officer with a salary of £1,700. There had been some strains on my relationship with Philip at Loudoun Road Mews and at the suggestion of Joyce Plesters, my old friend in the Department since 1951, I rented a small furnished flat in the street where she lived, Clifton Hill, St. John's Wood. It was still possible then to park my car in the road outside without restrictions, and I was able to drive to work and then enter by the loading bay directly to the Department, which had relocated to a new spot at the back of the building.

HELMUT RUHEMANN

Tacked on to our north wall was a sort of conservatory occupied by Helmut Ruhemann, the Gallery's consultant restorer. Helmut had worked on the paintings since before the War, having left Germany in 1934 with the rise of the Nazis. I am not going to allow myself here to be sucked in to any discussion of the so-called 'cleaning controversy'. Much of this was purely political and personal and now, with the public better informed on technical matters, largely ancient history.

Helmut always joined us for our tea and coffee breaks and one also had the opportunity to see him at work more or less up until the time of his death in 1974. Among the notable paintings needing major restoration was the *Rokeby Venus* of Velazquez, which had been slashed by a suffragette in 1914. The repairs and retouchings done at that time were starting to show and had to be undone and done afresh. Faint signs of the damage are still visible today, as was in fact intended, and the restoration has stood up well over time. Another major work he cleaned was Piero della Francesca's *St. Michael*. This was originally one of four side panels which flanked a central, now lost, image, probably of the Madonna and Child. Obviously panel paintings are likely to have suffered significant damage over the course of more than 500 years; there had also been alterations, presumably done before it was acquired by the Gallery in 1867, to make it look more of a 'stand-alone' painting. When it was back on display, after Helmut had worked on it, it struck me that the saint had a slightly quizzical expression from wear or damage to his left eyebrow. I suggested this to Helmut and he gave a characteristic response (which Joyce Plesters loved mischievously to imitate): 'O-o-o-o-h no. I don't think so.'

Later I noticed something else. St. Michael is wearing beautiful boots ornamented with pearling around the rim. On one of these a part of the rim is missing and the pearls float loose. Again I mentioned this to Helmut.

'O-o-o-o-h no. I don't think so [pause] but I tell you what I should have done. I should have retouched the eyebrow.'

Today (2016) things remain as they were and it doesn't matter at all. Let no mischief-maker try to make anything of it.

I hope the above does not give the impression that by now Helmut was an 'old dodderer': he was anything but. He remained interested in and receptive of the new and not only with what we were doing in the Scientific Department. In 1964 a group of us went down to the Whitechapel Gallery for the exhibition of the paintings and 'combines' of Robert Rauschenberg and Helmut came too. We were all excited and enthusiastic. When we came out into the street our eyes seemed to have been opened and we saw 'Rauschenbergs' everywhere we looked.

WORK AT THE GALLERY

Back at work I was at first quite uncertain as to where to direct my efforts. One perennial problem was open to investigation: that of finding a more durable and non-yellowing varnish for newly cleaned paintings. Garry Thomson had looked into and promoted the use of a synthetic material named MS2A and this had proved satisfactory. There were however problems with consistency as the suppliers were wont to change their methods of production. Moreover restorers still had a strong preference for using the natural resins dammar and mastic, which they believed gave a better final result. I looked into the effects of modifying them by hydrogenation (saturating the double bonds made them less susceptible to oxidative degradation) but this proved impracticable on the larger scale. Ultimately, it must be acknowledged that these efforts came to nothing. I decided to direct myself more towards analysis.

Paint is a combination of mostly inorganic mineral pigments and an organic binding medium, typically egg or drying oil in Western painting. The identification of the pigments was already established and was carried out by Joyce Plesters. Of course with pigments there is an immediate indicator of possible identity, namely the colour. There are no such clues for the identity of the medium, which any-way is far more complex in composition and has also changed with the drying process. It seemed to me that the only possible approach to the problem was the use of gas chromatography.

Since Archer Martin's initial experiments, which I had witnessed in 1951, the method had been taken up fairly widely. At first people made their own equipment but some was now produced commercially. It was very expensive, we had very limited funds in the Department and for long I was not confident that the outlay would prove to be justified. No other museum or gallery in the world had done this. I finally decided to press for it, the money was found (about £1,000; cf. my salary of £1,700) and a Pye Panchromatograph was bought.

I will try now to avoid details but I embarked on an investigation of the fatty acid composition of dried oil films. Surprisingly this had never been undertaken, even in the paint and varnish industry where one might have thought it was of some importance. The results were more or less as might have been predicted from the chemist's viewpoint but they provided a way to distinguish egg tempera from oil and were also an indication of which drying oil – linseed, walnut or poppy seed – this might be. This was a big advance in the study of paint media and has remained its basis since. In 1963 I presented these results at a conference in Leningrad and Moscow and they were later published more fully in *Studies in Conservation*, the IIC journal.

FRIENDS

I devote a succeeding chapter to the numerous and interesting café friends I made in Soho but I want now to update the histories of my long-standing ones. Before that I must mention the fascinating survival of an old-fashioned eating house of the kind which could have been described by Smollet in such novels about London as *Humphry Clinker*. It was located in the upper half of Whitcomb Street (since demolished for a garage and parking building) and was called The Old English Coffee House. It was not a coffee house but a restaurant with one large room with tables round the walls and a large central table where single people willing or desirous to enjoy the company of others would sit. On the way in one encountered a row of chefs in full chef attire standing behind large vessels containing the dishes of the day. These might include stuffed hearts, jugged hare, shin of beef, steak and kidney pudding and other such substantial fare. After making a choice one sat down and it would be brought to you with accompanying vegetables. Some clients had been regular lunchers there for many years and when it closed were quite at a loss as to where else to go. Maurer's in Greek Street had vanished so I would use this wonderful place when needing a heart-warming meal. One day it had special visitors. Michael Caine brought in his young friend Terence Stamp, still fresh from his success as Billy Budd in the Peter

Ustinov film and still with his bleached blond hair. Everyone knew who they were but studiously left them unmolested.

I have mentioned Keith Sutton as carrying out the interior decoration of Philip's mews flat. He had a talent for this and later, at the end of the decade, he did the same for David Sylvester's flat in Melrose Road, Wandsworth. His professional life as an artist was as insecure as for most of his generation but he had had a one-man show in 1958, while I was abroad, at a gallery in South Molton Street in which he had shown some twenty-four paintings and a portfolio of drawings. These were mostly landscapes done swiftly in a very impressionistic style but they also included some remarkable snow scenes, some of which still grace my walls. The show had good reviews and a few of the paintings were sold but it failed to launch a financially secure career. Depressed he had moved to Putney, living in some seclusion at first but then less so in the house of Ronald Alley, the art historian, in Deodar Road. He had also now changed his style, embarking on a long series of collage paintings which he was to show at the prestigious Hanover Gallery in 1962. Here again he was to suffer some disappointment, for despite some very good reviews only a few of the works were sold. He was particularly disappointed that David Sylvester, on behalf of the Arts Council, bought only a small work which Keith did not think one of his more important ones.

Well before this Keith's parents had moved from Blackheath to Cranleigh in Surrey and I would often drive him down there at weekends on my way to Guildford. This was more frequently the case after the Guildford to Cranleigh rail line closed in 1965, a victim of Dr Beeching's report. Keith's elder brother had been killed in the War, his plane shot down over Holland, so his parents, particularly his mother after his father's death, became increasingly emotionally dependent on him. This greatly constrained the teaching work which he could undertake. From the mid-sixties, as well as writing criticism for *The Listener* and taking on editorship of the arts section of the new but short-lived magazine *London Life*, he was teaching part-time at Stourbridge Art School but he gave this up when it became a full-time position.

DAVID SYLVESTER

By the early 1960s David was settled with Pamela and their two small daughters in a small house in Wandsworth, address now forgotten. Philip, who also knew them well, and I would sometimes be asked there to a meal. I remember that at one time David had a large felt sculpture by some American artist whose name I have also now forgotten. It consisted of long strips of felt, bunched at one end and suspended on the wall, the lengths of felt arranging themselves in variable ways down to the floor below. Obviously this was an irresistible hiding place for his two very young daughters and David would become almost hysterical when he saw this happening. I don't know what became of this work of art later when it was replaced by others.

On another occasion we four were due to meet at a small nightclub where I was to await the other three. As they were about to enter David halted and said (of me) to Philip 'But suppose he's making a *touche*!' I wasn't but David's hesitation was absolutely characteristic. He saw erotic adventure as paramount; not simply desirable but almost an obligation. This utterly French attitude must have been instilled or confirmed in him during his first visits to Paris after the War in the late 1940s. I think this was in a way acknowledged in the remark he sometimes made to me in later years: 'You're a fifties man, I suppose. I'm a forties man.'

During the sixties the BBC Home Service broadcast a weekly programme called *The Critics* (in the seventies, *Critics Forum*). New events in film, theatre, literature, music and the visual arts were presented by each specialist followed by general discussion. David was for a long time on the panel and of course had to go to the events. He must have been allowed tickets for two and as I was unattached and available he used often to ask me to go with him. I think he liked to have someone with him to test his ideas and reactions on. I have completely forgotten the films we saw but I do remember one or two of the plays. One was *East* by Steven Berkoff put on at the Regent Theatre during its brief existence in the Regent Street Polytechnic from 1974-9. David must have been tired and the play was rather boring.

He kept falling asleep and slumping sideways against me. After one such episode he demanded 'What did they say? What did they say?'

'I can't remember everything,' said I.

'But *you* were *awake*,' protested David.

David's love of making lists and ranking things in order of merit has been often remarked on. This extended to almost everything, even to trying to decide whether Typhoo or PG Tips was the better tea.

FAME IF NOT FORTUNE

In 1961, shortly before I started work back at the National Gallery, I was in that vicinity and on the way up to Soho for lunch. At that time a large temporary building, on a bombed site, stood on the corner of Wardour Street and Duncannon Street, adjacent to Leicester Square. It had been occupied by the store Debenhams who had now vacated it (it was later replaced by the Swiss Centre, itself now demolished and replaced). As I passed I saw that it was full of large, rather strident paintings including a *Last Supper* peopled with familiar media figures of the day. A poster announced that all this was the work of Andrew Vicari, whom I could just see within strolling importantly about. I could not bring myself to go in and resume our former acquaintance.

The exhibition attracted a fair amount of newspaper attention. It turned out that it had been put on by Jack Hylton, the band leader and impresario. There was an illustrated catalogue (price 2/6) which was being sold for the benefit of a charity. As well as in the *Last Supper* there were numerous portraits of well-known personalities including one of Aneurin Bevan which Hylton bought and gave to the National Library of Wales. Despite the media attention (I remember a photograph of Andrew, smoking an enormous cigar, next to Paul Getty at a dinner), it seems that few other sales were achieved and Andrew fell back into relative obscurity for the next twenty years or so.

I will very briefly summarise the situations of other old friends during the early sixties. Vic and Paula had ventured back to London and now resided in Albert Street, Camden Town with their three young children, Caroline (Cas), Victoria and Nicholas. Vic was painting, but for the most part rarely finishing, large pictures which sadly all too often got painted over. Many good things, which still remain in my memory, were lost in this way. Paula too was being copiously creative and was less subject to destructive doubts. Some of her work was getting shown, notably at the Institute of Contemporary Arts in Dover Street.

I had renewed occasional contact with Hazel. She had had, as they say, her ups and downs. Her relationship with Robin Cook had been, I think, fairly stormy, though they had had good times travelling together in France and Spain. She had also had some brushes with the law herself but in the early 1960s she was living alone in a flat in Eccleston Square where she still received old friends from Vic's Slade days. I visited her on one day, it might have been in 1962 or 1963, when something extraordinary was going on. About half a dozen of us were there, though I only specifically remember Euan Uglow, and a news event was being followed on the television. Robin Cook had branched out in his criminal career and had attempted, with certain of his Chelsea friends, an insurance scam. They had been in Holland and had claimed that a 'Rembrandt' painting they were in possession of had been stolen. I forget the details of their scheme but it had been met with disbelief from the Dutch police and the goings on there were being avidly followed by the media. They seemed to have been half under arrest but had been released and allowed to return on a ferry to the UK. 'I know he'll come here, I know he will,' Hazel kept saying. Indeed he did.

The doorbell rang and he came in. He could hardly have been anticipating such a large reception committee and his eyes darted piercingly round the room: friend or foe? I have only ever seen that look once again; at a wedding reception for a friend's son, given by the Maxwells. Robert Maxwell greeted the arriving guests. His look and assessment of me was like lightning: of no great account was his instant conclusion.

We, the guests at Hazel's, soon realised that we were de trop and made our departures. Outside I talked with Euan about all this and offered him a lift but he roared off on his motorbike.

REMOVAL

Early in 1965 I had two 'lifestyle' decisions to make. Firstly I had now had my big car with me in London for approaching five years and it was getting to be expensive to run and maintain. I decided to sell it, which I did for a very modest sum, replacing it with something at the other end of the scale – a Mini. Secondly I was tired of my small furnished flat and felt I deserved an unfurnished place which I could make more personal. My landlords offered a two bedroom garden flat in Abercorn Place, not far away from Clifton Hill, at £475 a year. Modest as this now sounds it was a big fraction of my salary so I decided initially to share it with my friend Ted. We worked hard on beautifying it and getting the garden under control. Initially we had almost no furniture but second-hand semi-antique items were very cheap then (it was before the *Antiques Roadshow*) and I soon acquired basic items as well as some better things which I still have. I bought curtain materials from Heals which my mother made up for me but the most significant embellishment was Paula's picture *Centaur and Harpy*, exhibited earlier that year at the ICA, which she most generously gave me.

NEIGHBOURS

At the end of the garden, on the other side of the wall, was a large studio with big windows. Within one could see paintings for this was, and had been for many years, occupied by Lilian Somerville, Director of Fine Arts at the British Council. Although we were often only a few yards apart, the large windows did not open and we never actually spoke, though we would acknowledge each other through the glass. Of course she often had visitors from the art world including Lucian Freud. I used to bump into him sometimes in adjacent Nugent Terrace. Once he came round the corner driving a large car (I think an old Rolls), took one hand off the wheel and waved vigorously to me, imperilling all in the vicinity. Another time I was waiting outside while my clothes rotated in the launderette and he appeared holding a bag of sweets close to his chest, the other hand poised half in it, and he remained like this throughout our conversation. He did not offer me one.

Hilda at East Dean, 1915
Lena and Hilda. A windy day at Bognor, 1921
Bachelor days with Guildford Rowing Club, 1920. Centre, Harry with cards. Left, brother Ted

ABOVE   Parents' wedding at East Dean, 1924

ABOVE RIGHT   June's christening, 1926

RIGHT   The Thornes visit to see June, 1926

BELOW   A picnic, Goodwood, with baby June and Grandfather William Stuart, 1927

ABOVE LEFT   Grandmother Anne Stuart at Oxted Green, Milford, 1931

ABOVE RIGHT   I am shown to my sister, 1928

LEFT   Lena, Hilda, June and the author at Bognor, 1930

BELOW   At Bury Street, 1932

ABOVE   Bognor, 1930. Goat carts are pleasant and exciting...

LEFT   But ponies are nice to

ABOVE LEFT   Madge, Lena and Hilda at Sandown, 1936

LEFT   With evacuees Ronny and Susan, 1940

BELOW LEFT   Swanage, 1939. Our last family holiday

BELOW RIGHT   With Susan in my little canoe, 1941

ABOVE   The author with June [...]
home, 1946

BELOW LEFT   Hazel, David Jones and [...]
author sitting on the l[...]
gates, Millmead, 1945/6. [...]
War finally over, at last [...]
seemed to be going well w[...]
the world for three 17-y[...]
olds

BELOW   A Sunday walk, 1945/6. [...]
author and Hazel

ABOVE   Catterick Camp with my fellow radio mechanic trainees, 1947
BELOW LEFT   By the lake in Rangoon, 1948
BELOW RIGHT   The great freeze at Catterick, February 1947

ABOVE LEFT   College boy, 1949
ABOVE RIGHT   Slade Ball. Vic, Hazel and (right) Keith Sutton
BELOW   Slade Ball, 1949. A face in the crowd

ᴠᴇ ʟᴇғᴛ   Hazel with Michael Andrews, 1957. After Vic's flight abroad Mike, a good friend to
               both Vic and Hazel, stepped in to give support

ᴠᴇ ʀɪɢʜᴛ   Hazel with Robin Cook. They embarked on quite a long affair

ᴏᴡ   Sunday morning coffee at Colville Square, 1953. Vic and the author

ABOVE LEFT   In the lab at the National Gallery, 1953
ABOVE RIGHT   Standing by the Detroit River with Windsor, Canada on the far bank, 1956
BELOW LEFT   American tour with parents, 1959. Motel in Yuma, Colorado
BELOW RIGHT   In the Rockies

ABOVE LEFT   At work: Syntex, Mexico City, 1958
ABOVE RIGHT   At play: Caleta beach Acapulco
BELOW   Avenida Polanco, with Riccardo Villotti

ABOVE   Zihuatanejo. The boy dug up these clams
BELOW   Puerta Vallarta. Red snapper ready for roasting on the beach

ABOVE LEFT   John Zderic, 1960. A good friend until his death in August 2016

ABOVE RIGHT   Bert Bowers. After rising to the highest position at Syntex, Bert sadly died aged only 60

LEFT   In the lab with John Edwards and our co-workers

BELOW   Back in the UK, in my much loved Chrysler, 1960

TOP	Pleased fishermen on the Gordon River, Tasmania, 2004
MIDDLE	Saltwater Creek Penal Colony, Tasman Peninsula
BOTTOM	Tony Werner

UPPER LEFT Goodwood Sculpture Park, 1998. Carl Djerassi sitting on the Bill Woodrow sculpture he and Diane later presented to the British Library

LOWER LEFT A view of my *Carpets in Paintings* exhibition, the National Gallery, 1983

A carpet-seeking trip to Portugal, 2007. Jacqueline and Michael Franses and the author at Sintra

ABOVE LEFT   Paula at home
ABOVE RIGHT   With Louis Sucheston at the British Library, 2000
BELOW   Ingeborg von Kusserow with husband Kenneth at their cottage at
               Houghton, W. Sussex, 1995

Lilian lived on until 1985 and in her later years I would see her sometimes on her roof, now a rather lonely and skeletal figure.

The house to my eastern side was also a Jellinek property and tenants there came and went as they also did in the four flats above me. On the other side of my garden wall, however, I soon became aware of, and friends with, its occupant.

INGEBORG

Ingeborg von Kusserow, to give her the name by which she was known during her career as an actress in Germany in the 1930s and '40s, was born and grew up (she always told me) in Silesia, though she said little about her parents. Something of her life, and much about her film work, can now be found on the Internet so I need say little about it. She would make light of it and say that 'they' always got everything wrong. The information is probably more accurate now but she was, in any case, far prouder of her stage work, for she had appeared as a dancer and singer in operetta (she had started at 16, she told me) and acted in serious plays including the role of Eliza Doolittle in in Bernard Shaw's *Pygmalion*. She met Percy von Welsburg in 1938 and they planned to marry but there were complications of nationality to be sorted out first: he, though of Hungarian parentage and with a Hungarian passport, had actually been born in England; she, a German, would become an alien on their marriage. They finally married in September 1940 with a plan of escape via Italy but this never worked out and they were forced to remain in Berlin throughout the War, enduring all its horrors. They were only able to get away to England, with their young son Patrick, in 1947. A year later she described all this in a book, *Enough, No More*, under her newly adopted name of Ingeborg Wells and translated (more likely ghosted from her narration) by one Lord Sudley. She never mentioned this book to me and I learnt of it and found a copy only in 2010.

But all this was a distant memory from a vanished world and was scarcely referred to when we first became friends, over the garden wall, in 1965. I believe she had lived there for many years but she and Percy were now separated and planning divorce. Taking Percy's place (they were able to marry in 1968) was Kenneth Slingsby-Fahn, a bluff but kindly and sensitive ex-air force officer who lived locally and had never quite found his way in civilian life. He was now working with an old-established wine merchants in St. James's. We too became very good friends along with one of his friends, Robert Rose, who came to live nearby and who was devoted to Ingeborg. We made a merry group, always entertaining one another at meals or in conversation over the wall. I also witnessed many visits from old friends and admirers of Ingeborg from her German life as she showed them round her little plot.

This continued until 1979. Sadly Robert Rose had died of pancreatitis and had left everything to Ingeborg (he had no discoverable living relatives) including his flat. She and Kenneth had also managed to buy a lease on their flat (I think for £3000!) and so upon selling both they were able to buy and move to a much-desired cottage in Houghton, West Sussex. I continued to visit them there for many years.

In the winter of 1968 Ingeborg was persuaded by old admirers to go back to Berlin and appear once again on the stage. The play was to be a German translation of Robert Anderson's *You Know I Can't Hear You When the Water's Running* which had been a success the year before in New York. I chanced upon an advertisement for a 'special offer' short visit to West Berlin by train which was too good to miss and so went off via the Harwich – Hook of Holland ferry and train across northern Europe that I had taken five years before (see below). That time I had only changed trains there but now I put up in a hotel on the Kurfürstendamm close to the Komödie theatre. Berlin was not then the vibrant, cosmopolitan city it is today but reconstruction had centred around the Ku'damm which was quite lively and the show was playing to good houses. The play was made up of four unrelated short pieces. In one Ingeborg made herself up and dressed on stage: she was very professional. Afterwards we dined together merrily and she told me how she had received calls and letters from people who had survived the War and who had seen and admired her thirty years before.

TRAVELS CONTINUED

I have mentioned that I was to present some of my findings at a conference. This was the Conservation Committee conference of ICOM, the International Council of Museums, which in 1963 was held in Leningrad (as it then was) and Moscow. As always I planned to take maximum advantage of the paid-for part of this outing by extending it further as part of my holidays. This would involve train travel so I decided to make the whole journey by rail. After the night crossing to Hook, where a great steam locomotive was waiting attached to all those through coaches to remote places in Eastern Europe, I was taken to Berlin, changed trains and went on to Warsaw. Here I met up with Professor Bohdan Marconi, a well-known figure in the conservation world, and he gave me dinner at the Hotel Bristol. Then it was on by sleeper through the Baltic Republics, all then a part of the Soviet Union, to Leningrad. Installed in the lovely, old Hotel Astoria I met up with colleagues who included Garry Thomson and Philip Hendy. I was delighted with my room which, besides the bed, included a divan and a niche with writing table stocked with notepaper. Of course, as continued for many years later, on each floor was a fearsome lady guardian of the keys and, 'incidentally', surveyor of who was going in and out.

Meals at the Astoria were served with almost pre-revolutionary formality but the service was intolerably slow. Even at breakfast there was a vast array of cutlery and glasses. The food was good, though the meat could be tough and one was introduced to classic Russian dishes such as chicken à la Kiev and beef Stroganoff – novelties then, today a degraded commonplace of the fast food shelves in supermarkets.

We, the delegates, were given some excellent tours of former imperial palaces surrounding Leningrad. With the War these had fallen into much decay but were now being lavishly restored to their Baroque splendour with much gold leaf and brilliant paint. The same was true of the Hermitage Museum where three rooms had been so treated. I was vastly impressed by the paintings collection and very moved by individual works, notably Rembrandt's *The Prodigal Son* and Titian's *Danae*.

The meeting was to continue in Moscow. Some of us were sent off on the train, as I would have preferred, and others by air. I have always remembered the small airport with its weed-strewn grounds and crumbling buildings in classical style. This had all changed when I was next there eighteen years later.

In Moscow it was the Kremlin and more museums but I was thinking more of my ongoing travels for I had obtained visas well in advance for Romania and Bulgaria and was headed for Istanbul. I obtained tickets for the sleeper carriage to Sofia, involving two nights' travel. I had a companion in my compartment – a Red Army officer who was kind and useful to me. I forget most details of the journey which went through Kiev and stopped for some time in Bucharest station where a Romanian conference delegate I had met had arranged to meet me and say hullo. I hoped we would go for a cup of coffee but I had no local currency and he had no money at all! On the train through Ukraine there had been a large visiting delegation of Chinese who would process down the corridor hand in hand to the restaurant car, filling it up and preventing me from entrance. I explained this to my officer companion who was indignant, took me back there and secured me a place. The food was not bad, I remember, and included a sort of soup with lamb's kidneys in it.

Having arrived in Bulgaria at the frontier station Rousse I had second thoughts about continuing to Sofia. I wanted to go to the Black Sea at Varna and thought there must be a more direct route so I got off the train. It was very quiet there, like a little country station with flower beds, but I found a ticket office with a single young man attendant and managed to make my purchase of a ticket to Varna though I have no recollection of how I paid for it. The Moscow-Varna through carriage, which had come with my train, was waiting in a siding. I tried to board it but was repelled by the stern conductress. No matter, it was afterwards hitched to the train which I did take.

In Varna I found a tourist office which fixed me up with a hotel room in one of those resorts just up the coast: Sunny Beach or Golden Sands, I forget now which. These were already beach resorts for tourists from the Communist countries and not long afterwards were taken up for cheap holidays by the washing machine entrepreneur John Bloom. I have mentioned that my mother even went on one of these at a cost (I think) of £30! I spent about three days there, relaxing on the beach and recovering from a streaming cold which had afflicted me on my journey. 'Luxury' goods were in short supply in Bulgaria and local 'wide boys' on the beach offered to buy things from me, even including my swimming trunks. I resisted denuding myself of them. In the hotel an elderly lady, very much a survivor from the time of the ancien régime, engaged me in conversation in French. 'This is a Communist country, you know; there are spies everywhere; we must keep our voices down.'

In fact I found the atmosphere rather relaxed. One evening I went into Varna to go, I thought, to the opera for which I had bought a ticket a day or two before. I must have mistaken the night for people seemed surprised when I entered the box (you could buy individual seats) as there did not seem to be a spare place. However a chair was found for me and my mistake dawned on me when instead of the opera it was *Swan Lake* again. I had seen this on the vast stage in Leningrad where great leaps could be made; here on a tiny one they had to make leaps more or less on the spot for fear of flying off into the wings. It was a charming evening none the less.

How was I to go on to Istanbul? I had hoped there might be some way of going directly round the coast, or even by ship, but there wasn't. I took a little plane to Sofia and there got on the *Orient Express* with a seat in one of the carriages that had come from Paris. It was so like the compartment in *The Lady Vanishes*! All looked up at me as I took my seat next to a Greek business man. He had, as he told me, already spent two nights there and was about to go through his third but he did not complain. To reach the dining car one had to pick one's way through the peasantry in the local carriages to which ours had been attached. At the frontier at night at those places with exotic names which had so fascinated me in Cook's Continental Timetable – Svilengrad and Üzünköprü – there was much delay with shunting and clanking. Eventually came the marvellous last stage along the Sea of Marmara, round the bend under Topkapı and into Sirkeci Station.

At last I was in Istanbul. I have been there many times since but these later visits have not entirely overlain my first impressions. To me it truly seemed like an oriental city and one whose main production appeared to be sugared almonds! They were everywhere in high glass containers. The shabby Western dress, enjoined by Ataturk for men, was universal. Women seemed hardly visible. The fishers lined the Galata Bridge, as still today. Taxis were all old American cars and the street leading from Sirkeci up towards Sultan Ahmet was lined with car repair spare parts shops. The clustering together of individual métiers was still the norm. I had found a cheap and none too clean hotel near there and I was soon up the hill to see the mosque and Hagia Sophia which, of course, astounds.

I forget now how many days I spent there. I think not many, for my money was short and I was uncertain what route to take to get home. I wanted to include Athens in my trip but the train journey there would be long and tedious. There was a range of small shipping agencies along the quay on the Galata side of the bridge and at one of them I secured a berth on a Russian ship coming from Odessa and on its way to Alexandria. This was mostly carrying engineers involved with the Aswan Dam, then being built. It was an agreeable one-night voyage to Piraeus and from there I took a bus to Athens. Apart from going up to the Acropolis I have no memories of my brief stay there. Sadly I have never been again but this may yet be rectified.

It's time to be done with this long journey. I took a bus to Patras (I remember the amazing Corinth Canal) and then the ferry to Brindisi – the reverse of the journey I failed to make in 1952. Then it was the train up Italy's Adriatic coast to Milan; another train to Basel to meet up with old friends from my Mexico days, Rolf and Margot Mauli. Thence on to Calais and so home.

1966

In September 1966 I made a tour to Yugoslavia with my friend Ted in my Mini, the first European tour by car I had attempted. We drove across Germany and Austria, stopping at Innsbruck and then on to Slovenia. Then it was right down the rather monotonous and unattractive Adriatic coast and a crossing to the island of Hvar. The little town is at the far end of the island and it was reached by a dreadful rough road but we made it and found a place to stay for a few days. Then it was back by the same route, having had to leave at 4 am to catch the ferry to the mainland, and eventually to Venice and then Milan to call on Riccardo Villotti. He had gone back to Syntex for a few years but was now with an important pharmaceuticals company in Milan. He was doing well and lived in a splendid apartment (1 Via Principe Amedeo) which had once been occupied by Arrigo Boito, the great librettist to Verdi. My friend Ted had to get back to work and went off on the train but I still had some time available. Yugoslavia was much cheaper than Italy so I decided to go back there. I sped down the autostrada to Trieste and on to Rijeka where I decided to leave the car and take the ferry down the coast. With some misgivings I abandoned my car in a small open-air unsupervised car park and caught the boat. I was down past Hvar again and landed at Korcula. While there I took a trip to yet another island, the delightful Mljet, which I see is now designated as a national park. Then it was Dubrovnik again, thirteen years after my first visit. It seemed completely unchanged.

Having returned to Rijeka I was relieved and somewhat amazed to find my car untouched. I called on Riccardo again and made my way home through Switzerland and France.

In 1967 I made my first visit to Portugal to stay with Vic at Maria Rego's house in Estoril. Her husband Jose, Paula's father, had died the previous year in London and Vic was now doing his best to manage Jose's electrical engineering business in Lisbon. By now he had more or less mastered Portuguese but of course he had no business experience. All his efforts and investment (which involved the sacrifice of the beloved family *quinta* at Ericeira) were ultimately brought to nought with the revolution in 1974 but at that moment affairs seemed positive. Vic took me to the famous club, the Gremio, of which he was a member, and we dined out one evening in Cascais – then little more than a fishing village – where strangely the one other occupied table was taken by the TV personality Bruce Forsyth with another man, perhaps his agent.

10
CAFÉ SOCIETY

The club- and pub-based bohemia of the Soho of the 1950s and '60s has had its due – some would say more than its due – of history and myth-making. I watched all this largely from the sidelines; occasional visits with friends to the Colony Room and the even more squalid Caves de France failed to persuade me that the kind of social life they offered was for me. The York Minster, known to its regulars as the French Pub, was fine for a short visit in the early evening, perhaps for a vermouth before the theatre or cinema, but I avoided more than a nodding acquaintanceship with the all-too-familiar faces of the laya-bouts who propped up the walls there and sponged off those (nearly all of them gay) who were 'in the money' and good for a drink or two or even perhaps a 'loan'. The advent of Colin McInnes, Johnny Min-ton, Francis Bacon or Daniel Farson would be eagerly awaited since their appearance gave promise of a round of pleasure until closing time or later.

But there was another and almost entirely separate bohemia (for want of a better word) that congregated in cafés and whose sociability was caffeine- rather than alcohol-fuelled. At the end of the 1940s, when I was first living in London, certain steamy cafés and dingy cellars in Rathbone Place and Charlotte Street gave refuge to a mixed bag of humanity: some of no fixed address; some escaping from cold bedsits and saving on shillings for the gas meter; a few with grubby notebook and pencil; some anxious to plumb the mysteries of the city and afflicted with the *nostalgie de la boue* (myself, for example?); some well-dressed late-nighters, showing their companions the lower depths. Here one might be alone and observational or one could make fleeting associations. But primarily these were assemblages of loners who showed little curiosity about one another and the whys and wherefores of their being there. Certainly I made no lasting familiarities, yet some of the more colourful (if such a word can be used of people so dowdy) individuals such as Ironfoot Jack and the 'Countess' sometimes turn up in other memoirs including those of Daniel Farson or Bernard Kops.

But from around 1953 or '54 there came a big change in the London scene with the explosion of the new espresso bars. Seemingly very little documented and now largely forgotten, these were an amazing phenomenon. They opened in their hundreds; every street had them, sometimes even side by side, each attempting to outdo the others with some new and extravagant decor. Nowadays it has become conventional wisdom that the fifties was a grey and dreary decade but it didn't seem so to those of us living in London at that time. 1954 saw the final end of rationing; concomitantly the War seemed to be finally over and a degree of exuberance and pleasure-seeking, as perhaps of the 1920s, was in order. Money was short but the espresso bars were a haven where hours could be spent in company with other habitués and 'o'er cold coffee trifle with a spoon'.

My own favourite was one called Chiquito's in Hanway Street, a little narrow dog-leg of a way connecting Oxford Street and Tottenham Court Road. The building is still there but long since turned into offices. The company was young and, to me, glamorous but it soon came to be evident, as they became more confiding, that many of the boys (they were hardly more than that) were small-time crooks. Quite starry-eyed they would sometimes mention with awe the names of the big-time gangsters of the day such as Billy Hill or Jack 'Spot', evidently hoping that their futures lay with them. Now probably long since dead or become old lags they were of no lasting interest but there were others whose activities were this side of the law. One such was the wrestler Peter Rann, an extraordinarily handsome youth, who usually had with him a small following of acolytes. I got to know him but before this I once saw him in the park, from the top of a bus rounding Marble Arch, heading his little train. Seeing him there in jeans and a check gingham shirt I was reminded of Melville's description of Billy Budd, the 'handsome sailor' who automatically becomes leader of the pack. We last met in the early sixties but I continued to see him sometimes in aggressive pose on posters, even once or twice on TV.

Concurrently with the evenings in the espresso bars there was the ultimately more rewarding lunchtime café life. During my first period at the National Gallery from 1951 until early 1956 I naturally sought out agreeable and inexpensive places for lunch. Two of these I have already described but there were others for more regular, lighter meals, where I might encounter existing friends or perhaps make new ones. The Café Torino, better known to its regulars as Torino's, on the corner of Dean Street and Old Compton Street, was just such a place. One could have a very decent bowl of minestrone and bread for about 1/6 (7½p) and if one was more flush some *spaghetti al sugo* for about half a crown (12½p). Friends from the Slade might sometimes turn up there, but for the most part I was a silent observer of the clientele. As it was only about fifty yards from the York Minster the regulars there (if they were up and about) sometimes appeared, for even they had to eat. A fairly regular attender was the grubby Paul Potts, the poet; another was Tony del Renzio, critic and writer. Victor Willing has beautifully described a meeting he had there in 1955 with Peter Snow (the first UK set designer for *Waiting for Godot*) and a man who turned out to be Samuel Beckett himself.

Another café which was eventually to yield me a fascinating circle of friends was one in Gerrard Street, long before its existence as the Chinatown that it is today was even hinted at. It bore no name over the entrance but was known as Legrain's, presumably after the two Belgian ladies (sisters?) who ran it along with the shop adjacent which sold roasted coffee and coffee-making equipment. The building is still there (Gerrard Mansions) but taken over by the expanding Chinatown. It has always surprised me that this establishment, frequented by European émigrés, artists, musicians, theatre people and those from the film industry in Wardour Street, has never, to my knowledge, featured in any Soho-oriented memoir. Maybe writers didn't really know what to call it for it always had an anonymous feel, and to someone newly approaching it, it gave the impression more of a private club. There was no menu, inside or out; one made known one's wants to one of the sisters who, when not occupied, remained behind a small bar at the far end. There were small round tables, the tops inset with dark plum-coloured tiles on which the crockery and glasses clattered somewhat and were rather unstable. Coffee was always served *au lait* in glasses and was very delicious but hot, and one had to develop a technique of initially holding the glass up near the rim. Lemon tea was also much drunk and again was served in glasses though held in metal holders with handles, Russian style. I can remember little of the solid food available; there were certainly sandwiches and, I think soup and some simple breakfast-style egg dishes. Some elderly patrons had known the café before the War and said that then there were newspapers available attached to wooden rods, as is still often the continental custom today.

I was myself only an occasional visitor in the 1950s and didn't then make many acquaintances but I well remember the rather static clientele, mostly males, many of whom seemed always to be there. They were waiting in hope of being chosen as extras for the rather dreadful, B-quality films which Wardour Street produced at that time and I would sometimes recognise them on the screen. Only when I came back from my periods in the USA and Mexico and was once again employed at the National Gallery from 1961, did I go regularly to Legrain's. By now I was a less inhibited person and in any case appreciated that café *moeurs* allowed – indeed encouraged – conversation with someone sharing your table, especially if you recognised a regular. The first person to take me up was indeed a regular and a gregarious one who already had quite a circle around him. This was Fritz.

Fritz Kuhn was born, as he used to say, with the century, so when I first knew him he was in his early sixties. He was then, and indeed remained, a well-built and handsome man for his years. I rarely question people directly about their personal histories so all that I got to know about him came out gradually over many years and certainly does not constitute a continuous or consistent biography. It is possible that he was illegitimate since he never mentioned his father but he did mention that his mother could not afford to look after him and he was put into a children's home for some years. They lived in Berlin and he must have been there through the First War and the 1920s. How he lived then did not fully appear though he spoke of having been an actor and even of playing Hamlet. I imagine that in those *wandervogel* years he made a living as best he could, his good looks perhaps playing a part. He claimed that he was active politically and so with the rise of Hitler to power in 1933 he very soon realised that there was no future in Germany for a homosexual Jewish Communist and he left the country for Paris. Again I don't know how he supported himself there but his lot was one shared with a good many other exiles. With the approach of war, in 1939, he came on to England.

In 1940, with the panic about fifth columnists, Fritz, along with so many other wholly anti-Nazi refugees, was arrested and sent off to internment, first on the Isle of Man and then to Canada. He never expressed any resentment at this treatment; it was simply another of life's vicissitudes. But towards the end of the War he was released and went with the American army to Germany as an interpreter. If I remember correctly his work there included translating during interrogations of Nazi officials from liberated concentration camps. Released from this and back in London Fritz eventually got a job supervising the packing at Lawley's, the china store in Regent Street, and he was still working there when I first knew him. It seemed to allow him plenty of time for long lunch hours at Legrain's, moreover he had financial prospects to look forward to as I will explain later.

Conversation with Fritz and the others I shall mention was very much about the arts and especially music. At that time, the sixties, it was easy to get into Covent Garden Opera and not impossibly expensive. One could simply wait in Floral Street or at the front until someone appeared waving spare tickets that they wanted to sell. I myself went frequently on the spur of the moment after work. Fritz often went too though later he acknowledged that he couldn't any more sit through a whole Wagner opera and might leave at the interval. He could be very critical of singers and indeed of conductors. He couldn't stand Solti, for example: 'He drowns the singers.' Tremendous arguments on these matters could take place, not least with another friend, Philip Wrestler, who had equally strong opinions, forcefully expressed. Philip really only liked Italian opera and Verdi in particular: *Don Carlo* was his favourite (he was right there). He did not care for Britten and especially *Billy Budd*, which he would refer to rudely as 'Buggery on the Bounty' (he was wrong there). He and Fritz would sometimes fall out over singers' merits to the extent of not speaking for some days. 'He's a horrible old man,' Philip would say.

Philip was in films but he seemed always to prefer our mixed company to that of his fellow cinematic workers. For the most part he made only minor, usually educational, films and he liked to tell me about those on aspects of chemistry that he had directed. I gathered from others that his unguarded opinions of many in the film business had made him enemies which may well have adversely affected his career. However, in 1969, when he was 48, came his big break in feature films: he directed the second unit in *The Italian Job*, filming the famous car chase in the streets of Turin. It seemed that his future in films was assured, yet it was not to be. He was involved with the Bond film *Octopussy* (1983) but nothing else of note, though he still found work in various aspects of film-making. But he never gave up and even in the nineties, after he had recovered from a quadruple heart bypass, he still told me of projects that he had with scripts he had written himself.

Philip Wrestler was born into the Jewish East End. He rarely spoke of it but from the little he said it seemed that he experienced the common impoverished childhood in a cramped two-up, two-down terraced house. I have forgotten his father's occupation, if he ever told me, but he certainly had a brother who also died of a heart attack. Philip had a lady friend with whom, at a happy stage of his life, he shared a cottage in Sussex at weekends. It had a large orchard of apple trees and they made cider. In London by the mid-nineties Philip was living in a small flat in Trinity Square while she was largely flat-bound in Dolphin Square, Chelsea. Even then, when he could hardly get about himself, he would drive down there to do her shopping. When I last spoke to him on the telephone at Christmas 2002 he was still doing this and, on his behalf, I protested. 'Well, what can you do?' he said. The following year I got no card and no answer to my call; the same the year after and I assumed he had died. Through the wonders of the Internet I found that he had indeed, of a heart attack, on 4 February 2003.

As well as amateur music-lovers in our circle there were also professionals. One on the periphery was Karl Haas, the well-known founder and director of the London Baroque Ensemble. A fellow refugee from Nazi Germany (he came to England in 1939), he and Fritz knew each other well and may indeed have been fellow internees for a while. But by 1943 Haas and his ensemble were already contributing concerts to the wartime series at the National Gallery and after 1951 his first recordings were issued. During the 1950s and early '60s his name was constantly heard on the Third Programme, for he was essentially the first to bring much eighteenth-century music to the public, although he did not confine himself to that. His ensemble was not a regular orchestra but an ad hoc group of players got together as needed for the music to be played and it often included many distinguished individuals such as Dennis Brain, Leon Goossens, Gervase de Peyer and even Carl Dolmetsch. He would wander into Legrain's looking round to see who was there, acknowledge Fritz but then usually join some musician friend. 'Women have been his undoing,' Fritz would say, though what exactly he meant by that I do not know.

Very much one of us was Allan Gray, the composer. All the time that I knew him, from the early sixties until his sudden death in 1973, I was never fully aware of his very distinguished career in film music for he never talked about it, though we did know that he had written the music for *The African Queen*. It was also known that he had studied with Schönberg in the 1920s and I designated him, in my flippant way, The Pupil of Schönberg. He lived in Amersham and, indeed, had a wife there, though she never appeared in his company. I think he had an office in Denmark Street and he would often come in with his friend and secretary, Peggy. At this time the peak of Allan's career had passed but he was still writing and devising many schemes for musicals with, of all the unlikely people, Tommie Connor. Tommie was a small, sweet-natured elderly Irishman, lyricist and composer, who had perpetrated (I use the word advisedly and he would have taken it in good part) such popular successes as *The Biggest Aspidistra in the World*, for Gracie Fields. When we happened to be alone together our talk sometimes fell on music hall, the venue for many of Tommie's successes. My father had been an addict of music hall songs, the words of some of which had stuck in my head and all of which, of course, Tommie knew:

> *I'm following in Father's footsteps*
> *I'm following the dear old dad*

To escape constant badinage from Fritz, he and Allan would move to another table to put their heads together and devise their scenarios. What became of these plans I do not know but I rather think nothing.

In about 1967 came the dread news that with the ever advancing tide of Chinese restaurants and groceries in Gerard Street, Legrain's was closing. We were out on the street but chance meetings spread the word that the Patisserie Valerie in Old Compton Street, already known to most of us for many years, was the favoured new venue. Soon many of the familiar faces re-established themselves there among its existing clientele and lunch hours went on much as before. During 1968 I was away for a year in California but when I got back there they all still were and our intercourse was resumed. One day in September 1973 Fritz announced to me that he had heard that Allan was no longer in the land of the living. It was true for he had died quite suddenly of pneumonia following flu. This was a shock for Allan was only 71 and had always seemed in the best of health. It seriously dashed Tommie Connor's plans but he was an old pro with many irons in the fire and he went on to write songs for such sentimental songsters as Val Doonican.

Many years later, in 1999, I heard a talk on Radio 3 by one Thomas Gayda about German cabaret songs from between the wars, and Allan's contributions to these were mentioned. Brief biographical details were given including Allan's original Polish name, Josef Zmigrod, and his birth date, 1902, neither of which had I known. I wrote to Gayda and told him about Allan's café life in London. He replied but was not able to add much to what he had already reported in his programme but he thought that the two German films for which Allan wrote the music, *Berlin Alexanderplatz* and *Emil and the Detectives*, might well not have achieved the status they did without him. Of course this made me look into Allan's contribution to British cinema and I found that he had worked with Powell and Pressburger and written for such major successes as *The Life and Death of Colonel Blimp* (1943), *A Matter of Life and Death* (1946) and *I Know Where I'm Going* (1945) as well as many other less well-known films. He had also done much work for television during the first half of the fifties, royalties from which must have largely provided for the comfortable lifestyle which he seemed to enjoy. He sometimes expressed concern for my own, urging me to get married. This was the right policy, he implied, regardless of personal inclination or the availability of a suitable partner. More immediately practicable was the recipe he gave me for hamburgers. I was to use the best tartare mince from Benoit Bulcke, the high-class butcher in Old Compton Street, dilute it with a proportion of white breadcrumbs and add other ingredients that I have now forgotten though I did follow it, with notable success, for some years.

But back to Legrain's in the 1960s and some of the minor players. A regular with whom I sometimes found myself sitting was Michael Geen. He worked for a major theatrical costumiers and his manner was appropriately yet discreetly camp (at this time the word had yet to come into open parlance). He had stories to tell of his customers, some quite risqué, and he sometimes hinted at early adventures of his own: he had known Ivor Novello *awfully well*, he averred. Male ballet dancers were sometimes concerned that they showed insufficient embonpoint in a certain region. 'Oh stuff a sock in it,' he would advise, 'After all, many *do*.' He used to distress me by mashing up the lemon in his tea to a state of suspended pulp, and I would protest but he insisted that he liked it that way. He was engaged in writing a little book on costume for amateur theatre but confessed to concern about a heart condition from which he was suffering. The book did indeed appear while I was away during 1968 but when I got back I found that Michael had succumbed.

There was another loner who regularly attended and whom I did eventually get to talk to even though I never learned his name. His lunch invariably consisted of two slices of toast with jam and a pot of tea so he did not loom large as a physical presence. He was a clarinettist and played mainly in dance bands, including those on luxury transatlantic liners and cruise ships. But this was rather a dispiriting experience, he told me, as the passengers were nearly all elderly who had no stamina for late night dancing and early drifted off to bed. He lived at home with his old widowed mother who, he explained, needed looking after. It seemed a sad life.

A large, overweight but carefully turned-out, past middle age man would come in from time to time smiling round at the company in what seemed a self-satisfied way. He affected a debonair manner with his overcoat hanging over his shoulders like a cloak and he even sported a monocle. For a long time I had no idea who he was and I designated him Baron Ochs after the character in Strauss's *Rosen-kavalier*, a cognomen which greatly tickled Fritz and stuck. Much later I learned from Philip that he was a well-known photographer named Hans Casparius. I have discovered that like Fritz he too was born in 1900 and had also lived in Berlin but what a different life he had enjoyed! From a well-off and cultivated Jewish family, he had been successful as a photographer in Germany in the 1920s and early '30s but had also been involved in the making of silent films, even playing bit parts in them, including one in the famous *Pandora's Box* with Louise Brookes. His photographic commissions had taken him on extensive travels in Canada, Palestine and Egypt. In 1936 he and his wife left Germany to live in London and managed to settle quite comfortably and take up similar work but his mother and one of his brothers could not be persuaded to leave and both died in the camps. He himself was lucky enough to be spared internment in the War as he had a useful supply of photographs of foreign parts which were in demand by the military. After the War he had forty happy and successful years in London, living in Hampstead and finally dying in 1986. No wonder he seemed pleased with himself.

Hans was no part of our circle but he would often join a woman of about his own age who was a regular at Legrain's though I don't remember whether she moved on to Valerie's. She was usually on her own and commonly studying and annotating a handful of manuscript while smoking a cigarette held in a long holder. She had a marked cast in one eye which possibly was the cause of her manner being very slightly prickly. I remember once asking her a question about one of the regulars whom I had not seen for a while: she knew nothing about him, said she, he was 'simply a café acquaintance'. So who was she? Again, Philip turned out to know her quite well as she was in the same profession as he and moreover lived in the same block of flats (Dolphin Square) as his lady friend. She was Julia Wolf, film editor and subtitle writer for all the 'art' films from the continent which, in the 1950s and '60s, we ardently attended at the Curzon, the Academy and Studio One in Oxford Street or the New Gallery, a long disappeared and largely forgotten cinema in Regent Street (though apparently the actual premises survive). She had been born of Austrian parentage in London in 1901 but had spent childhood years in Dresden and was caught there when war was declared in 1914. Back in England in the 1920s she worked for a trade film newspaper and was sent back to Germany to survey the film industry there, meeting Fritz Lang and the other silent filmmakers and no doubt Hans also. She considered most German films to be far too long for English tastes and so they were cut, usually by her. When the talkies came in she had the added task of writing the English subtitles and did this for all the films shown at the Curzon until it was bombed during the Blitz. After the War a part of her work involved making small cuts and modifications to get some films past the censor, something at which she proved to be quite an expert. Long disappeared from Soho she lived to be 93, dying in 1995.

I must not fail to mention Teddy Schwarz, a big, shambling man and seemingly enigmatic character in whom both I and my friend

Peter Dunsmore (another regular habitué) quite independently found affinities with the character Schigolch in Alban Berg's *Lulu*. In fact this was a complete misreading of him for which really he had only himself to blame. He could have told us more of his early life and background about which one only got to know after his death. He too, of course, was a 1930s refugee and he had known Fritz in Paris before they both came to London. There always seemed to be a degree of friction between them which I never got to the bottom of. Fritz would show signs of irritation if Teddy joined us at our table, and downright contempt for his opinions if he joined in the conversation. It may have been a question of money, of which Teddy was chronically short even though he did have modest gainful employment as a photographer. On the whole, though, I think there was more to it than that; something that went back to their Paris days.

Teddy's photographic activities principally consisted of providing attractive scenes for brochures of European travel but he would turn his hand to other subjects also. I arranged for him to photograph the paintings of my friend Paula Rego; this in the days before she became famous. He also dabbled in Far Eastern art, forming a collection of ceramics and paintings and engaging in a small amount of dealing. By the 1990s his health was increasingly uncertain; he was living in some squalor in his single room in Notting Hill and was sometimes in hospital. He was largely tended by Peter Dunsmore during his last months and, seemingly having no relatives, in the end he left him his pots and other things. At his funeral and interment in Kensal Green cemetery one bitter cold day in 1994 I was surprised at the number of his friends attending, none of whom had ever been seen with him at Valerie's. Several of them spoke of him most respectfully as an old and valued member of the German exile community. A year or so after his death some of these friends published a slim volume entitled *In Memoriam Freimut Schwarz* and from this I garnered more information. He had been born in Sotterbach bei Waldbröl, Rheinland (a tiny place as seen on Google maps) on 28 April 1913. He studied modern German literature and later ethnology at Cologne University where subsequently he became private secretary and co-worker of Professor Julius Lips, a distinguished ethnologist, who himself also left Germany for Paris on Hitler's rise to power. A year later he moved to England and apparently worked among the unemployed in Liverpool for some time. With the outbreak of war he was interned and sent to the Isle of Man. He told me of how he knew the artist Kurt Schwitters there and, like everyone else, thought him quite mad. He now much regretted having no keepsake from him! So then it was to Canada, like all the others, but after seventeen months he was released as an anti-Nazi and made ends meet in England with multifarious jobs: washer-up, decorator, labourer, language teacher and translator before settling on his photographic activities. Both before and after the War he managed to write and publish essays, short stories and a poem or two, and he even did some editing of transient émigré literary magazines. Teddy was well read and we discovered a common liking for Conrad and especially *The Secret Agent*. The commissioner's defining catchphrases ('Be lucid. No details please.') became a sort of joke between us.

At Teddy's funeral we (myself, Peter Dunsmore, Ron and Lilian of whom I write below) were upset and hurt to learn that Fritz had also died only a few weeks before and had been buried with none of his old café friends present. I had seen little of him recently as the few of the old circle who survived rarely turned up at Valerie's. He did, however, once or twice invite me and others to a meal at a favoured Chinese restaurant adjacent to where he was living, now in days of relative affluence, right by the canal in Little Venice. How had this come about?

Over a long period in the 1960s and '70s, when we were alone together in one or the other café, he would sometimes go into a sort of reflective mood, talking more or less to himself and referring to someone named Peter who had bequeathed him money. Apparently this was the subject of litigation, primarily by Peter's mother who was trying to overturn the will. He never seemed overly concerned about it despite its seeming more and more like a new Jarndyce and Jarndyce. One day, I think in the early 1980s, he announced, chuckling, that the mother had finally lost her case: she had been declared a vexatious litigant! He was to get the money – of the order of £200,000 – a very large sum at the time. Only now, when I have been looking into it, do I more or less know the full story.

Peter Fuld was born in Germany on 12 February 1921 of German parents. His father, of Jewish origin, was a wealthy man with a flourishing business in Frankfurt where Peter was brought up. In 1939, some years after the death of his father, his mother sent him to England to study but after the outbreak of war he was, of course, interned and in 1940 sent to Canada. It was during this internment that Fritz came to know him when he was still only eighteen or nineteen. The extent of their intimacy can now never be known but evidently it engendered a lasting affection and friendship. In 1942 Peter was released from internment but he stayed on in Canada and entered university in Toronto as a law student, only returning to Europe in 1946. He had acquired Canadian nationality and he then lived both in London and Frankfurt, factors which complicated the question of his actual place of domicile and hence the system of national law under which the later probate case should be settled. But, to be brief, he contracted a brain tumour in February 1960, was successfully operated on and partially recovered but eventually died on 21 March 1962. In July of the previous year he had made a will and in October a first codicil to it. By these his estate was put into a trust from which, for twenty years following his death, the income was to be paid as follows: one third to his mother and the remainder in varying percentages to some nine other beneficiaries among whom Fritz Kuhn was to receive five percent. At the expiry of the twenty years the capital was to be distributed to the beneficiaries in the same proportions, with some other provisos.

Probate of the will was opposed by the mother and an enormous court case ensued before Lord Justice Scarman in 1965. The hearings covered ninety-five days; twenty-two counsel represented the plaintiffs and defendants; eight firms of solicitors were involved. After sixty-one days the mother abandoned her opposition to the will and codicil (the judge said she should never have commenced it and had other harsh things to say of her) and eventually probate was granted. There were three other later codicils, not affecting Fritz, which were not approved. Presumably from then on Fritz received the income, allowing him to live comfortably. As the time approached for the distribution of the capital the mother must have renewed her litigation, resulting in her being declared vexatious as stated above.

So Fritz bought his flat in Maida Avenue. Only now do I realise that it was on the opposite side of the canal and almost facing 8 Blomfield Road, where Peter Fuld had had a flat. Some old memories and sentiments yet remained, it would seem.

RON AND LILIAN

Ron and Lilian were a couple whom I would never have chosen for friends on first principles, as it were, rather than by the workings of chance. Yet in fact they proved to be loyal and fascinating friends until their deaths in sad circumstances which I will recount. They were a presence in Legrain's of which one was at first rather vaguely aware until they gradually became incorporated into Fritz's, and so my, circle. They were a childless couple (entirely by choice) and Lilian was the dominant partner though Ron was in no way henpecked. He was a fairly senior civil servant, part of whose duty being to give advice to ministers answering awkward questions in Parliament. He hated his work and looked forward to retirement promptly at 60. They were consequently fairly well-off and able to indulge their ruling passions which were travel and good food but they were also great readers and theatre-goers and so able to contribute largely to the conversation.

Yet sometimes their *idées fixes* could be quite baseless and maddening to my scientific mind and I could lose all patience. This was especially so on matters of food, on which Lilian in particular held rigid and uncompromising opinions which were in part to lead to her downfall. In the seventies and into the eighties they were reporters to the Good Food Guide and, I suspect, rather too severe in their judgements even for that august body, as eventually there was no more mention of it. Not that they ceased staying, from time to time, for weekends in country hotels noted for their food. Indeed they seemed almost to live for this and, I think, survived on rather short commons at home. Lilian could cook; she did occasionally entertain, though more usually in the way of afternoon tea (taken with a rich Dundee cake and Lapsang tea with lemon) at their elegant but rather spartan flat in a 1920s apartment block in Muswell Hill (which Lilian preferred to be referred to as Fortis Green). The problem was, as Lilian constantly lamented, that she could not get the quality of foodstuffs that once she did and which she absolutely required: the bread, for example, that she could buy locally was now uneatable (I have to some extent come round to her view) and good cheese could only be bought at Paxton & Whitfield in Jermyn Street. And she needed food to be freshly bought, for one of her bugbears was refrigeration. They never possessed a refrigerator ('it takes away all the flavour') and so had real problems in summer with milk and butter.

If heat was the problem in summer, cold was in winter, for the flat had no central heating and, being on the corner of the building, was very exposed. Lilian demanded the comfort (?) of open fires, before which to roast, and consequently even when they had both arrived at their eighties Ron had to carry up coal by the outside back staircase. For the flats had been designed and built in the days when even such a small household would have had a maid or at least a daily general servant. Indeed Lilian had confessed to me once that in their early married state she had expected that they would live out their life with servants. When an open fire was not practicable they resorted to multi-bar electric heaters but here too there was much to complain of. If they did not glow as brightly as was expected Lilian accused the electricity company of lowering the voltage and defrauding them of the heat for which they were paying. It was in vain that I would explain that less electricity would be used and that consequently they would be paying less. This did not console her.

Lilian always dressed (and dressed Ron) with meticulous care in a distinctly old-fashioned way. Everything had to be 'correct', even down to the wearing of gloves, though I don't recall that she wore hats. But any impression given by this that she was prim or prudish would be entirely mistaken. In fact she loved the quirky, even the outré, and she often recommended films to me that they had greatly enjoyed: *Blast from the Past*, *The Purple Rose of Cairo*, *Farewell My Concubine*, and especially *Withnail and I*. I later heard that in the early days of her marriage she had scandalised her new in-laws by outrageous cavorting in scanty clothes and apparently she had even once published a novel though I have been unable to secure any details of this.

As our café circle gradually dissolved through retirements or death, and particularly after my own retirement at the end of 1990; Ron, Lilian and myself met less at the Patisserie Valerie and arranged our meetings for coffee at a variety of other places. In town we often gathered at the café at the Royal Academy or sometimes at a restaurant they favoured in Jermyn Street. But often we preferred not to meet in the West End but chose places in Camden Town, Highgate or at Kenwood.

As mentioned above, their great passion was getting away from it all through travel. In 1976 Ron reached the retirement age of 60 and so they promptly put their plan for world travel into execution. They put their best things into storage, shut up their flat and set off by train (they eschewed air travel, as one might suppose) to Moscow and then on the Trans-Siberian to its terminus at Nakhodka. From here they took a ship to Yokohama, did Japan and subsequently Korea and then proceeded to I know not where. In all they were away for nearly a year, Lilian sending many postcards written in her small, neat script. I forget whether it was during this trip or later that they went to America, travelling across and around it by train. Again, as one might expect, they did not greatly enjoy the experience and never repeated it.

Once settled back in London their travels were largely confined to Europe, Morocco and the Near East. They were especially fond of the less-developed Eastern European countries; Plovdiv in Bulgaria was a favourite place and later, inexplicably, they took to Bucharest in Romania. They often toured around Turkey. Italy and Spain were regularly visited, always travelling by train and bus and staying in the smaller places. I myself was doing much the same during the eighties (though in my case by car) and I could recommend towns that I felt they would like. They did in fact take to several of these for repeated stays: the upper town at Bergamo, Orvieto, Sulmona, Palestrina, Trani. In their turn they introduced me to little-known places on the railway south of Naples that they had dropped off at: Agropoli, Palinuro, Sapri. Once I actually ran into them. On arriving at a small hotel in Palermo I found them sitting reading in the entrance lobby, on the point of departure. Egypt they had loved but now found too touristic; Morocco, however, was still a great favourite and they would get there overland through Spain and make their way to particular small towns for prolonged stays. Lilian loved heat and desert places, detesting humidity and anything which seemed to her too green and lush, so they avoided the tropics. Only a year or so before the Anglo-American attack they got as far as Baghdad and had talked of their trip with enthusiasm.

Apart from the common unfortunate incidents of travel they had got through all this unscathed. It was at home in Fortis Green that disaster struck. In 2002 Ron phoned to tell me that Lilian's dressing gown had caught alight on brushing against one of her beloved electric fires and her leg was badly burnt, far more so than they first suspected. She was now in the specialist burns unit at Stanmore and he was himself staying in accommodation there to keep her company. Skin grafts and everything else were tried but she was now impossibly thin – grossly undernourished in fact; the doctors had been urging her to eat *anything* but her obsession with only eating the 'right' foodstuffs had taken a firmer hold in later years. The grafts would not take and eventually they had to admit defeat. She died, I think of septicaemia. She retained her sense of dignity, but also a refusal to acknowledge the truth, to the end. When I went to visit she wished I hadn't: she didn't want to be seen in that condition. As she was dying (Ron had been told and knew it) she asked him to book a nice hotel where they could go away and stay together.

That was that then. Ron was told he should now go home, which he did; aged 86 back to his cold (it was winter), lonely and cheerless flat. He was uncertain what he would do: there could not be an immediate funeral as an inquest was called for on account of the accidental nature of Lilian's death. I phoned him a few days later but there was no answer and I thought that perhaps he had gone into a hotel or possibly to stay with his nephew Tony (almost his only relative) in Chester. Another day or two and again there was no answer and no message of any kind came. Then I had a phone call from a policeman (he had got my number by dialling 1471 from the flat) who told me that Ron was in the Whittington hospital and very ill with pneumonia. Apparently his neighbours in the adjacent flat were concerned at not seeing him about and had looked through the letter box to find him lying unconscious on the floor. The police had had to break in the door to get him out. For some reason they suggested that I take charge of the flat, to sort through and deal with letters and take things to Ron in hospital that he might need. I went there and was given the key of the padlock that they had now fitted. Inside I found the flat far more run-down than I remembered. The virtually unaltered 1920s kitchen no longer seemed as charming as once it had; its deficiencies and blatant inconvenience now thrust themselves on me. The old four-legged gas stove; the stone sink with a geyser over it; the perforated zinc-fronted meat safe which substituted for a refrigerator and which contained only a bit of hardened cheese and a block of halva (which Lilian supposed peculiarly nutritious). In the bedroom the two single beds, set against the wall without headboards, bedside table or lamps, reminded me of a monastery.

Ron was at first too ill to receive visitors and barely conscious. When he finally came round it was evident that much had been wiped from his memory. He made no mention of Lilian and responded only with blank looks when she was referred to. How much came back later was hard to tell but he certainly never raised the subject of his life with her, let alone the final bad weeks at Stanmore.

The sequel, though extended, can be briefly told. His nephew and heir Tony took over management of Ron's affairs and as it was clear that he could not go back to live alone in his flat it was sold and its contents dispersed. After several weeks in hospital he was moved to a nursing home in Golders Green where he was well enough attended but had to endure the depressing company of patients mostly more infirm than himself and in some cases alarmingly demented. In consequence, apart from during visits by Peter Dunsmore or me, he got little stimulating conversation and we found that his ability to respond progressively diminished. The words would not come; he would dry up. After six years the end came. At the crematorium (just down the road) a very few friends gathered but both Peter and I were disappointed that neither of us was asked to say a few words about Ron and Lilian's long London life. I hope this short account may in part compensate.

To some it might seem that this life was one of perfect selfishness. In our circle some hardly knew what to think. Fritz had mocked their constant talk of food but it was good humoured, while Philip, I suspect, did not really like them. He probably envied Ron's comfortable pension, as well he might. Harry Hoff (the novelist William Cooper), who quite often joined us, expressed the opinion that they were quite mad, though this was a characteristically impulsive rather than a considered judgement. Tommie Connor was, I think, completely baffled by them, or else he kept his own counsel. But was it a selfish life? I rather think not. From the hints that Lilian sometimes gave I understood that her early life was not a very happy one, her father not usually being at home – however that was to be interpreted. Ron too never spoke much of his early life and I don't know how the two of them first got together. But they had had to make their own way in life and, having done so, were intent on enjoying the fruits of it in the ways that pleased them best. So in fact, until the end, they were never dependent on others; they did not consume that much of this world's resources, eschewing modern life's conveniences, and they could be thought of as being early and unconsciously 'green' in their lifestyle.

HARRY HOFF

Harry Hoff (William Cooper), mentioned above, became a friend whom I met occasionally almost until he died. I wrote earlier that back in 1955, before I went off for my first stay in America, I applied for the permanent post at the National Gallery and that he was on the Civil Service Commission examining board. Years later, at Legrain's, I am sure he didn't remember the confrontation and I never reminded him of it. Nor did we ever speak directly of his own work, though I had read some (now all) of his novels and thought well of them. They are strangely innocent works showing a simple appreciation of life's pleasures and a kindly amusement at individuals' foibles. How very different from the sententious and thrusting characters of his mentor C.P. Snow. Harry went rather astray in his middle period (*You Need the Right Frame of Reference; You're Not Alone*) but returned to his natural, autobiographical style later.

Carl Djerassi often lamented the large absence of authentic science in fiction but would cite with admiration the rare exception of Hoff's *The Struggles of Albert Woods*. A year or two before Harry's death I was able to introduce the two to each other at a meeting of the Royal Society of Literature. This was in fact the last time that I met Hoff but I did send him one of Carl's novels and he approved of it in a letter.

11
CALIFORNIA *ET SEQ*

By 1967 my work had become rather uninspired and routine, though I had resumed some work on natural resins in collaboration with one Laurie Gough at the Borough Polytechnic. The Department, moreover, had suffered some fallings-out and tensions. There had been some mingling of business with pleasure and the female staff member at the centre of this, who was supposed to assist Garry Thomson, no longer seemed to have any well-defined role. We were all tending to retreat into solitude in our offices.

I had met up with Carl Djerassi in London from time to time and he often told me I was welcome to come back to Syntex for a year if I could arrange a sort of sabbatical. Its research department had by now moved from Mexico City to Stanford, California. This sounded like a welcome refresher course to me. Our director Martin Davies kindly gave his agreement and it was arranged.

What to do about my flat? My co-occupant Ted had got married and left but Ingeborg had become friendly with a middle-aged American couple who were staying two doors away from me in a large maisonette. They wanted a smaller place and were happy to take over my flat for the year. My complaisant landlords agreed to this.

I flew off to San Francisco in late November. An apartment was soon found for me on Hollenbeck Avenue, Sunnyvale – quintessential Californian suburbia with its pool and sauna. The other essential, a car, was also soon found from a campus wife who was getting a new one. It was a 1960 Dodge Polara which had done 80,000 miles but it took me for another 20,000 without a hint of trouble. In fact it was a rather better car than my Chrysler though not, alas, a convertible.

At the splendid Syntex laboratories on the Stanford Industrial Estate I met up with several of my former colleagues from Mexico along with the many new ones. I had a place in the lab of Belig Berkoz, an amiable and kindly Turk with whom I would exchange reminiscences of Istanbul and Turkish food. He and others seemed mainly to be working on making new derivatives of my old Synalar in order to extend its patent life. I worked on one or two interesting problems which I need not go into here.

In the same lab was Belig's assistant, Graham Lewis, with whom I soon found myself much in sympathy. It was now 1968 with all its liberal and social revolutionary attitudes and Graham was involved with a project called the Free University. He was unhappy in his work with Belig and one day, 8 April, we decided to play truant and join a *pradakshina* of Mount Tamalpais to celebrate the Buddha's birthday. This had already set off from Muir Woods by the time we got there but we followed on and soon caught up with stragglers. It was a truly extraordinary occasion graced by most of the literary lights of the Beat Generation and luminaries of the City Lights Bookshop in North Beach. It was a warmish day and several decided that the pilgrimage would most appropriately be carried out naked. Allen Ginsberg was one of these. This mostly took place on the summit where there was a halt for refreshment but some persisted throughout the walk. Neither Graham nor I felt inspired to go that far. In late afternoon, with the sinking sun, we all walked back down the hill. It was a wonderful, unforgettable day.

But that was when I was well into my stay. Back in December, during the Christmas and New Year holidays, I had set off towards Los Angeles on the dramatically scenic coastal road starting just beyond Monterey. I had read of Big Sur on account of Henry Miller's one-time residency and decided to break my journey there. By chance I happened upon Deetgen's Big Sur Inn and secured a room. It was still cheap then and Deetgen himself was there to entertain the guests. A very convivial evening was passed not only with guests but also with local residents who dropped in. The following day I took in William Randolph Hearst's 'Castle' and stayed the night at Santa Barbara. At dinner there I particularly remember noticing that no one drank wine. Instead big jugs of that fearsome cocktail Santa Margarita were placed on tables to be poured into the salt-rimmed glasses.

In LA I found a motel in Hollywood and explored downtown, primarily to see the buildings. These included the then new Hyatt Regency Hotel with its startling glass-sided elevators which shot through the atrium roof and up the outside of the building. Another was the Bonaventure where I had a good meal in the top floor restaurant with its amazing views over the city lights. On Christmas Day itself everything seemed to be closed up and I found myself having my Christmas lunch in the coffee shop of the Biltmore Hotel near Pershing Square!

I went to see the Simon Rodia towers in Watts. These had been saved by enthusiasts from demolition by the city authorities in 1959. Now they are a designated monument. After this I drove back to Sunnyvale by the fast but dull inland route.

A NEW QUEST

My collaborator on natural resin work, Laurie Gough, had been working on a project: the chemical taxonomy of the *Cupressus* genus, i.e. an attempt to divide it into individual species on the basis of the chemical composition of the exuded trunk resins rather than on grounds of morphology. Western America, and particularly California, boasts a large group of these cypresses of which the most famous, the widely cultivated *C. macrocarpa* or Monterey cypress, occurs naturally only on the Monterey peninsula. The others are widely scattered, sometimes occurring as single, isolated strands. This afforded me the interesting – even quite challenging – objective for my outings of finding them and collecting samples of the resins, which led me in all directions. One trip up north was to Mendocino County and on to the beautiful Klamath River then back down inland. A favourite trip was to the foothills of the Sierra Nevada and Route 49, the region of the Gold Rush of 1849 ('…was a miner, 49er') and its charming old towns such as Copperopolis and Murphys. The latter was where I would stay as it had good accommodation and meals and in fact I went back there on later visits to California. Another trip took me more south-eastwards and was extended to Death Valley with its many fascinating features and sudden flowering if one is lucky enough to catch it, as I was in the spring.

My most adventurous trip took me across the Mexican border at Tijuana and into Baja California. An isolated species, *C. montana*, was supposed to occur in the Sierra San Pedro Martir so I made my way there and found a delightful house to stay the night in, the cultivated family taking in the occasional guest. Of all things they had a complete recording, on albums and albums of 78s, of most of Wagner's *Ring* cycle, which their two young sons appeared to know almost by heart. They gave me delicious trout caught in the adjacent stream and also lent me their jeep to pursue my search further up the mountain. I was not successful in finding the trees and moreover had to curtail my trip; the dirt road on the side of the hill proving just too poor. I had then to turn the jeep round while some local rancheros further down watched with interest to see if I would go over the edge. Back at the frontier the border people did not want to let me in: my visa was for a single entry into the USA. I forget now how that difficulty was overcome but obviously it was.

And then aside from these lengthy outings out and about the state there was San Francisco itself with the amazing Haight-Ashbury phenomenon. How had this come about? I went there many times and was very touched by the sight of all those young people, many of whom had come long distances after having heard that *this was where it was at*. And there they were, sitting on doorsteps or on the grass in Golden Gate Park, bemused by the company they found themselves in and also, in some cases, by marijuana. Usually their money had run out too and many were hungry. All sorts of enterprises had sprung up in this essentially residential district, all of which had totally vanished when I was briefly back there on a visit nine years later. I went to some theatrical performances including some small plays by Antonin Artaud, also one called *The Beard* by a local writer much celebrated at the time, Michael McClure.

My mainstream cultural activities were relatively few but a notable one was a fine production of *Tristan und Isolde* at the San Francisco Opera. At the end of Act 2, when Melot stabs Tristan, all the colour was drained from the scene and the stage turned to grey. The effect has remained with me and I always see it when I hear the opera on radio or discs.

THINKING OF HOME

Despite these great experiences, and the kindness and hospitality of many of my colleagues, when I was alone at Hollenbeck Avenue the inevitable question would sometimes arise in my mind: 'What am I doing here?' Essentially I knew that the Californian – the American – way of life was not for me permanently. I would return to London and stay there for the rest of my career. I had also to think of my parents who were now getting old, though in fact they were to live for many more years. My father was approaching 82 and when I eventually came home said to me 'You won't go away again, will you?'

My quest for the resins of all the local cypresses was still incomplete: I needed samples from *C. arizonica*. These grew along a river not far from Phoenix so I decided to go there on my way to New York and home. I sold on my wonderful Dodge to a technician at Syntex. He obviously failed to register the transfer as threats of fines, even imprisonment, for a parking violation, were redirected to me in London for months. In Phoenix I rented a car and successfully made my little expedition. Then it was on to New York and home.

BACK IN LONDON

My American sub-tenants had themselves just departed back to the US and my flat was in good shape, though the garden was greatly overgrown. Next door Ingeborg and Kenneth were now joined in marriage. A month or two later I was to make the journey to Berlin to see Ingeborg on the stage as I have described earlier.

In Guildford Mills & Sons Printers Ltd was being wound up. Father and his three younger brothers had had enough, both my male cousins Ted and Peter had long left to work elsewhere and it could not be sold as a going concern. Some of the machinery and moveable type was so old that it was given to a museum, the rest discarded. The premises were sold and the modest proceeds divided between the four. This sum (I believe it was no more than £3,000 each) formed the sole capital to provide a pension alongside that provided by the state. It was put into a building society account and was, of course, diminished to insignificance by the great inflation of the seventies. But my father did not really take this in and was happy enough. The mortgage on the house had been paid off by now and expenses were modest. He had another twenty years to live.

At the Gallery I resumed work on the natural resins; the *Cupressus* resins providing some interesting new compounds which led to a paper or two. When collecting these resins I had also thought to collect the seeds of the trees and I offered them to Kew. They were accepted with enthusiasm and many plants were raised both there and at Wakehurst Place. A small grove of the various species was planted at Kew, which I often went to visit in later years. Some did well but others, used to the dry conditions in California, grew too high and spindly in the wetter UK and tended to blow over in winter.

Staff changes in the Scientific Department had led to a better atmosphere and also allowed the appointment of a new senior scientific officer to assist me. This was Raymond White, who proved a great boon and collaborator. He was to remain for the rest of his career, taking over the practical organic work entirely even before I left.

Quite soon we had to move within the building. The North Extension, with us on the top floor, was to be built on the old Barrack Yard and would also incorporate our present space. A temporary laboratory and offices for us were adapted from what had once been a gallery space called the Dutch Cabinet, at the extreme south-east corner of the building (now the main restaurant), and we were comfortably established there for about five years.

CARPETS – STIRRINGS OF INTEREST

I had noticed some beautiful Caucasian rugs decorating walls in the Biltmore Hotel in LA and had also been envious of a fine example in the home of Syntex colleague Bert Bowers. I returned to the UK with a small capital of about £600 and after buying another (second hand) Mini I still had some cash to buy a few rugs. Philip Gundry told me of a specialist dealer/auctioneer concern on Cromwell Road called the Persian Carpet Gallery. It was the business of one Jean Lefevre and it held its auctions once a month. It offered very good rugs, mostly consigned, as I learnt later, by other London dealers, so by the standards of the time there were no bargains to be had. Prices were however very low compared with what they were to reach only a few years later. I bought three items; one of which, a beautiful Kurdish rug which was described as Sauj Bulak, I still have and admire. It cost only £100.

I soon learnt that much cheaper, if dusty and battered, old rugs could often be found un-regarded on the floors of antiques shops in provincial towns. This led me to a greater interest in UK travel, so I made no foreign trips in 1969. Philip Gundry had become very friendly with the family of (largely 'resting') actors Sarah and Tom Colmer. I had also known them for some years and so this year decided to join them on their annual holiday in Cornwall. As usual they rented a cottage in Mousehole and I made the long drive down there taking one or other of them with me. I much enjoyed this return, for me, to the atmosphere of 'family holiday'. We made outings to various beaches but a particular highlight was when we stayed up late to watch the moon landing. We also entertained local friends. I helped with the cooking (I had been an Elizabeth David fan for years) and I might also prepare some special luxury dish. I forget whether it was this year or another when I made Nesselrode Pudding, a disgracefully indulgent ice cream filled with crystallized fruit, dried fruits soaked in sherry or brandy, pints of double cream and much else. I had to go into Penzance to get ingredients but it was a great success.

One evening we had very special guests: Caspar and Mary John who lived in retirement up at Hayle. Caspar, second son of Augustus, had been an Admiral of the Fleet and he was First Sea Lord for several years up to 1963. They sounded intimidating but in fact were delightful, friendly and informal people. My contribution to dinner was only to prepare salad and I carefully divided up the *coeurs de laitue* in what I had read was the approved way. 'These are far too big,' said Mary, and pulled them all to pieces!

156

Years later I heard a radio talk by Mary on the bohemian life of the girls when she was at the Slade. One sentence has always stuck in my mind:

'Our beds were like old dog baskets.'

Well, *plus ça change…* But at least they didn't put them on exhibition as works of art.

12
THE SEVENTIES

Nineteen seventy did not start off well for me. In December 1969 I went down with flu but just before Christmas I decided I was well enough to drag myself to Guildford to spend the festive season with my family. On Christmas Eve I developed severe pain in the abdomen which was unrelieved by antacids. Eating was impossible and the following day the doctor was called in. He diagnosed appendicitis and I was whisked into the old Royal Surrey County Hospital close to us in Farnham Road. I was operated on immediately; the appendix, I was told, was at bursting point.

That should have been all but I continued to be slightly feverish. After a few days I was doubtfully allowed to go home but as it turned out I had some sort of viral lung infection which was to last for nearly three months. Though feeling pretty rotten I felt obliged to go back to London and to work. January passed and in February I felt I needed somewhere to recuperate. Vic said that it could be relatively nice in Estoril in that month and I went there to stay with Paula's mother, Maria Rego.

It did me no good. I dragged myself about, including into Lisbon whose hills almost defeated me. I remember only one enjoyable event. I found a huge old second-hand bookshop and rummaged about in its English section. A cardboard box contained a large number of letters, the notepaper headed by the words 'Osborne House'. They described the monotony of Queen Victoria's daily routines: 'drawing rooms' and other receptions and drives out. I could not however discover by or to whom they were sent and dates were given only as month and day, no year. They were too bulky and I was too ill to take charge of them, which I still rather regret.

I very gradually started to feel better and recover my strength towards mid-March. The rest of that year was unremarkable. I toured about at weekends looking for rugs and holidayed again in Cornwall.

The following year was better. I had remained in touch with Louis Sucheston, my friend from Detroit days, and now he had just taken a new wife. They were holidaying in France in May and I went over to join them for a week or so in the flat they had rented near Saint-Malo. In September I went on one of those long car journeys through Spain which were to prove my principal travel experiences in that decade. I did not then keep a travel diary, apart from noting my main stopping points, so I do not remember the journey in detail. I drove across France and up to Luchon in the Pyrenees. French people then were still given to taking 'the cure', so there was much company at the central spa where I stayed the night. I recall the large communal dining table and interesting conversation for which I had to really practise my French. Then it was down into Spain and across to Cordoba, staying in a *pension* near the mosque. I crossed into southern Portugal at Huelva and drove up through the Algarve to stay with Vic and Paula at Estoril and at the *quinta* at Ericeira. Here I learnt for the first time that Vic had been diagnosed with multiple sclerosis. His symptoms were not then too severe, nor always in evidence, so I was probably unaware of the prognosis and what was eventually to be the dreadful outcome.

I set off back into Spain heading for the region known as Las Hurdes (Caceres). I had known about this remote and impoverished region since my first Spanish travels twenty years before. I had then brought an old Cook's handbook to Spain which described the terrible backwardness of the inhabitants in the early years of the century. Since then there had been several initiatives intended to relieve the suffering but to little effect and in the Franco period complete stagnation and partial depopulation ensued. I spent a night in the small town of Coria and then drove rather randomly about the area, not always easy on account of dam construction: the roads on my old maps sometimes came to a dead end. At one point I came to an abandoned village, Rio Malo de Abajo. I stopped and looked at it from the road. A notice enjoined *Prohibida la entrada* and I was little tempted to disobey. The straggling dirt 'street' stretched away from where I stood lined with hovels – little more than single-storey, makeshift shacks with flat roofs barely six feet high. There was no sign of life.

I went on to La Alberca. This jewel of a small town had been declared a national monument in 1940 and had, in effect, remained untouched since then. To walk about it was like being back centuries before. The houses were all constructed with accommodation for domestic animals at ground level and were still so used, gentle sounds of lowing emanating from them. There were no cars to be seen, only a few carts, nor do I remember noticing many shops. A small hotel had been built on the periphery and I had a bite of lunch there and talked with the waiter. There were no other visitors. Now, forty years later, and its being only an hour's drive from Salamanca, I see that it has become quite a tourist centre with many small hotels and flower-decked balconies. This should not be lamented, I suppose.

So then it was on to Salamanca, the great university town, for the night. After that I went to the beach town of Laredo on the north coast, anxious to see the original of Laredo, Texas and Nuevo Laredo. It was an unremarkable but pleasant enough place. And so on to Calais with overnight stops at Bordeaux and somewhere on the Loire.

Travelling in 1972 proved to be even more exciting. It might seem from my narration that I was very little at work but in fact this was going well, if in a rather routine way; more interesting developments were to come later in the decade. In February there happened to be two conference meetings in Delhi, India at almost the same time. One was on the chemistry of natural products, the other on conservation in the tropics. I prepared a little paper for the latter and Martin Davies, the director, agreed that both Garry Thomson and I should be funded to attend. The long flight to Delhi was broken with a stop in Tehran for refuelling. Outside the flat-roofed reception lounge everything was covered in snow and ice; it was bitterly cold. Years later that flat roof collapsed under the weight of snow killing many people.

In Delhi we were put up at the old Central Hotel and I enjoyed walking about New and Old Delhi. Twenty-five years after independence it still had, to me, some of the indefinable feeling of its former colonial status, which I had known from Colombo. It had not quite lost dependency and gained self-sufficiency as now, forty years later, it clearly has.

The chemistry meeting afforded little of interest apart from meeting up with Derek Barton and, for the one and only time, Robert Woodward of Harvard, then considered the world's pre-eminent organic chemist. The other meeting was more rewarding, not least because it was followed by the standard triangular tour to Agra and Jaipur. I enjoyed the latter city very much. We went to Amber, taking the elephants up to the top, and also to Fatehpur Sikri. This marvellously preserved hilltop palace seems to have been abandoned for its lack of a reliable water supply.

By most felicitous chance the Maharani of Jaipur had invited us delegates to tea at her palace and there I was introduced to May Beattie. May was at that time the foremost worker on carpets in the UK outside of the Victoria and Albert Museum and she was in Jaipur to catalogue the large array of old carpets in the Jaipur family collection. I told her of my interest and my hopes of making a scholarly contribution one day. We often met up at conferences after that until she finally retired in the 1990s. She bequeathed money and her archive to the Ashmolean Museum in Oxford to create the May Beattie Foundation for the study of carpets and textiles. The other great experience in Jaipur was to see the famous, and the best, sixteenth-century Persian 'garden carpet' in its museum.

As usual I was not going to waste my opportunity for further travel and I went by a small Royal Nepali Airlines plane to Kathmandu where I found myself a room in Green's Hotel. I was charmed by the town. The airport was still too small for jumbo jets so mass tourism had not arrived yet. The people all seemed very happy and some could be seen smoking large joints of marijuana, which was still legal there. This was, of course, the final destination on the 'hippy trail' through Afghanistan and India and there were, in fact, a good many young Western travellers in evidence. Several hung out in a hole-in-the-wall tea room cum restaurant where I went for its tolerable food. An

161

ambulant dealer offered me a great block of cannabis resin stamped with the official seal of approval but I had no use for it.

I took to cycling again for the first time since boyhood. I rented a machine and cycled the ten miles or so to Bhadgaon (Bhaktapur). I had had the sense to get a hat, for the UV is very strong there, but my hands on the handlebars did get quite burnt. At the site a small bright-eyed boy took me in his charge and conducted me, often by the hand and warning me of low doorways, through the buildings which were still in an unrestored state. As the tour finished, he suggested tea in a smoke-blackened vendor's place. I must have given him something but it would have been very modest and perhaps he also got commission from the chai-wallah.

I enjoyed the cycling so much that back at work I took it up permanently, cycling daily to and from the Gallery through Regent's Park and along Regent Street.

In September the International Institute for Conservation of Historic and Artistic Works (IIC) held its biennial congress in Portugal. Southern Ferries had, the year before, started a car ferry service to Lisbon from Southampton on the *Eagle* and I thought this would be a good way to go, returning overland. It was a two-night crossing arriving at breakfast time and it was quite stormy. I stayed with the Willings in Estoril and went into Lisbon daily for the lecture sessions which were held in the wonderful new buildings of the Gulbenkian Foundation. Although we could not know it, the Salazar regime was to come to a revolutionary end in two years' time and meanwhile the entertainment provided was almost shamefully lavish for a fairly impoverished country. The puddings resembled the coloured plates in an early copy of Mrs Beeton and remained a fond memory and talking point for long afterwards.

My long journey home included a first visit to Ronda in Spain. I stayed in the Hotel Reina Victoria and found, when I had gone on to my next stop, that I had left my suit in the wardrobe there where it was still hanging when I went back. This was a lesson to me not to put clothes away on overnight stops.

The following year, 1973, I thought it was about time, given my interest in Turkish carpets, to see something of Anatolia. The cheapest way of getting there was via Cyprus so I took a return flight in June to Nicosia. Although it was now independent, Cyprus was still riven by Greek-Turkish divisions and also by division within the Greek faction. Nicosia was itself divided and the blue-capped United Nations peacekeeping forces were in evidence. I rented a car and went immediately to Famagusta, still very popular with package tourists. The beach was lined with hideous newly-built hotels, in one of which I stayed; but more attractive, and most extraordinary, was the little Turkish community enclosed and isolated in the old fortress.

I went on to Patras, then undeveloped as a tourist resort probably because it lacked a good beach. One of my objectives was to find certain trees – *Pistacia atlantica* – and collect a sample of the semi-liquid resin which they yield. I had reason to believe that this was a material much used in antiquity, particularly in Egypt, and I needed to determine its chemical composition. I did find the trees and obtained some resin and later was able to show that it was identical with resin found in amphorae recovered from a Bronze Age shipwreck which had been excavated at Kaş.

I also toured to other parts of the island, including Kyrenia, before returning to Famagusta to take the regular overnight ferry to Mersin on Turkey's southern coast. It was like a furnace there and I made haste to take a bus to Kayseri where I found a pleasant hotel with a rooftop restaurant. Then it was on (always by the excellent bus services) to Cappadocia, staying in Ürgüp and Nevşehir, to visit the extraordinary subterranean cities for which the area is famous. And then on to Konya (passing the great Seljuk palace of Aksaray) where I finally got to see some early carpets in the Mevlana Museum. After stops at Eğirdir and Pammukkale I journeyed back to the coast at Antalya, a delightful and undeveloped town. Now, I believe, it has received the full tourist makeover. I rented a car to drive up to the fabulous hilltop Greek city of Termessos where the sides of the hill are littered with monuments and sarcophagi. Continuing to Alanya, from there I took an overcrowded minibus for the very long drive along the corniche road back to Mersin and the ferry to Cyprus for my flight home.

FRIENDS

I have mentioned that Keith had felt obliged to give up his part-time position at Stourbridge, rather than take it on full-time, so as to be more available to his parents at Cranleigh. This left him in a difficult position financially and initially he made ends meet by doing decorating jobs for friends including me and Philip but more extensively for David Sylvester at his new bachelor establishment in Melrose Road. It struck him that David's flat needed some good rugs and carpets like the few that I had already acquired. This was the start of David's own interest in carpets, which he was to take up enthusiastically. I often called in on him while en route to Guildford at weekends so carpets became a major shared interest. David soon got to know all the main carpet dealers in London and would visit their shops and spend time in their back rooms looking over the stock. He made many purchases, several he subsequently considered mistakes and disposed of, but he developed a marked tendency to buy extremely worn and faded pieces if they were of an important type. Keith and I referred to them as 'David's ghosts' and later still a worn rug was sometimes referred to in the trade as being in David Sylvester condition. Later in the seventies and the eighties David knew, and had an exaggerated respect for, certain fashionable interior decorators and he was given to following their 'shabby chic' ethos. Everything should look old. Of course that did not apply to works of modern art but in fact he had rather little of this apart from his Giacometti sculpture and a Francis Bacon painting, each a gift from the artist. He already collected antiquities including a massive Roman head. He became fascinated by organising his small front garden and the part of the back allotted to him. For years during the eighties when I called in he would not allow me to talk of anything else, always demanding my opinion of his new arrangement for he treated it like an exhibition and continually moved the plants about. Of course they could not thrive under this treatment and although he would promise me that this was the final arrangement the next time I called I would find all changed.

To return to Keith, his father died in 1976 and his mother in 1979. After selling the Cranleigh house and settling all affairs he found himself to be in relative financial security and was able to resume painting. Throughout the decade we had often dined at mine or gone out together, commonly to Mustoe's Bistro in Regent's Park Road, where we were usually joined by Philip Gundry who now lived nearby in a house he had bought in 1972. Of course this was too big a living space for himself alone and he partly divided it into flats. A strange turn of events was that through some sequence of acquaintanceships the Hollywood actress Gloria Grahame ended up moving in to one of these in 1974. She also brought her old Scottish mother and would madden Philip by leaving her on her own, more or less in Philip's care. Another distressing trait was her tendency to make long calls to California on Philip's phone in the dead of night hoping that Philip would not hear, but he did. Gloria took up with a young actor, Peter Turner, who was now part of our circle (via Sarah and Tom Colmer). He later published a little book about their friendship and her sad end in Liverpool before being flown back to die in New York.

Philip had also acquired a remote hill farmhouse in Wales not far from Lake Bala. It had electricity though no running water but there was a stream and rainwater for the latter. There was also plenty of wood for fires so it could be quite cosy. I stayed there by myself once or twice and on two occasions was awoken by what seemed to be a loud knocking on the door in the early morning. I rushed downstairs to open it but found no one there. I later discovered that the noise was made by a crow pecking at its reflexion in a roof window.

During the first half of the decade Vic and Paula lived with their family – Caroline, Victoria and Nicholas – in their house in Albert Street, Camden Town and they both worked at their painting at home. However, Vic was finding it increasingly difficult to cope with stairs and after some searching they sold the house and moved in 1975 to a spacious flat in The Pryors, a large block of mansion flats on the edge of Hampstead Heath. Vic could still get out and he drove a large car with modified controls. He was still going to Portugal to deal with the electrical firm but after the revolution of 1974 it was no longer viable and eventually closed. Paula's mother Maria still had the house in Estoril but more and more she preferred to live with the family in London.

WORK AT THE GALLERY

In 1975 I was asked if I would take on the editorship of the journal of the IIC journal, *Studies in Conservation*. Garry Thomson had been editor from the time of his arrival at the Gallery in 1955 until he had handed it over to Dolf van Asperen de Boer in 1968. In 1975 the editorship had passed to Nigel Seeley at the Institute of Archaeology but he had shown little interest in it, saying that he was disappointed with the quality of the contributions. My appointment was, for unknown reasons, opposed by Norman Brommelle, long-time Secretary General of the IIC, and this led to a long estrangement between us, but he was over-ruled by the Council.

The quarterly journal was nine months – three issues – in arrears. To make this up efficiently required that nine issues should come out at a rate of one every two months for eighteen months and I resolved to accomplish this. It was not easy, as contributions had rather dried up and those that were on hand were indeed rather poor and needed much careful editing before being fit for the printer. Perry Smith, who ran the IIC office and had herself done considerable editing of IIC conference papers, was an invaluable help in this. Of course this was before digital compositing and I had to spend long evenings pasting up the proofs, along with the headers and footers and numbering, on to forms for the final printing. In the end my objective was achieved and to look at those issues now is to see no sign that they were not published regularly each quarter. Contributions had resumed and difficult ones were sent out to referees but they were often very slow in coming back. It was clear to me that things would be speedier if we had three editors of differing specialisms so that more of the papers could be assessed 'in house'. This became the policy and in fact the number of editors increased even further in later years.

By now the Queen had opened the North Extension to the Gallery in Orange Street and we were established in our new laboratories on top. Garry had been closely involved in the design of lighting and climate control systems for the exhibition rooms and he was now working on his book *The Museum Environment* (published 1978). This involved a good deal of mathematics and he increasingly felt the need to get into computing. We were also just beginning to hear a new expression: 'word processing'. All of us in the department did our own typing of letters and papers for publication whereas the curatorial staff dictated theirs for typing up by the typing pool. If we could type on a computer and easily correct mistakes and formatting all would be that much easier for us. A Wang microcomputer was bought. This had what now seems an unimaginably small amount of memory – 32 kilobytes – and a cassette system of program and data storage later upgraded to an eight-inch disk system. There were only a few programs available; we had to write our own in Wang Basic. This was an exciting new activity but could give one many a sleepless night trying to work out which line of code was causing a malfunction. Garry devised a very primitive word processing program which in fact I did use in writing up one of my papers, but it was a pain – no automatic justification or line return. The most complex program which I wrote was for compiling a cumulative index to *Studies in Conservation* and it demanded careful thought on the logic involved in putting entries in alphanumeric order. A proper word processing program never was available for that machine. It was only in the early eighties with the BBC Microcomputer that that immense convenience became available to me.

Raymond White and I were beginning to find that gas chromatography (GLC) by itself had its limitations for the analysis of complex organic materials. Mass spectrometry (MS) and the combined technique of GLC-MS were already widely-used techniques in academia and industry but still unknown in the museum and gallery world. The equipment was very expensive and learning to handle techniques quite new to us would be challenging but we decided to go ahead with it. Somehow the money was found and a Kratos MS25 GLC-MS apparatus, together with its enormous computer, was installed in our laboratory. Today these are compact, largely automated devices but this one certainly was not and it required careful maintenance and operation. The computer had to be pro-grammed ('booted up') in octal via a set of keys on the front panel and data was stored on huge removable disks which had the capac-ity (1.4 MBytes) of later 3-inch floppies. Over the next couple of years we got interesting and useful results and a first report of these came out in the *Technical Bulletin* (an annual publication started in the Department in 1977) in 1982.

DEVELOPMENTS IN THE CARPET WORLD

In the early seventies I became aware of some carpet activities in my adjacent street, Nugent Terrace. Robert (Bobby) Franses was one of four Franses brothers who were among the foremost London carpet dealers and he kept his stock and also had some repair work done there. His young son Michael was also sometimes there and so that was where I first met him. Michael went on to be not only the most adventurous and successful of international dealers in important an-tique carpets but also a major writer and entrepreneur in the world of carpet scholarship, as I shall explain.

About this time I already felt the urge to write something about the carpets to be seen in the National Gallery's paintings. That approach was not new – it had been important in the early work of the late-nineteenth-century carpet historian Wilhelm von Bode and the twentieth-century Kurt Erdmann – but I felt that it could be done more systematically and completely. But I would start with what was afforded by the Gallery collection which is rather rich in examples. It so happened that a series of little booklets called *Themes and Painters in the National Gallery* had recently been published, authored by the curatorial staff – Cecil Gould, Michael Levey and Christopher Brown, among others – and I thought I could produce a little book that would fit in well with these. In fact the series of six was complete but it was agreed that there could be a second series of which my little work should be the first. I much enjoyed writing something so completely out of my former sphere and which necessitated a vast amount of interesting background reading. It was probably too ambitious but I don't believe I made any serious mistakes, even if the history of early carpet-making has been much modified since then. The booklet was published in 1975 as *Carpets in Pictures*.

Writing about the advances of the Turkmen carpet-making peoples from east to west through Central Asia inspired me with the wish one day to visit those regions, not at the time feasible. I had the romantic notion that if I learnt Turkish I would be able to cope with other Turkic languages spoken there and I started taking evening classes. The small group which I joined consisted primarily of the English wives of Turkish men and we had a very good teacher. I was delighted by a language totally different from any I had tried before and made fairly good progress. I continued the following year and in 1977 but had to miss about three weeks of lessons while I was away in America. On trying to resume on my return I found that the course had dissolved with the defection of the other students so at that point I gave up. The little I had learnt did prove useful later and at least my pronunciation was good.

Also in 1975-6 I started to see Michael Franses, along with a new acquaintance, Robert Pinner, working at something in Nugent Terrace. They were planning several things: a society devoted to promoting the study and love of carpets; an international conference at which specialists could come together; a publishing company for issuing occasional books otherwise unlikely to find a publisher; and a magazine which would publish the conference papers and other worthy articles. In the end all these ambitious projects came to pass. Robert became one of my most stimulating and valued friends until his death in 2004.

The first International Conference on Oriental Carpets took place as soon as 1976 in London with exhibitions and the valued participation of the appropriate departments in the Victoria and Albert Museum and the British Museum. On account of my booklet I was asked to present a paper on the carpets with animal motifs which appear in Italian paintings of the fourteenth and fifteenth centuries. This then appeared in the third issue of the newly-formed magazine *HALI* (the Turkish word for carpet) in 1978. Many of the representations, and particularly those in the Sienese paintings, had features which made it impossible to designate them *Anatolian* animal carpets as they had been by Kurt Erdmann since 1929. Professor Marco Spallanzani of Florence, working with the Sienese archives, has discovered that there was in fact a carpet industry in Siena, yet the descriptions of its products do not fully accord with what we see represented in the paintings. A mystery still remains there but my own belief is that most of the carpets with animal designs shown *on the floor* are in fact reed mats either painted or wrapped with coloured wools.

To jump forward a few years, the second conference, which I did not attend, was held in Munich in 1978 and the third, which I did, in Washington in 1980. I did not give a paper this time but I much enjoyed the special exhibitions and reception at The Textile Museum as well as visits to Dumbarton Oaks and the major museums.

ALBERTO

I first met Alberto de Lacerda in the mid or late seventies. He was a long-time friend of Vic and Paula and I suppose we met up at The Pryors one weekend. He had been probably the first person to appreciate Paula's work in a published critique and was very supportive of her. At that time Vic was very impressed by Alberto's poetry and urged me, should we become friends and correspondents, to keep all his letters.

Readers, if they are interested, can now find his biography elsewhere and I shall give only a few salient points. He was born and brought up not in Portugal but in Mozambique in East Africa, only moving to Lisbon in 1946. Loving English literature, especially Shakespeare, he came to London in 1951 and found work with the Portuguese section of the BBC. Somehow he got to know the Sitwells, Edith in particular taking him up and introducing him into literary circles. This led to his friendship with Arthur Waley, the great orientalist, who collaborated with him in translating his *77 Poems*, published in 1955. These brought him modest fame but not, of course, fortune. Poverty, in some degree, was to characterise his whole life and was no doubt the prime cause of his ultimate bitterness. But he made ends meet in London until 1967 when he took up an academic position at the University of Texas in Austin and he was also, briefly, at Columbia University in New York, a city he loved. In 1972 he was made professor of Portuguese at the University of Boston and he remained there until his retirement in 1994.

Alberto and I were almost the same age; born in fact within three weeks of each other in September 1928. We found we had many interests in common and soon took to meeting for meals or visits to the theatre or, more rarely, the cinema. This, of course, was only during academic holidays, primarily the summer vacation, for he did not always come back for Christmas or Easter. He had a small flat in Primrose Mansions on the south side of Battersea Park and sometimes he gave me a meal there, or we ate out at a particular Indian restaurant he favoured, but more often he came to me and I pride myself that I always gave him a very good meal. It's a long way back to Battersea from St. John's Wood; public transport to there is inconvenient and taxis would be an extravagance so it was usually up to me to drive him back. I did this willingly for many years but eventually it became burdensome, even unwise if we had enjoyed (as we normally did) a bottle of wine and perhaps whisky afterwards.

Alberto naturally had affairs that needed attention in London during the long periods he spent in the US. Somehow I was gradually more and more roped in to cope with these. The main duty was to go every three or four weeks to the flat and sift through the pile of mail on the doormat. He wanted me to put it all in a large envelope and send it on to him but there was so much that this was impracticable. I would put aside (but I was on no account to throw away) obvious junk, open recognisable bills that had to be paid (I was left a handful of signed blank cheques) and send the rest to him. Making the payments was complicated: I had clear instructions only ever to pay the minimum allowable but sometimes there were unreasonable estimated utility and telephone bills (with threats of disconnection) which had not been allowed for, or some problem with the mortgage payments. It was a tricky business and made more difficult by Alberto's policy of secretiveness. He would not, for some reason, communicate directly with his bank to change direct debits and such like. I was to tell them to do so (which of course they would not allow) and then he would send a letter under cover to me, which I was to post to them from London.

These were not my only duties. Alberto was an obsessive collector of LPs which, it seems, were often remaindered or heavily discounted in shops he frequented in Boston. He would send *sackfuls* of these (apparently making use of some university postal concession) to The Pryors, from where I would convey them to Battersea. He later added these records to those already filling the shelves lining one side of (and half blocking) the long, narrow corridor through the flat. I was in permanent fear of these shelves collapsing or even eventually causing the floor to give way.

Another faithful friend of Alberto's, often commissioned with tasks, was John Sims, the St. James's bookseller and one day we were asked jointly to collect and transfer to Battersea boxes and boxes full of unsold copies of his *Sonetos* (Sonnets). They were collectable from somewhere in Jermyn Street and I think we must have taken them by taxi. Carrying them upstairs and finding anywhere to put them was no joke.

This all went on for years and years; through the eighties and into the nineties, by which time I was retired. Despite this I continued to value Alberto's friendship and particularly our common interest in and conversation about the arts, music, literature and theatre. We were both delighted with Paula's increasing success and reputation. He himself kept up old and valued acquaintanceships. He would from time to time go to stay at Renishaw, the Sitwells' family home; he would meet up with the poets Anne Beresford and Michael Hamburger; in Paris he would stay with the foremost Portuguese painter Vieira da Silva and her husband Árpád Szenes (d. 1985). When she died in March 1992 it struck me that Alberto was probably the best person in the UK to write her obituary and I urged him to do so and submit it to *The Independent*. At first he was doubtful they would take it but he did write it and dictate it to me to type up on my computer. The paper was delighted with it and it was duly published.

Sadly Alberto's calls from Boston on my time and patience became too much to bear. I forget which exact straw it was that broke this camel's back but it was just before his retirement and permanent return to London. I think it was when new requests came just as I thought I had done everything before leaving on a trip to Istanbul. I did them but said I would do no more and that ended our intimacy. With Alberto one perceived offence cancelled out all past obligation. For the rest of his life we did occasionally meet – at Paula's shows; at Paula's mother's funeral – but distantly, as it were. I was not alone in this. If one met his friends and the subject came up the cry was always the same: 'Oh, Alberto's so impossible!' One friend, John McEwen, did stick with him through his last years and after his death in 2007 wrote a wonderful obituary for *The Independent*. A cluster of us, including one of his former students who had come over especially from America, gathered in Brompton Cemetery for his interment in a plot that he had himself reserved. Little was said and like Laertes I felt like asking 'What ceremony else?' At a small Italian restaurant with a Portuguese proprietor near Waterloo which Alberto had favoured we all shared our memories of him and found they had much in common. We had all felt real affection and respect for him and done our best but in the end 'He was so impossible'.

Since then Alberto's long-term friend, legatee and executor Luis de Sousa has done wonders in promoting his memory and the availability of his work both in Portugal and the UK.

TRAVELS CONTINUED

In 1974 I took two delightful holidays. In June I drove in Brittany for ten days or so, mostly on the south side of the peninsula including Concarneau and Belle Isle. In September I set off along what later became a well-known route, stopping in Dijon and Aix-les-Bains on the way to my first visit of the Riviera. I stayed a few days in St. Raphael and Eze sur Mer before continuing on what later became to me to be a rather dreaded route round the Gulf of Genoa with the endless plunging into and out of the *gallerie*. The changes from brilliant sunlight to dark tunnels get to be very trying but, once through, I made for the delightful Cinque Terre. I stayed, I think, in Levanto but I certainly took that wonderful walk over the clifftops to Monterosso and on to Vernazza. By now very hot, I stripped down to my underpants to take the most delicious bathe ever from the jetty. Without road access the place was very quiet and un-touristed but thirty years later when I attempted to drive down into Monterosso the road was lined with parked cars for a good two kilometres outside the little town. I was unable even to stop and I turned round and went away.

That was my first brief foray into Italy since the debacle of 1952 but the following year it was back to Spain and Portugal again, this time taking a different route. Starting at Cherbourg I went through Nantes and down the Atlantic coast through La Tranche and Royan. I had a night in Bordeaux and then one in Pamplona where I was struck by its un-modernised appearance, still having the windowed balconies in the centre of the town which were so reminiscent of the Spain I had seen in 1949 and 1950. Then it was Burgos, my first stay of several, with visits to the Cartuja de Miraflores and the monastery of Las Huelgas with its wonderful collection of medieval textiles and garments. I stayed then and later at the old-fashioned but conveniently central Hotel España also patronised, they told me, by Ron and Lilian.

After a couple of days in Madrid, where it was still possible to find somewhere to leave one's car, I took the long, long road to Guadalupe, where I stayed in the monastery in an appropriately spartan cell. After a few days relaxation with Vic and Paula in Estoril and Ericeira I resumed my long tour, stopping memorably one night at the wonderful parador at Oropesa. I crossed the central Pyrenees via the remote and empty Val d'Aran and returned to Luchon for a night. On the way down from there I stopped for lunch at St. Bertrand de Comminges with its enchanting small cathedral. I went on for a night in Cordes at the ancient hotel on the summit but the rest of the journey remains vague as I had caught a flu-like infection and actually had to put up for a night in Dieppe to partially recover. I had probably rather overdone it.

In March the following year (1976) I renewed my engagement with Italy on a modest scale, this time travelling by train after flying to Milan. Memories of that trip have been much overlaid by many subsequent ones but I was first in Bologna then once again in Florence. In Siena I stayed at the Pensione Palazzo Ravizza, recommended to me by my curatorial colleagues. I liked it on that occasion but less so on a later stopover. My first rather brief stay in Rome was enjoyable and I found a nice hotel on the Aventine. My subsequent visits have been rather few and I don't feel I know Rome as well as I should. Then it was back along the same rail route but with a stop in Modena. The cathedral there is my favourite in all Italy. It was in a poor state then with plants, even trees, growing out of the masonry, but I found it restored years later. Back in Milan I made my first visit for ten years, with Riccardo still in his magnificent apartment at 1 Via Principe Amedeo. We had met on his visits to London however.

That summer in England we suffered prolonged hot weather and severe drought. Gardens and field crops went brown and died as it was impossible to keep them adequately watered. I recall that down at Guildford for weekends I found the heat at times so unbearable that in the evening I would go down to swim in the river at my old boyhood bathing places. In September I drove down to Cornwall for a week but by then the weather was breaking up.

I have mentioned that my Turkish classes broke up during my desertion of them during a visit to California in 1977. This was in April-May and I find it hard to recall now the impulse for my visit. I did however give two lectures, one to Carl's students at Stanford on my National Gallery work and the other to the local rug society on carpets in paintings. In all I stayed about three weeks, initially in Palo Alto, saw old colleagues and got about in a hired car. I couldn't resist a night back at Murphys and then set off down the old coast road again. I stayed again at Deetgen's Big Sur Inn but he himself was now dead and the atmosphere, though still agreeable, not the same. I visited Hearst Castle again and after LA went on down to La Jolla and San Diego. I have to say that there is a blandness, a sameness about travel in America that now makes it difficult for me to distinguish this trip from that of nine years before and also that to come in 1990.

By contrast I do remember vividly the short holiday I took in September to Corsica. Earlier that summer I had a painful accident in Gower Street. I was running to catch a bus and tripped over a raised paving stone, twisting my ankle. I hardly knew where to put myself for the pain. I just half lay there on the pavement in agony while passers-by asked if I was 'all right'. I wasn't but eventually I got a cab to UCH where a severe sprain was diagnosed and a crepe bandage applied before I was back in another cab and on crutches to the NG. It was weeks before I could do without the crutches but by the time of going to Corsica I was much better and able to walk almost normally again.

Part of the reason for going was to visit the gallery in Ajaccio, which my library research had revealed to have some interesting paintings with carpets in them. The quest for these was already becoming a powerful motivation for particular visits. Apart from the gallery I don't remember anything special about Ajaccio itself and I soon took a bus up the coast to Porto, a dramatic spot with a river full of mullet running down through it. Then it was further in a clockwise direction until I reached the northern end of the wonderful railway which runs down through the mountains back to Ajaccio. I, however, stopped halfway to stay overnight at Vizzavona in the heart of the forest. The proprietress was out in the woods collecting fungi to incorporate into our excellent dinner. Back in Ajaccio I rented a car to visit the east coast and look over the dramatic cliffs at Bonifaccio to Sardinia which I have never actually visited.

The next year, 1978, was to prove a wonderfully busy one for both professional and private travel. In January I had my first experience of Italy in winter as Raffaella Rossi of the Bologna conservation centre invited me there for consultation. As usual I was not just going to come straight back but went to Ferrara and then on to Venice. The gondolas were all shrouded in mist but the residents were not deterred from their evening *passeggiàta* and took the opportunity to show off their elegant winter clothes. I went to a piano recital by Emil Gilels at La Fenice.

I was currently preparing another article for *HALI*, this time on the so-called 'small pattern Holbein' carpets. A strangely untypical one appears in a painting by a relatively minor artist named Giovanni Francesco Caroto in the parish church in Tisoi, a village near Belluno, so I rented a car to drive up there. The church was closed, of course, so I looked around for the padre. Small boys soon gathered to advise me and point out his house, one immediately ringing the bell and running away to hide. The Father appeared at an upstairs window and I explained my mission. Alas, the painting was not there, he said, it had been removed to Venice for conservation. I never have seen it but my trip was not entirely wasted. On the way back I called at Vittorio Veneto and saw the beautiful *Annunciation* of 1505 by Andrea Previtali. This has one of the finest representations of the above-mentioned carpet type.

In April I made a trip to New York and to Washington, the former to give a talk at the Conservation Center, the latter to visit Robert Organ, formerly of the British Museum and now head of the Conservation Analytical Laboratory there.

In September I set off on a cycle tour of Normandy starting from Cherbourg. I had underestimated how empty of small towns that western coast of the Cotentin Peninsula is and almost found myself benighted. I was not carrying camping gear but reckoning on small hotels. I did find something eventually and for the rest of a delightful trip had no problems. The freedom to stop wherever and whenever one wants inspires a wonderful sense of liberation. I had my fiftieth birthday lunch in Caen including a delicious dish of *lotte de mer* (monkfish) *au poivre rouge*, which I have never been offered again. The following year I made another cycle tour, this time along the north coast of Brittany from Roscoff to Saint Malo. I had learnt by now that it was best to ride from west to east!

Back to autumn 1978, the IIC had a conference in Oxford and we had accommodation in Keble College. Everyone, though notably the American delegates, enjoyed this, particularly the service of breakfast. In October there was yet another conference, the ICOM conservation meeting in Zagreb which turned out to be an attractive city with an upper and a lower town. The post-conference tour was to the coast ending in Split, where I had not actually stopped on my previous trips to the Dalmatian coast. It's an extraordinary town with the modern part integrated with the remains of the Roman Palace of Diocletian. Some of us were unwise enough to swim there despite smells from the sea which didn't seem quite right. A horrible gut infection resulted. I had arranged to go on from Zagreb by train to Budapest but once there I found myself largely confined to the room I had rented. Despite this I did manage the main museums and saw the significant carpet collections. I went on by train to Vienna (the rifle-carrying guards on the train were very suspicious and rather intimidating) but my illness did not relent and I had to abandon my plan to continue my journey home through Germany by train and take an expensive flight instead. Once home I continued to be ill for fully another week.

In January the following year (1979) I was tempted by an advertisement for a cheap week's stay in Istanbul at the famous old Pera Palace Hotel. I found that by now it had fallen on evil days and was distinctly run-down. However, I had an enormous room and a bathroom the size of a normal bedroom, even if the bathwater flowed somewhat thinly. At that time Turkey was rather turbulent politically with unexplained deaths and kidnappings taking place and sometimes there were disturbing noises outside at night. My room, moreover, was at one corner of the building where roads crossed. There was no indication of priority and of course no traffic lights so my sleep was broken by cars screeching to a halt and raised voices.

It must be said that winter is not appealing in Istanbul. It is cold, damp and foggy and the streets are covered with fine mud. There were times, walking the bleak streets, when I wondered if I could stick out the whole week. Fortunately I was hospitably treated by Professor Oktay Aslanapa, then the foremost authority on Islamic arts there. He kindly had me to lunch twice at the university and also arranged for me to see carpets in store at the Turkish and Islamic Arts Museum; then in its old location, the *imarethane* (soup kitchen) of one of the mosques (I think it was the Suleymaniye). The famous so-called Seljuk carpets, discovered in Konya early last century, were got out for me and unceremoniously unrolled in clouds of dust. Although no longer considered by everyone to be of the Seljuk period these rugs are certainly of the thirteenth or fourteenth century and now, well mounted and conserved, are displayed as part of the treasures of the museum.

In late April I spent ten days in Sicily, flying to Palermo and travelling by train. As I mentioned earlier, arriving at my small hotel in Palermo I was delighted to find my friends Ron and Lilian sitting in the lobby reading. I will not go into details of this trip, which included Segesta, Agrigento and Syracuse, as I made several others later and will come back to the subject in another chapter. It had, however, an unfortunate conclusion. Back in Palermo I was walking across the big, empty main square to catch a bus to the airport when I was the victim of a well-known form of attack as two men on a Vespa came up from behind and seized the bag I was carrying. I very nearly managed to pull off the pillion passenger, who made the grab, but alas not quite. Then it was a repetition of the experience with the police that I had had in Naples twenty-seven years before, though this time, at least, I had not lost my documents. I made my *denunzio*, taken down by a fearsome *carabiniere*, who clearly saw me as an equally guilty party to the offence, and I got away as quickly as possible afraid that I would miss my flight. As it happened this was several hours late and it only got to Luton at about 4 am. A kind fellow-passenger gave me a lift to town but once arrived at Abercorn Place I realised my keys had been in my stolen bag and I had to awaken Ingeborg next door for a spare one to get me indoors.

After my cycle tour in Brittany in September, in October it was back to Italy again to go with Raffaella Rossi to Ferrara where the facade of the cathedral was under restoration. Once upon a time this had been vividly painted but, as with all others, had lost almost all its paint over the centuries. Some survived in sheltered spots and a technical examination of it was to be made. We clambered about on the scaffolding and I took a few samples to examine for the paint medium. Unfortunately the whole of the facade had been treated, sometime in the past, with a coating of linseed oil, intended as a preservative, and this was the only thing I could identify in my samples. I went on to Mantua and then for a day or two with Riccardo in Milan. I tried to stay in Genoa but could find no accommodation, so as the weather was dreadful I went back to Pisa and got home on an earlier flight. Airlines were far more accommodating about that in those days.

In the last year of the decade, 1980, my travels were slightly more restrained. In May I toured France by train with a two-week long ticket allowing more or less unrestricted travel. My aims now were centred on seeing as many museums and galleries as possible and to add to my catalogue of paintings with carpets depicted in them but I was also concerned to see major historic places which I did not know. I went to the main towns of Provence, then to Lyon, Strasbourg and Colmar, Metz and Nancy, among others. October found me back in the USA to talk again in New York but also in Washington at the Smithsonian Institution. This was followed by our carpet conference as I mention above with events at The Textile Museum.

I have failed so far to mention Charles Grant Ellis. At that time he was the most prominent early carpet scholar and enthusiast in America; an amateur and independent but loosely attached to The Textile Museum. He had contacted me after I had published my booklet in 1975, encouraged me to further studies, corresponded and met up with me when he was in London. We were friends. I don't know exactly how long he had been engaged with carpet work (his main field, I believe, had been architecture) but he had met Kurt Erdmann and he had translated a well-known German book into English which became standard reading on the early carpets. He had, however, uncritically adopted certain theories of Erdmann's on a particular carpet group and also formed an eccentric theory of his own as to the place of weaving of another. Later I was to find myself in complete disagreement with him, as I shall explain, and we had interesting correspondence, but I was never able to shake his adherence to his adopted positions. I turned out to be right but by the mid-nineties when this became clear Charlie had already passed away. I think he would still have been fighting a rearguard action.

13
INTO THE EIGHTIES

Comprising the final ten years of my life in paid employment, the eighties were to prove a varied and active period with both successes and sadnesses. At the Gallery our work on mass-spectrometry was opening up various lines of enquiry, one of which was to try and solve the problem of the nature and composition of Baltic amber. Amber is known to be a fossil tree resin surviving from some fifty million years ago. Not all of it is suitable for use as jewellery and the poorer quality material has sometimes been used in the past for making oil-resin varnishes. We wondered if it would be possible to identify these by detecting any surviving characteristic components. First it had to be determined whether there *were* any such components surviving in amber itself: curiously, despite a good deal of work on it in the past, nobody had really looked to see. Eighty per cent of amber consists of a highly insoluble, cross-linked polymer, the composition of which I need not go into here but the remainder dissolves in ether and so could be examined by GLC-MS. Amazingly I found numerous identifiable components including a range of familiar conifer diterpenoids. Apparently these had been preserved from oxidation by the tough and impenetrable polymer matrix. A paper on this was duly published by myself and Laurie Gough, with whom I had collaborated since my California days.

Another fascinating and unexpected discovery concerned the technique of the eighteenth-century painter George Stubbs, famous for his animal studies. Some of his paintings are notorious among conservators for being difficult to treat. The paint is sometimes very soluble in the normal cleaning solvents and may also be very heat sensitive so that some lining procedures become dangerous or impossible. My colleague Joyce had also noticed that cross-sections of some paint samples, instead of showing the normal regular stratification of layers, appeared all muddled up. Examination for the paint medium now showed that Stubbs had apparently added other ingredients such as wax and resin to, or instead of, the usual linseed oil and had experimented with a sort of encaustic technique in which the paint was blended together by briefly exposing it to heat. Such a technique had been devised and published by the Comte de Caylus in 1755. Raymond and I published our findings in the *Techical Bulletin* in 1985. Stubbs was known to be interested in new techniques including enamel paints on copper and ceramic but so far as I know no historical reference to his working in encaustic has been uncovered.

EXOTIC TRAVELS

Early in 1981 I spotted an advertisement for a week's tour to the Caucasus region, still then part of the Soviet Union. It was very cheap (I think £200) and irresistible. There were no international flights to the region then and all such tours started in Leningrad (as it still was) or Moscow. In March Leningrad was still snowbound and it was no longer the Astoria for us but a more austere hotel on the other side of the Neva River but I still managed to walk across the bridge to the Hermitage Museum. We were flown to Baku where it was more spring-like. There were carpets to be seen in the local museum, housed in a small disused mosque, but nearly all of recent, post-revolution weaving. Baku was a large city – I think the third in size in the Soviet Union – and it already had an extensive metro system. Old parts and a fortress survived however; as well as the Zoroastrian Fire-Worshippers' Temple, in the northern suburb of Surakhani, visited by travellers since the nineteenth century. This is located on a large natural gas and naphtha field which once used to vent spontaneously and was often on fire. Commercial exploitation, largely by the Nobel brothers, was well under way by the 1870s and was very much in evidence at the time of our visit and still is today.

We were a small group and we had a delightful Intourist guide who did much to oblige us. She managed to get me an interview with Lyatif Kerimov at the university. Kerimov was the local great authority on Caucasian rugs both as an author and also as a designer of what we collectors in the West saw as horrible Soviet-inspired portrait rugs. However, he was believed to be reliable on the towns of origin of earlier rugs with particular characteristic designs so I was glad to talk with him. He preferred to speak Azerbaijani rather than Russian and this was translated for me by a charming local Intourist girl.

Among our group was a pair of East End boys whose presence at first seemed unaccountable. All became clear, however, as we were flown towards Tbilisi in a neat little Russian jet plane. They were West Ham supporters and had conceived of this tour as a way to get to a game between their club and the Georgian national team in Tbilisi. It became evident that we would not arrive in time for them to see the game, already in progress, but the pilot and crew entered into the spirit of the thing, listening to the radio broadcast of the match and reporting back to the passenger cabin. I do not remember the result but rather believe it was a home win. At the end of our trip, back in Leningrad, I took these two boys on a tour round the Hermitage, pointing out to them many of the great things there and I found them very responsive.

The following year, 1982, a similar irresistible opportunity arose for a week's tour in Central Asia. Once again it was back to Leningrad where, although it was a week earlier than the previous year, the weather was slightly milder and free of ice and snow. A four-and-a-half-hour night flight, and a three-and-a-half-hour time change, brought us to Tashkent at 10 am. We were all desperately sleepy but a relentless round of meals and city touring kept us going until the evening. The hotel was full of delightful track-suited young athletes from the Soviet bloc, there for some sporting contest. Those who spoke English (a good many of them) were only too pleased to talk to us.

Tashkent looked rather grim and it was not helped by the still leafless trees. Much had been rebuilt in bright modernistic style following the serious earthquake of 1966 and it had not lasted well. I believe there was another serious quake in 2011.

We flew on to Bukhara in a small twin-engine propeller plane and were put up in a crumbling hotel in which all the fixtures and fittings were broken. The food was interesting though and it was wonderful to see the town. One really felt one was back in the world of Beys and Khans. At night sleep was difficult as the roaming dogs barked all the time.

A similar flight took us to Samarkand and a better hotel for three nights and here I was free to wander about at will among the monuments. The great buildings in Registan Square had already been restored by the Russians but other buildings were still partly ruinous, including the Gur Emir ('Tamerlane's tomb'). The high point of my visit was the fabulous mausoleum complex with its glorious tiles known as the Shah-i-Zinda.

We flew back to Moscow, arriving late at night. We were urged to go out and promenade with the people in Red Square but I took to my bed. There was all the following day however to make a tour and I did, as well as making an inspiring visit to the Pushkin Museum. We flew back to Gatwick that evening.

AN *ANNUS MIRABILIS* FOR CARPETS

Another international carpet conference (ICOC) was due in 1983 and it was to be held in London for the second time in June. The lecture sessions were to be at the Barbican Conference Centre while in the Barbican Gallery there would be an exhibition of mainly nineteenth-century 'collectable' carpets from all the main regions organised by Jon Thompson and called *Carpet Magic*.

David Sylvester had organised a carpet exhibition at the Hayward Gallery in 1977 drawing all the exhibited pieces from the collection of Joseph MacMullen, which had been bequeathed to the Metropolitan Museum of Art, New York. Now the Hayward was to hold a major exhibition, with important carpets borrowed from major museums worldwide and selected by David along with Donald King of the Victoria and Albert Museum. Its title was *The Eastern Carpet in the Western World* and it was to be accompanied by a well-illustrated catalogue including an article by me, 'The coming of the carpet to the West'; this I duly produced. It was well received and I think is still useful today. Additionally I was asked to prepare an audio-visual presentation to be available to the exhibition visitors. This was long before digital imagery and Powerpoint presentations and so consisted of the mechanical cycling of my slides with my commentary spoken by a well-known BBC presenter whose name, I fear, I have forgotten. It must have been run through hundreds of times yet never, I believe, broke down.

I was in the Hayward Gallery when the carpets were being hung or laid out for exhibition and so had a view (and hearing) of David's proceedings. He could get almost hysterical if things were not going as he wished and poor Susan Brades, the overall co-ordinator, was almost reduced to tears at times by his demands. The positioning of large carpets in a given space is more or less predetermined by the dimensions of both yet David would often insist on these heavy objects being rotated through all possible orientations for his assessment until they finally ended up in the obvious position.

MY EXHIBITION AT THE NG

In addition to this work for the Hayward Gallery show I had proposed to Michael Levey that we put on a small exhibition of paintings showing carpets alongside actual carpets of the same types. He raised no objection and the problem was now to locate and arrange to borrow suitable carpets. Michael Franses told me of a recent discovery of three early Turkish carpets in the old cathedral of Sion in the Valais, Switzerland, two of which would be ideal for my show and would also make their first appearance in public. I arranged to go and see them and in April went off by train to Brig to spend the night. The following morning I went back along the railway to Sion and up to the cathedral, perched on its hill. I was kindly received by the verger who had got out the rugs so that I could see and photograph them which was soon accomplished.

It was still early and I was determined not to come this far and not go on to Italy. I went back to Brig and caught a train to Milan, changing there for an express to Verona where I arrived about six o'clock. Walking in from the station I took a room at the Albergo Siena and continued to the town centre. I went straight to the Museo del Castelvecchio, which I knew to be open until 7.30 pm, and as I arrived there I gradually became conscious of an extraordinary change and enhancement of mood. I felt immensely happy; everything that I looked at was transfigured. The paintings on the walls, the sculptures on the gleaming marble floors were the most beautiful I had ever seen. This was surely the most beautiful museum in the world. Outside, crossing back over the bridge I was ravished by its structure and the views between the battlements. This too was the most beautiful bridge in the world. Walking back into the centre of Verona, in what can only be described as a state of bliss, I asked myself, can this go on? It did. I found a small restaurant and had a meal outside. A crowd of young Italians revealed themselves as the happiest, most delightful and beautiful young people I had ever set eyes on. As the evening went on the mood very slowly subsided and I made my way back to my *albergo* and a good night's sleep.

The next morning I was more or less back to normal but still very happy. I have never had another such experience and of course wonder what brought it on. It could be thought of as a sort of Thomas Traherne semi-mystical experience ('the corn was oriental and immortal wheat…') and though I would not deny that, I would also like a scientific explanation. I can only think that it stemmed from my having passed a completely successful day in which everything had gone right and nothing remained to disturb me.

Back in London arrangements for my little show went well. Two of the Sion carpets were borrowed and, along with others, arranged on a long table in what was known as the special exhibition room in the North Extension of the Gallery with the paintings on the walls as normal. I prepared an updated, slightly larger version of my 1975 booklet, now called *Carpets in Paintings*, to accompany the exhibition, which opened in June and ran for a few months. It got some good mentions in reviews and I still meet people who remember it. The booklet is sought after now and quite hard to find, selling for about £20 or more on the Internet. Its original price was 60p.

The following year Professor Oktay Aslanapa set up a little conference in Istanbul, the 1st Turkish Carpet Conference, and I was asked to contribute. It was a delightful affair, well-organised and with splendid exhibitions of carpets from the stores which we were free to photograph. When it finished I flew to Trabzon – the famous Trebizond of old – which had survived for a further eight years after the fall of Constantinople to the Turks in 1453. The overgrown citadel was still visible, if hardly visitable, but among other sites that I went to was the mountainside monastery of Sumela. Sadly damaged and with its murals defaced following the wars and 'exchange of populations' of the 1920s, it remains impressive. Some years later, following the collapse of the Soviet Union, I heard that Trabzon became flooded by Russians from across the Black Sea intent on buying and selling.

I went on by bus to Sivas and Ankara before returning to Istanbul and home. A year or two later Oktay put on another small meeting, this time on Turkish tiles, and this took us on further wonderful travels to İznik and other parts.

ANDREW VICARI

For more than two decades after that remarkable exhibition in 1961 the question was sometimes raised among his former friends and acquaintances, 'What happened to Andrew Vicari?' but no one had an answer. On Sunday morning 5 June 1983 I got a phone call from David Sylvester: 'Have you seen *The Observer* supplement?' I had. 'Now you know what happened to him. *Now you know what happened to him!*' he chortled, almost choking with the joy of it. Of all possible eventualities it was indeed the least imaginable. The article, 'The Court Painter of Riyadh' by Alan Road told the story, later endlessly rehearsed and elaborated by other journalists and by Andrew himself, of his series of paintings, *The Triumph of the Bedouin*, glorifying the Saudi regime and created to decorate a new conference centre. Andrew was now rich and commuted between Riyadh and a home in Nice and/or Monaco.

Henceforth Andrew was to prove an unfailing source of news items for the press, amply encouraged by his own pronouncements and shameless boasting and by a lavish book which he published: *Andrew Vicari. Vie et Oeuvres* (Parma 1986). He falsified the year of his birth as 1938 which continued to appear in articles for the next thirty years and which meant that he had to claim to have been the youngest student ever to enter the Slade. He was 'The King of Painters'; he had exhibitions in Geneva, France, Russia, China, the USA and was photographed with the rich and famous; he entered the *Sunday Times* rich list with an estimated fortune of £40 million, later upped to £90 million; he was buying Picasso's old villa at Antibes and would start an academy there; he was writing his autobiography. This last project never materialised and would have been tricky to write given the way that biographical details he had already released had been 'embroidered' (to put it kindly).

This continued well into the 2000s by which time he had been adopted as a national hero in his native Wales. But there were hints of financial problems which included the great expense of creating, storing and insuring his numerous large, unsold paintings. Out of the blue in 2014 came reports that he was in bankruptcy proceedings. It would seem that he had over-reached himself and it had all ended in tears. The rest was silence until on 3 October 2016 came the news that he had died of pneumonia in hospital in Swansea aged 84.

Well the newspapers mostly got that right even though most still peddled the old myths and some still gave his birth year as 1938! Perhaps all this will one day be the subject of a careful biography and the many mysteries clarified. I found the ending very sad indeed for we had been friends once. His early work still shows a great talent; he certainly worked hard and with dedication and the Riyadh project was a real achievement.

14
ANNÉES DE PÈLERINAGE

I have always been attracted to the idea of the quest, the pilgrimage. It is almost a cliché that research is a pursuit of that kind and a particularly important result is often spoken of as the 'holy grail' of a project. Even in my teens I sometimes consciously dedicated myself to study and achievement. I often fell short in perseverance but on the whole this attitude has allowed me to carry through my small projects to successful ends. In the arts too I am touched by works on this theme. Liszt's wonderful piano cycle to which he gave the name I have used for this chapter touches me. Poems and operas on a like theme are among my favourites: Tennyson's 'Sir Galahad', Wagner's *Parsifal*.

By the start of the eighties it struck me that I only knew Italy very incompletely and I resolved to pursue my quest for carpets in paintings by scouring museums and churches in all those small towns with famous names, from Lombardy down to Calabria. I didn't intend to abandon Spain entirely, and most years went there for a week or so in spring, but I was resolved to spend the bulk of my vacation allowance (a generous six weeks) in Italy in September/October. I was still doing all my travelling in my Mini which I found adequate to carry me and my baggage over the Alps. It was only later, in 1995, that I needed a somewhat larger car when I drove Tony Werner to Italy to visit Joyce Plesters. I did not initially keep a diary but in 1982 started recording each day's events on a small cassette recorder for eventual (?) transcription. In fact I have transcribed the Italian entries which form a book in themselves. Obviously they cannot be inserted here, even abbreviated, and I mean simply to pluck out a few incidents of particular interest or charm.

Colour pictures of paintings were still hard to find in those days before the Internet and in my efforts to get photographs I would have to battle with obstructionist vergers in churches or guards in some museums but this was my aim; yet these were spiritual journeys too.

TEA TIME IN CORTONA

In 1981 my first extended tour in central Italy was a rich and rewarding one but I shall report only a single episode. Knowing of my plans, Alberto said to me: 'If you go to Cortona you must call on the Conte Morra and give him my kind regards.' Apparently they had met at literary functions, had corresponded by letter but had now lost touch. I did indeed plan to go there as there was an important painting by the Sienese artist Stefano di Giovanni (known as Sassetta), of course with a carpet in it, that I wanted to see.

Cortona in Tuscany is one of those ancient hilltop towns of immemorial origin and a history going back to Etruscan times. Like other such it also has a modern town down below clustered around the railway station. Alberto had not been able to give me any address so after a successful visit to the upper town I returned below to make inquiries. A newsagent came up with the address, the Villa Metelliano, so I promptly went along to it and rang the bell. A servant took my message and came back to say that I could not be received that day but if I cared to come back to tea the following day the *conte* would be very happy to see me.

Next day I duly returned at the appointed hour and found a gracious old man along with two local friends. One was a formidable English lady, the other a young man whom I took to be his amanuensis. I failed to catch either of their names. All spoke English. The *conte* asked after Alberto and I gave some account of his life in the USA. I explained what I was trying to achieve in the way of carpet scholarship but I hardly seemed to get that across. After our tea I was asked if I would like 'to go upstairs'. I thought it a slightly strange question but said yes and the young man took me up to the *conte*'s bedroom. Hanging over the head of the bed was an enormous photograph of King Umberto I of Italy. Nothing was said as to why it hung there. He is now said to have been the *conte*'s Godfather but the whole atmosphere – and I have also heard it hinted – suggested that the relationship was a closer one; that he was in fact his father. The *conte* was born in 1897. King Umberto was assassinated in 1900.

When I was back in England I wrote to Umberto Morra di Lavriano e della Montà, to give him his full name, thanking him and sending him a copy of one of my papers. I did not get a reply and it was only years later that I learned that he had died only two months after my visit, on 5 November at his home.

ANGELS TODAY

The Gargano is that strange 'spur' jutting out into the Adriatic just above the heel of Italy. It's quite mountainous, of course; that's why it's still there. The coast is not very interesting but inland there survives a remnant of the oak and beech forest, the Foresta Umbra, which once covered much of Italy and indeed Europe; driving through it one experiences darkness and a sudden and marked drop in temperature.

Somehow the town of Monte Sant'Angelo, with its sanctuary dedicated to Archangel Michael, seemed like the place to visit. Arriving up there in my Mini I was shocked and disappointed by all the ugly modern buildings but I had had a long day, it was late and I needed to stay there. I went all over looking for a hotel. A modern hotel at the end of town looked empty, dark and depressing but back in the centre I found a humble little *albergo moderno* where I took a room. I was the only guest so I had the bathroom and other facilities to myself.

It was evening and the *passeggiàta* was already in progress. How could there be so many people in this small place? Certainly every one of them was out on the main street and overflowing into adjacent ones; old and young, they were there. A cluster of the boys, spotting a stranger, accosted me for conversation, their leader a captivating Piero della Francesca angel of curls and smiles. Already knowing everyone in the town, at least by sight, and every nook and cranny that could be explored he looked further afield and wanted to know all about me, what I was doing there and where I was staying. It was easy to talk with him as he spoke pure Tuscan Italian almost as a second language and consequently more slowly and carefully. 'We usually talk in dialect,' he said, 'see if you can understand me.' And he chattered away to his friends. Of course I couldn't which much amused them. They danced away into the throng. I walked uphill to look for somewhere to eat. The restaurants near the Sanctuary, used by pilgrims during the day, although still brilliantly lighted were now all empty and uninviting so I sought a trattoria. On my way I witnessed a painful scene. A man was berating a young girl of perhaps thirteen or fourteen, presumably his daughter. She stood there in her cheap flowered frock cowering against the wall. '*Veti a casa! Veti a casa!*' he shouted and walked away. Suddenly turning round he went back and gave her a terrible slap on the face. Those around looked silently on, then all melted away and the flow of people resumed.

I found a cavernous trattoria and peered in. Two tables were already filled with parties of locals. The proprietress urged me to come in and I did so. I had a wonderful meal taking everything recommended by the Signora – delicious antipasti followed by a small mountain of tiny chops – goat not lamb – which were very tender; a salad and fruit; and, of course, local wine *ad libitum*. When the *conto* was brought to one of the other tables a storm of protest immediately ensued with fists thumping on the table. A vigorous argument was carried on. The Signora went into her kitchen and brought back raw materials to show off the quality of what she had provided. Gradually it quietened down and seemed to end amicably. Exactly the same happened with the second large party. Perhaps such protests are de rigueur, demanded for the honour of the father of the family, but I certainly made none. My bill was a modest 8,500 lire, I suppose about four pounds then. I felt a great sympathy with the Signora and her tough life. It reminded me of Gissing's sympathetic encounter (*By the Ionian Sea*) with the poor old overworked servant woman ('*Ho tanto, tanto lavorato*').

I walked back down the street which was still crowded. My new young friend waved to me and mouthed 'Ciao'. What was to be his destiny in this backwater? Now, more than thirty years later, has he become a frustrated table thumping, even violent, paterfamilias? Perhaps not; times have changed and there is now greater scope for escape. Or perhaps yes; 'Full many a flower…'

MEALS IN SYRACUSE

While eating alone in restaurants, especially if they are rather empty, can be depressing, it does allow one to observe the company more closely. I notice that many of the incidents I shall describe stem from that circumstance.

I was in Syracuse (Siracusa) during my tour of Sicily in 1979 which ended disastrously in Palermo. While there I visited the remarkable Greco-Roman remains on the mainland but I also had a good look at everything on the peninsula, or rather island, of Ortigia. On that side of the bridge that links the two parts there was a nice open space and a restaurant, the Darsena, with tables outside. After a busy morning at the museum I decided to lunch there. I had bought some postcards of Greek vases depicting erotic scenes. The young waiter spotted these on the table, picked them up and blew kisses at them in sympathetic participation. *Evviva* paganism! Later I became conscious of two men a few tables away. Lunch was nearly over, it had grown quiet and I could occasionally hear a few of their words. One of the men was sleek-looking, slightly plump and dressed in a smart suit. The other was more casual, lean and rather mean-looking, somewhat resembling the actor Clint Eastwood in his earlier roles. They were speaking in English and rather intensely. The lean man suddenly became animated and said very clearly, 'Shall I kill him now? Shall I kill him now?' I 'froze in my seat', as they say, and took care not to look in their direction but out of the corner of my eye I could see the sleek man raise his hand in a calming gesture, lean forward and, I suppose, urge patience. I stayed on over my coffee until they had gone, quite shaken really. *Evviva* the Mafia?

MEALS IN SYRACUSE 2

Back once again in 1986, I stayed at the old Grand Hotel in its prime position overlooking the mole. With the decline of the town as a port, what must once have been its glory days were well over and it was run-down and dowdy[1] but it was pretty well the only hotel on Ortigia. A room was cheap and if the hot water supply was minimal and it took half an hour to (partially) fill a bath there was compensation while waiting in enjoying the fine view from the window.

I was back there primarily in quest of a particular painting, said to be in the Palazzo Arcivescovile in Piazza Duomo. My first efforts to gain entry to see it were on a Sunday and they were unsuccessful. I was told to try the following day. I had a good look at the cathedral, a remarkable building which partly incorporates an original Greek temple. I had noticed with some alarm a platform out in the square with instruments and an array of loudspeakers but I thought, it's Sunday, they will not play today and I entered a restaurant for lunch. I was quite wrong: the loud pop music started up and went on relentlessly during my meal; it was too late to escape. However, within the cathedral a counter attack was afoot. The bells were rung! They were truly deafening; the musicians struggled on for a while but eventually they looked at one another and by common agreement packed up their instruments and left the stage. Satan was resoundingly defeated.

SYRACUSE 3

In 1991 I was once again in the city as I was intending to take the ferry to Malta where my sister June and brother-in-law Arthur were now living. I stayed once again in the old Grand Hotel which was in much the same state as it had been five years before. The lobby was small and uncomfortable so one did not linger there long to observe the guests. At one point however I noticed a middle-aged Italian couple conducting themselves, as it appeared, rather grandly towards the staff. It seemed out of place to be putting on airs in this decayed hotel and I wondered if perhaps they were themselves survivors of the decayed local aristocracy who had perhaps known it in its better days.

The Trattoria Darsena where I had had that interesting lunch was still in place but I decided to choose somewhere more stylish for my dinner on this evening. The Trattoria Archimede looked good and I turned up there unfashionably early as usual. Provided with wine

[1] The hotel has since been completely refurbished.

and titbits I was in no hurry to order before more company should arrive. Rather strangely a single man in ordinary workman's clothes was among the first. He was seated alone near me and was treated offhandedly by the waiters at first but they became more respectful as he ordered and ate a copious meal: the usual *primo* of pasta followed by a large fish.

A slight flurry at the entrance heralded the advent of my couple from the Grand. She, the dominant partner, wore a huge stole – almost as grand as the *stola veneziana* once affected by Venetian senators. They looked all round, not quite satisfied with their reception, and then walked through to a farther room. Still not satisfied they came back and stood by a side table bearing antipasti, she smiling and helping herself to choice morsels while the *patrone* was fetched. He finally got them seated to their satisfaction.

As I was getting through my own meal there was a sudden influx of a large group of people all carrying big red notebooks, evidently attenders at some course or symposium, and confusion ensued as to where they were supposed to sit. Two young men, looking quite lost, approached an elderly man, who had already defiantly seated himself, to ask his advice. '*Non so niente!*' (I don't know *anything*) said he, and so vehemently that it made me burst out laughing.

The 'working man' near me finished his meal and left. He had been given no bill.

The minor character of my Grand Couple left his table and approached the *patrone*, flourishing his wallet as if offering to pay (if he had asked the waiter he would have got the bill immediately). '*No, non pagare, non pagare!*', was the response in what sounded to me like despairing tones. Nonetheless he was taken at his word and the two swept out with gracious smiles.

I asked for my own bill. The *patrone* wrote it out with almost vicious sweeps of his pen. It was bigger than it should have been (45,000 lire) but after all *somebody* had to pay. I didn't care; I had been richly entertained even if some of what I had seen remained open to explanation.

LITERARY PILGRIMAGE

I think it was Norman Douglas's generous appreciation of her in *Alone* (1921) that started me reading Ouida. I still have about a dozen of her books on my shelves and although I am glad to have read them I cannot say that I have very vivid memories of them apart from *In Maremma*. This has wonderful passages of nature study but the story, like others of hers, eventually sinks into melodrama. As Douglas remarks, her essays and critiques are superior but they, of course, never did nor could make her the money she needed for the extravagant lifestyle she always felt was her due. She ended up living in poverty and undernourished in Viareggio and died there in 1908. She says somewhere that she hated Bagni di Lucca: it's in a valley and in winter the sun never showed over the hills before 10 am and disappeared behind them by 4 pm; nonetheless that was where she was buried, courtesy of her friends.

I have often stayed in Lucca itself. It used not to be crowded with tourists like Florence; it was relatively easy to park and if one arrived by train there was a handy *albergo* nearby and only a short walk through the walls to the centre. Despite its name Bagni di Lucca is a considerable drive from Lucca with no obvious connection with it. It's to the north and getting into the foothills of the Apennines in beautiful country. I went there to find Ouida's grave.

In the nineteenth century this small town, or rather large village, was a fashionable spa and place of resort, especially in summer when it was no doubt cooler than the cities. I believe the Brownings went there after their escape from England and Mr Barrett; perhaps taking the waters was also a consideration for permanent invalid Elizabeth. Although it still functioned as a spa, it was a very quiet place indeed when I went there in the early nineties.

Ouida is always said to be buried in the 'English cemetery' so that is what I enquired for. I got puzzled looks but eventually obtained the direction that I should cross the river and walk about a kilometre along the road there. I did this but arrived at what was the main cemetery. Renewed enquiry sent me back to just across the river from the town where I found the walled and gated enclosure I was seeking.

It had a rusty padlocked iron gate but the wall was broken down in places and gave easy access to the picturesque, rather overgrown grounds.

It turned out that this was by no means just an English cemetery but a burial ground for all non-Italians for whom the waters had not proved curative or whose survivors had chosen the place. It was quite sparsely 'populated' and I soon spotted Ouida's tomb, a rather grand sarcophagus with, on top, herself recumbent in marble with a dog at her feet. I have now forgotten how it was inscribed.

Well, that was it really. What more can one do? I took some photographs and looked at some of the other monuments but the names meant nothing to me. I made my way back to Lucca. A year or two later, when in Bury St. Edmunds, I sought out the little semi-detached house where she was born and also the memorial in the form of a drinking fountain for the animals she loved so much. It was neglected, dry and dusty just as Douglas had found it ninety-odd years before.

While on this topic of literary pilgrimage I might just mention a greater hero of mine, George Gissing. He too is said to lie in an English cemetery in St. Jean Pied de Port, at the western end of the Pyrenees, where he died. In fact his grave is just 'in some corner of a foreign field' given over to foreigners in the general cemetery at St. Jean de Luz on the coast. Here H.G. Wells attended his interment having arrived just too late to bid him farewell in life. This was of course before the simple headstone had been put up.

VISIONS OF THE BAROQUE

I once remarked to a very distinguished connoisseur and collector that I was beginning to like, perhaps to 'understand', the Baroque. 'It happens as you get older', he sagely responded. Is this true? If so, why? I have no answer but will recount two instances of 'revelation'.

Piazza Armerina in Sicily is best known for the fabulous Roman mosaics of the Villa Casale some two miles outside it. They are indeed a marvel and most visitors come from elsewhere to visit them, missing the town. I stayed a night there so had a chance to wander about the

197

old streets and I ended up in early evening sitting in the square in front of the cathedral. Both are on an eminence, so the westering sun fell full on the facade. I took no photograph and so now have nothing to remind me of exactly how it was but somehow the stolid, almost clumsy, piling up of heavy decorative elements seemed to make sense; seemed to reveal a defiant striving towards an affirmation of faith – in an age of uncertainty? The effect was touching and beautiful. This is a very minor example of seventeenth- and eighteenth-century architecture, yet it could move me more than supposedly far greater works – St. Peters in Rome, for example.

Taranto in Puglia is set on an extraordinary site. The old town is compressed on to a small island which half blocks the narrow entrance from the bay – the Mare Grande – to the large, round inner bay – the Mare Piccolo. Bridges at its north and south ends link it to the mainland. The modern town is to the south and, as the home of a large training establishment for the Italian navy, is animated and cheerful. Smartly turned out cadets walk up and down in pairs and there are bands and ceremonies. I had no special interest in being there though I did know that in antiquity it had been famous for production of a fibre, byssus, obtained from certain species of mussel, which was used to make very fine gauze-like cloth. This was still being made when the Scottish traveller and writer Craufurd Tait Ramage was there in the 1820s. He had also seen a small hill of whelk shells, relics of the extraction of the famous Tyrian purple dye. There was no evidence of any of all this now; at least I did not find any in my short stay.

There are some parts of southern Italian towns that are so dark and decayed that they give one the creeps. It is all too understandable that they have been abandoned and it seems unlikely that they can ever be brought back to life again. I had felt this at the very end of Ortigia, Syracuse when I walked up there on my first visit in 1979. Again, in Cosenza, I walked up through the narrow, old main street between the towering, dark small-windowed tenements and had to turn back. Surely, I thought, no one could now live in these. In Taranto in the afternoon I walked over the south bridge into the *città vecchia*. There was not a soul about and though I persevered for a while, creeping about through the hopelessly slummy streets and alleys, I found the cathedral closed and retreated back to the mainland. I was not at all sure I would go back again in the evening but fortunately I did, walking briskly along the *via duomo* to avoid groups of youths who were not reassuring. Inside the cathedral I found it completely deserted and with only some, very dim, lighting. I spotted the chapel of San Cataldo, a small freestanding (as I recall it) structure within the nave and went in. Just inside was one of those coin-in-the-slot light switches and I inserted the required coin. An astounding interior, like some magic grotto, exploded into view, every surface embellished with coloured marbles, images or decoration and frescoes on the ceiling. Round the walls were niches, each with its statue of a saint and all with the most varied, exaggerated and tormented gestures and expressions that I had ever seen. It seemed to be in wonderful condition, as if it had been completed yesterday; a perfect and unitary work of art. I believe it is quite late, even early eighteenth century, and it certainly seemed more in the spirit of Rococo than Baroque. Dare I say it, more feminine than masculine. But these are subsequent reflections; then I just gazed in wonder putting coins into the light box until I had no more.

I made my way back over the bridge in quest of dinner and thinking about San Cataldo. Very popular in Southern Italy and Sicily (there are several small towns named after him), it seems he was a seventh-century Irish monk, originally from Lismore. He went on a pilgrimage to Jerusalem and on the way back was shipwrecked near Taranto, there eventually to become bishop and archbishop.

EARTHQUAKE COUNTRY

In 1989 I was mostly in the Abruzzi and those wonderful small towns in Central Italy south of Rome for which I have a special affection. I had been in Scanno and from there made my way to Alatri where I decided to spend the night. The church was closed and would not open until later so I went off to nearby Ferentino where I found the duomo open. There was the wonderful Cosmatesque pavement and the *sedia* behind the altar; perhaps not quite as striking as the one in Anagni but very lovely with its two *leoncini* at the base.

The following day I went on to Subiaco and later called in on Olevano Romano. This once held a thriving artistic community and was a haunt of Norman Douglas between the wars but was now sadly decayed and completely uninteresting. I went on from there and at lunchtime found myself in Genazzano, where I parked and (as I remember) walked up a long slope. Every building seemed to be covered in scaffolding. An earthquake had resulted in extensive damage and massive efforts were now going on to repair, or at least stabilise, the historic buildings. I asked a solitary gentleman walker if there was a trattoria nearby.

'Oh yes', he said, 'up the hill and on the left.'

'And what is it called?' I asked.

He giggled and replied, 'Trattoria Terremoto' (Earthquake Trattoria).

I found it and went in. It was very busy, several of the tables being occupied by the building workers who were enjoying substantial meals lubricated with great flagons of the local wine. I ordered *salsiccie* (sausages) and *fagioli* (beans) which turned out to be rather good.

They seem to be particularly sensitive in Italy in their way of treating physically and mentally disabled people and you often see groups of these with their carers taken for outings to parks or restaurants. Moreover this seems to be well accepted by the ordinary customers despite the sometimes disturbing behaviour. A youngish man was sat down at a table adjacent to mine. He seemed to be at least partially deaf and dumb and well known to the proprietor of the restaurant who squatted down by his side to try and persuade him to choose something from the menu. His suggestions were irritably rejected until it came to the sausages. I impaled one of mine and held it up. '*Eccolo!*' said the proprietor and the suggestion was accepted to general relief all round.

Meanwhile at the workers' tables the wine flagons had given way to bottles of grappa. I could not imagine that work could be resumed on the sites but eventually they all rose and trooped off, apparently none the worse. Perhaps I underestimate the capacity and resilience of the Italian worker.

I drove straight on to Palestrina, which I like and whose little hotel I already knew, for a restful afternoon and evening and to catch up with writing postcards.

OVERDOING IT

After that Sunday afternoon in Syracuse and the battle of the bells I went the following morning back to the Palazzo Arcivescovile and, after some discussion and explanation, a kindly prelate allowed me access to the *Sala* where hung the painting I was in quest of: a large enthroned *Madonna* of around 1500, possibly by Antonello da Messina. For me the important thing was the careful depiction of a so-called 're-entrant' design Turkish carpet. This was the earliest, and an unpublished, example and I wanted to acquire it for the big article on the group which I was preparing. I managed to take some photographs using flash; not easy when you have no one with you to hold the flash-gun at an angle to avoid flare but they came out successfully. Much elated at this achievement I left town and drove at speed up the coast to Messina and took the ferry across to the mainland.

I very much wanted to see the famous abandoned hillside village of Pentedattilo (five fingered), named after the rocks which rise behind it and famously depicted by Edward Lear in one of his watercolours. I made my way round the 'toe' of Calabria and up the dead-end road. All the residents had long since been moved out and access was prohibited but one got a good view of it from below; impressive but not quite as dramatic as Lear had shown it. I believe that now (2015) there is a group of enthusiasts dedicated to its preservation and re-vivification.

I drove back down to the coast road and then almost immediately turned north towards Gambarie. The road went up and up through forest, incredibly winding and more and more deteriorated. Just be-yond Croce di Romeo I saw a makeshift notice saying no entry! But I was low on petrol and there was no alternative to going on over humps and potholes and even some roadworks. There was nobody else on the road and I was afraid at moments that I wouldn't make it. I did however and got some petrol in Gambarie which is a resort and boasted two modern hotels. I was really in an irritable state by this time, rejected both as too expensive and reluctantly set off down to the coast again leaving the bosky surroundings and refreshing coolness. I drove back up the coastal road past Villa San Giovanni and scoured several little dusty villages for a hotel, without result. It was 7 pm and getting dark when I spotted a roadside *albergo* designed primarily for truck drivers. I peered inside, noticed food laid out on clean white tablecloths and took a room with bath at 25,000 lire. It was all perfectly decent yet I did not sleep very well. It can't go on like this, I thought. This is not the way to take holidays. You must find some other way.

After breakfast coffee next morning I felt differently of course and resolved to see more of Calabria. I set off up the coast road and then took a main road back over the Aspromonte through Tauriano and Cittanova. Then it was up, up, up through wonderful woods of chestnut and beech and pine. Over the top it became hotter and drier and more like maquis before down I went to Gerace. I found all the churches closed, including the huge fortress-like Norman Cathedral. In cafés I asked when it might be open. Oh, perhaps by midday, I was told, so I waited for an hour or two but to no avail.

I continued down to Locri and bowled along the Ionian coastal road. I went up to Stilo to see the exquisite ninth-century Byzantine church, the Cattolica, a national monument. It still has remains of frescoes but it is the building that is the treasure.

Again I passed along the coast and up to the quite large and busy town of Catanzaro. I had thought I might stay here but the hotel was prohibitively expensive and I went on again towards Taverna.

It was now about 5 pm and the entire population of this small place seemed to be already out on the streets. I wanted to stay to see the churches. It was the birthplace of Mattia Preti, a *seicento* painter of whose work the National Gallery has a single example. I don't in fact like it very much but I felt it incumbent on me, as a rare visitor, to see the works by him which are said to be in the churches. These were all closed however so I made inquiry as to hotels. There isn't one, they said, you must go up to Villagio Mancuso, a resort where the hotels are.

I set off again up the winding road through pine forest to a clearing, apparently deserted, with wooden buildings in a Swiss alpine style. In the Grande Albergo something or other I bargained for a room, getting it down to 40,000 lire.

I was filthy and soaked in sweat. I showered and washed my shirt and underclothes: they would be dry by morning. Dinner was promised for 8 pm. As usual I was the first in. I ordered my meal which was more or less table d'hôte. A litre flagon of wine was brought and the *contorno*, a huge cauliflower covered with steaming white sauce, brought in and set on a side table to cool. Hot cooked vegetables are such a rarity on commercial Italian tables that I was not going to lose this one and demanded some immediately. After a while a distinguished-looking party of six came in including a woman, who appeared to be the guest of honour, who looked my very idea of the countess in *The Marriage of Figaro*. I wondered if she was indeed that, brought in from some local provincial production or perhaps, more likely, she was acting in a film being shot nearby. I did not find out but the group gave tone to the room and the dinner.

I had had no lunch and was very hungry so applied myself to the food and drink. The basket of fruit brought for desert contained two bananas, four peaches, four pears, apples and a bunch of grapes and I ate a good proportion of these. The wine too was good and though (truly) I did not drink all of it, the proprietor offered to show me to my room afterwards. I did not accept yet the room proved strangely hard to find.

Alas, I did not have a good night. The dogs barked as I had not heard them since Bukhara four years before. Again I resolved: I shall not go on travelling in this way. Of course I did.

15
Upwards and Outwards

In 1984, following the mainly carpets-in-paintings-oriented activities of the previous year, I turned my attentions back to more scientific matters. I felt strongly the need for proper word processing facilities as I was doing a good deal of writing. The BBC Microcomputer had appeared a year or two before and I felt this would answer my needs: the PC had not then arrived. One was granted me in the Department and I bought another for myself. Thus, with the aid of the five-and-a-quarter-inch floppy disks then in use, I was able to pursue projects seamlessly at work and at home. For so long now this has been the norm that it is hard to recall how transformative that was and it was very useful indeed for me since as well as articles for our *Technical Bulletin*, I also had a book in mind.

For a while now Garry Thomson had shown some signs of illness. He did not speak of it but it appeared to be Parkinson's disease and this was later confirmed. He was still working on methods of 're-cording' colours in paintings in a permanent way so that in future it could be seen whether there had been changes. To this end he had even acquired one of the very first experimental digital cameras. His assistant in this work had been Sarah Staniforth but she had departed to the National Trust and been replaced by a brilliant young man, David Saunders. I am still proud to have been in part instrumental in his appointment. Garry had favoured a woman applicant already known to us.

In 1985 Garry announced he would retire at the end of the year. Was I in line to succeed him? This was by no means certain, for the post was advertised and there were other applicants. I certainly want-ed the position (I had recently declined the offer of another appoint-ment which included a professorship) and I would have been deeply humiliated if I had not got it. To cut the story short, in October I was successful and so due to be the scientific adviser to the trustees in January 1986. I think that on the whole the other staff members were happy with that; retaining the status quo is reassuring.

I took over most of Garry's commitments in advance of his leaving so new and wider responsibilities were added to my personal expertise and projects. These were primarily environmental matters, especially lighting. I now had far more contact with the rest of the Gallery staff as well as with heads of conservation departments in the other London galleries and museums. I also now saw much more of our director, Michael Levey, both at our weekly meeting and in the meeting of department heads. Michael was very much a stickler for tradition – things should continue to be done as they always had been done – and he could be quite prickly if one tried to deviate from this principle. At this time he was especially exercised with the controversial designs for the Hampton site extension, now the Sainsbury Wing. He was even nervous about the viability of the project and once said to me that he feared Mrs Thatcher would take back the Hampton site if the design and funding were not soon settled. Before the final choice was made there was particular concern as to whether the designs would allow for natural light as the main source of illumination. To inform myself of how such things had been tackled in several new galleries in Germany, in April 1986 I went on a short tour of them – in Cologne, Dusseldorf, Stuttgart, Munich, Frankfurt and other places. They were a mixed bunch, in my view, and included some lessons in how not to do it. I made a careful assessment of the various designs for the new building and submitted it to Michael. I never heard anything further of it and I don't know if it was ever shown to the trustees. In the end the Venturi design was chosen and, of course, was financed by the munificence of the Sainsbury family.

In my new position I was sometimes asked in to the monthly trustees' meetings, an informal buffet lunch followed by formal business. Following his notorious criticism of one of the designs (not the final chosen one) the Prince of Wales had been co-opted on to the board to involve him in the selection process (and perhaps to limit his public pronouncements). After one such lunch, which I attended, we all trooped over to the Scientific Department and I showed the Prince round. He seemed a bit bemused by it all and when I offered him a bound volume of the first few technical bulletins he felt he might find them rather too technical and declined it. He does have a genuine sense of humour and this was shown in the speech given when he declared the Sainsbury Wing open. 'In the Bible,' he said, 'it says "They asked for bread and were given a stone" but Lord Sainsbury has given us bread and stones.' I thought Lord Sainsbury looked a bit po-faced, as they say.

On that occasion, which was conducted outdoors, I was standing with Michael Andrews. He had been appointed as the 'artist' trustee a few years before, in part, though not uniquely, on my suggestion, but he never was really comfortable in the position. At the time he was living in Norfolk; he found the journeying to London tiresome and much of the matters discussed at the meetings remote from his experience or interest. He resigned not long after and then another had to be suggested. Euan Uglow was now the general choice but he too was not very happy in the job. He told me that he had been particularly opposed to the purchase of a painting by Jacques-Louis David, *Countess Vilain XIIII and her Daughter*, which he did not think worthy of the Gallery. I think he was offended that his view was disregarded and he did not stay on much longer.

I have run ahead somewhat so, returning to 1987, Michael Levey, now Sir Michael, decided to retire on his sixtieth birthday. He bought a little house in Louth, Lincolnshire where he was to care for his wife Brigid Brophy, who was another sufferer from multiple sclerosis, until her death in 1995. A new director was advertised for and to general surprise and, at first, some bewilderment and resentment, Neil MacGregor was chosen. Neil was young (41), was editor of the *Burlington Magazine* and without any experience of museum work or administration. Michael had departed totally, leaving a complete *tabula rasa* for Neil who said to me that he would not have resented some initial guidance with the ways of the Gallery. He soon settled in however and his seeming light-heartedness and enthusiasm engaged him with all of us. Or nearly all, for one member of staff, who had confidently expected to step into the position himself, made his resentment all too clear and became antagonistic and obstructive. It was some time before this situation was resolved. Neil's success in his fifteen years at the Gallery and in his subsequent position directing the British Museum is so generally acknowledged that it would be presumptuous of me to say more.

A MAJOR PUBLICATION

Garry had published his important book, *The Museum Environment*, for the Butterworths Museum Conservation series and I had decided that I must write one on my own subject. I initially thought to call it *The Organic Chemistry of Museum Materials* but as this could be confused with the chemistry of materials for museums I changed it to *The Organic Chemistry of Museum Objects*. It seemed a formidable task touching on the whole range of organic compounds so I broke it down into chapters dealing with types of raw materials with others on analytical methods, deterioration processes etc. treating these as separate 'papers' with their own references; thus it became more manageable. Raymond White undertook to write the chapters on proteins and carbohydrates and we set to work on our BBC Micros using its View word processor program. Not everything could be accomplished using that; one had to revert to typewriters for some things and in the end the publisher still wanted double-spaced hard copy. But it was finished and was published in 1987. When it came to producing a second, revised edition in 1994 it was now the time of PCs and WordPerfect and I somehow had to transfer and convert the files by a lengthy process via a late version of the Sinclair ZX Spectrum home computer.

In 1999 the book came out in a softcover format and amazingly still (2015) continues to sell, as no one has written a replacement. As an account of historical results it is still valid but much new material has been published in the last twenty years and it should be revised or re-written: that is now beyond me.

In June 1987 I spent a week in Prague, arranged by the British Council, to give two lectures on my work. It was still under Communism, of course, and rather grey and lacking in many comforts, but the young people whom I met were all longing for contacts with the West and thus friendly. I loved the city, which is very beautiful, but have never found the opportunity to return to it in its now long-since liberated state.

Also in 1987 Joyce Plesters, my much-loved friend and colleague from my earliest days at the Gallery in 1951, announced she was retiring. Her husband, Norman Brommelle, was older than her and after retiring from his position as keeper of the Conservation Department at the Victoria and Albert Museum in 1977 had taken on the directorship of the Hamilton Kerr Institute of the Fitzwilliam Museum, University of Cambridge where Joyce also went at weekends. Norman retired from that in 1983 and they both wanted to escape to their Umbrian farmhouse on a hillside near the village of Morra, itself not far from Trestina and Città di Castello, which they had been refurbishing during summer holidays for some years. They sold their charming detached house in Peckham and moved, literally lock, stock and barrel, out there. I wrote an appreciation of Joyce and her work for the *Bulletin* and I think this must have melted Norman's heart for I frequently got messages from Joyce to the effect that Norman was repentant (of his earlier opposition to my editorship of *Studies*) and much wanted me to pay them a visit. In September 1989, in the course of a long tour, I did so. All went smoothly, the past was not referred to and relations were restored to the status quo ante 1975. But not for long; a couple of months later I had a call from Joyce at the Gallery: Norman had died, in an ambulance on the way to Rome for an emergency heart operation. He was buried at Morra where Joyce stayed on by herself.

FIRST VISIT TO AUSTRALIA

Returning to 1987, in September of that year the Conservation Conference of ICOM (International Council of Museums) was held in Sydney and I attended. I stopped over in Hong Kong (my first visit) and stayed two nights in a luxurious hotel in Kowloon at £40 a night. I remember that my breakfast was wheeled into my room on a trolley by a young waiter *supervised* by a higher dignitary. By now readers will know that it has not usually been my lot to enjoy such attendance.

I was charmed by this outpost of empire with its British ways and I recalled that I could well have been posted there back in 1948. A little incident particularly touched me one evening. As I stood on a pavement a grand car containing a party in evening clothes came by. It bore the governor's crest but was unaccompanied by security motorcyclists or any screaming sirens. It stopped at a red traffic light and then went on.

In Sydney I stayed in one of those little apartment hotels where one has a small kitchen and facilities for preparing one's own breakfast. The meetings took place in the Hilton Hotel, an unattractive venue where the hotel proper only started on an upper floor, the ground floor comprising other commercial activities open to the public. However, I loved Sydney itself and here too I was surprised by how British it still seemed; I had expected it to be more Americanised. I enjoyed the Manly ferry, the National Gallery of New South Wales and the Botanic Gardens, to all of which I seemed to go back on later visits.

Together with several other British delegates I caught some sort of flu-like infection (we even suspected Legionnaires' disease) and after a dreadful fourteen-hour flight to Los Angeles I arrived at my hotel in poor shape. It was morning and hours before I could get into my room. Although I did manage to get to the Getty Conservation Institute to meet up with fellow conservation scientists, I found myself too ill to make a proposed side trip up to San Francisco and so flew straight home from LA.

FRIENDS

Through the seventies and early eighties Vic's reputation grew as new work appeared in many exhibitions, including one-man shows at the Bernard Jacobson Gallery in Cork Street and, in 1982, the Serpentine Gallery in Kensington Gardens. These shows culminated in 1986 with a large and impressive retrospective put on by Nicholas Serota, then director of the Whitechapel Gallery. It was accompanied by a beautiful catalogue, still sought after. Vic, now in a wheelchair, attended the show and gave many interviews. I was myself asked to take a group round and talk about the paintings. I hung my little cassette recorder round my neck so that Vic could later hear what I had said and I am proud to say that he phoned me after he had done so, clearly very moved, and thanked me.

But he was very ill. At home at The Pryors he was most of the time in bed, often in pain and very depressed. It was hard to give him much comfort.

Paula's reputation too was growing apace. She had also had many exhibitions including, in 1985, a huge retrospective at the Gulbenkian Foundation in Lisbon. I went to this and was simply astonished at her range and fecundity. It was marvellous. A few years later, in 1990, Paula was appointed the first Associate Artist at the National Gallery with a studio in the building. It was almost surreal to see her name blazoned along the outside of the building.

As for my friend Keith, he was on his own now, his mother having died, and he had enough money to live on but he was showing disturbing symptoms and an inability to cope. He had been deeply upset by being forced out of his flat in Belsize Avenue by his landlord and moved to a smaller one in Gloucester Avenue. He seemed unable to do any more work and was much reliant on us, his friends. Fortunately his new place was very close to Philip Gundry's house in Bridge Approach so he had help available nearby. Every Sunday he would go up to The Pryors for lunch and if I was back from Guildford I would drive him home.

FAMILY

In 1986 my father had his 100th birthday at home with the usual ceremonies: the letter from the Queen, a visit from the mayor wearing his gold chain and a piece in the local newspaper. His sight had almost gone now and he did not walk outside. That winter he was ill and had to go into hospital which he found a great luxury. He hoped to remain there but of course they needed the bed and we had to find a residential home for him as my mother would not have been able to look after him. We found a very attractive one at Bramley – a handsome old house in large grounds – and he moved in. The system was a rather strange one in that the occupants stayed almost entirely in their rooms; they were not even taken out to a dining room for their meals. But he did not seem to mind and continued to listen to endless talking books on large cassettes. We visited as often as we could, as did such few of his friends as still survived. His 101st birthday came and went there.

My mother remained alone in the house and through 1987 I think I went down almost every weekend. She was now showing early signs of dementia, at least if absence of short-term memory is an indication of that. She would ask me the same question over and over again. On Sundays I would cook a roast chicken and I think she more or less subsisted on the pickings for the rest of the week. A doctor would come sometimes but no sort of carer and of course she could not be relied on to remember to take pills at the right time, if at all. One day that winter when I went down I found her in bed in her stone-cold bedroom (which had no central heating and she would leave the upper window open 'just a crack') and her lungs making gurgling noises as she breathed. I called another doctor who pronounced pneumonia and sent her to hospital. She recovered from that but once home again she fell and broke her hip bone and was back inside.

Nineteen eighty-eight was to prove a difficult year for all of us. My mother slowly recovered but being away from her usual routine and surroundings ensured a further deterioration in her mental health and it was clear that she too would have to go into a home. There would be no point in putting her into the Bramley home and we found another on the Hog's Back Road, easier to get to. It was in an attractive location with good views to the south but it had just the characteristics that she had so disliked when she had visited other friends in nursing homes and one in particular: the high armchairs ranged around the walls. She, however, was now usually in a wheelchair so could be put in a good vantage point near the window when I went to visit.

Money now had to be raised and so we had to sell the house. There was a bit of a housing boom at the time and we had no difficulty in doing this. It fetched £165,000, half of which was Mother's and the other half Father's as they were joint owners. Curiously I did not feel any great sadness at seeing the house go or at the fairly ruthless way in which it was cleared of furniture. June and I chose a few items for ourselves, some others were put into auction but much of the old furniture (mock-Jacobean of the 1920s) was of no value and a firm of house clearers made bonfires of it in the garden.

The sale was completed in April and only a few days later we got a phone call with news of my father's death. About two days before I had visited and found him dressed and in his chair but in a catatonic state and unresponsive. A very old friend of his from days before his marriage was also there and also tried to rouse him without success. We left together suspecting this was probably the end. It was, as a day or two later we heard that he had died in his sleep.

Following the phone call I drove down to Guildford, met up with my sister and we went over to Bramley. She did not want to view the body but I went upstairs to where he had been carefully laid out. In his youth he had read Edgar Allan Poe on the subject of being buried alive and years ago he had asked me if, when the time came, I would check that he was really dead. I had no doubt that he was but I put my hand on his forehead which was indeed 'as cold as any stone'.

Mother was brought to the funeral but seemed a little confused as to whose it was for she and Harry had not seen each other for months.

Only a few weeks later, in early morning, Paula phoned me to say that Vic had died in the night. At The Pryors he was still lying on his bed. We sat there awaiting the arrival of the undertakers. Vic's eyes were still partly open; Paula closed them. I put up on the computer screen a last message which I knew he had written and we read that. When the undertakers rang the bell, the others went to another part of the flat and I saw the body carried away. Then I went into work.

Paula wanted a proper church funeral and a grave; I was asked to give the address. All Vic's old Slade friends came: Mike Andrews, Euan Uglow, Keith of course and others whom I cannot recall or did not know well. Hazel came; David Sylvester, rather shamefully I thought, did not.

At Fortune Green Cemetery I found myself with uncomfortably divided loyalties, for I had to stand by Hazel at the graveside, who had no other friend present, rather than by Paula.

That summer I noticed something going wrong with my left eye. A dark cloud appeared in the upper part of its field of vision and seemed to be moving downwards. My new young doctor, Dr Rosenfelder, suspected a detached retina and immediately sent me to hospital. It was not that but after endless appointments and tests the only diagnosis the various specialists could come up with was idiopathic optic neuritis. During all these tests I had been given no treatment of any kind and I was desperate as the darkness seemed to be spreading. Hearing the words 'inflammation' and '-itis' I put myself on large doses of soluble aspirin. I was gratified, but silent, when at a second test for leakage of blood from an artery into the eyeball I heard the words 'It seems to have stopped'.

Many years later (2012) the same thing occurred in my other eye, though much worse. The diagnosis now was anterior ischemic optic neuropathy. I was given massive doses of prednisolone but it was not caught in time.

My eyesight, until 1988 almost perfect, was spoiled and I found it difficult to adapt. The bad eye spoilt the sight of the other and I tended to close it when reading. An eyepatch was suggested but I felt that would be giving in. Eventually, over years, I did adapt and what sight I had seemed like normality, but I always had at the back of my mind the fear that it would happen again.

On 7 September I went to visit my mother in her rest home. We moved the wheelchair to a position with a good view over the Surrey countryside. When I told her that I was now 60 she could hardly believe it. When I told her she was 92 she couldn't believe that either but supposed it must be so. She was not happy though: she complained of the pain she suffered in bed at night from the blocked vein in her leg and wished she could just go to sleep and not wake up again.

Later that month I took a trip that should have been a real highlight and taken my mind off my troubles yet it failed to do so. I had been co-editing the preprints for the IIC conference on conservation of Far Eastern art and so attended it. I flew to Tokyo via Moscow and immediately took the 'bullet train' to Kyoto. Wonderful though it was to see the famous sites there, it was terribly hot and humid and one was deeply grateful for air-conditioned interiors. I did get about though and certain little scenes impressed me. I saw a bunch of little children leaving school and watched as they punched in numbers on telephone ranks outside to call their parents to come and fetch them – this was before mobiles. In the evenings I found myself unable to join others in the quest for restaurants and I just stayed in my hotel.

For some reason, now forgotten, a number of us had been invited to Taipei, capital of Taiwan, and I flew there from Osaka which is very close to Kyoto. Taipei seemed a strange town with wide open undeveloped spaces. We were put up in a large hotel with cavernous bedrooms and also, for a couple of nights, in a resort hotel in what seemed to be the middle of a steamy jungle. The director of the National Museum gave us lunch, or rather a sumptuous Chinese banquet. He did not speak a word of English but compensated for it by eating well and raising his glass of rice wine for a toast every five minutes.

It was altogether a strange, rather unreal experience. I continued to Hong Kong for a second short stay. I took a ferry across to Lantau Island, then undeveloped, and walked about quite alone between vegetable gardens. At a deserted, litter-strewn beach I looked across to the variegated skyscrapers of Hong Kong Island.

Back home, for the next three months I visited my mother often but I did have another brief getaway during the first week of December. I went to Portugal with Robert Pinner to visit the holdings of carpets in Lisbon and Coimbra. I rented a car and we drove around in fabulous weather: sun and blue skies the entire time, with striking carpets of white frost-like snow on still shaded spots in the morning.

On Christmas Day June drove Mother to Merrow for dinner. She said she had not expected ever to drive through the town again. Curiously at this time her memories of the house in Wodeland Avenue had become quite vague and she had reverted to thinking about the house in Bury Street, left fifty-four years before!

214

On 30 December I had a call from the home to say that she was going to be sent to the hospital, though no special reason was given. I went down and found her in bed being examined by the doctors. She seemed perfectly normal, certainly not ill. The following morning, New Year's Eve, I had another call from the hospital: 'Your mother is not communicating. You may wish to come down.'

I found her unconscious under an oxygen tent. Her lungs were full of fluid. She had been given an opiate for her leg pain and this was the result. I sat by her for some time. I heard her last gasp. A doctor confirmed her death.

At the funeral she was remembered by many of her fellow Women's Institute members who gave a handmade wreath. Naturally *Jerusalem* was sung.

I was far more affected by my mother's death than I was by my father's. Unlike his it was so sudden and unexpected. It is hard now to recall how exactly I felt for the year or more after but I know that both of them were in my thoughts all the time, day in and day out. This is grief, I suppose.

Travels helped as usual. A month or so after the funeral I spotted an advertisement for a week's vacation in Luxor at the Sheraton Hotel and took it. By wonderful good fortune the delightful small team of restorers working on the Nefertari tomb were staying there and I soon was friends with them. They included Stephen Rickerby from The Courtauld Institute and he invited me into the tomb to see it, an extraordinary privilege. To get around I rented a bicycle and it was delightful riding along to the Valley of the Queens past the Colossi of Memnon. Donkey riders greeted one and in a pond a man was washing one of his sheep. He laughed and waved. Egypt was wonderful and I was to make three more visits.

Retirement

Around this time I started to feel rather unhappy at the change in managerial style that was gradually taking over at the Gallery. For some reason an administrator had been brought in – I think from the Ministry of Agriculture and Fisheries – to bring us more into line with ministerial ways rather than continue in the relaxed style which had served us so well. This meant a greater emphasis on hierarchy and the production by heads of departments of regular staff assessments. In a small group such as we were in the Scientific Department (six people), where we all felt equal and equally committed to our work despite our different grades, I found it very embarrassing and even offensive to have to do this. I know that Martin Wyld in the Conservation Department felt the same. During 1990 I started to feel that I could do without this and, though I was only 62, I decided to retire at the end of the year. Added to my motives was the fact that I was preparing a long and quite important paper for *HALI* magazine on a group of carpets and I wanted to be free to finish this in my own time. A competition to select my replacement was held and won by Ashok Roy, already a long-standing member of the Department who worked on the electron microscope and also edited the *Technical Bulletin*. He stayed on in the post for many years but has now himself retired.

So I was now unemployed. It did indeed feel very strange and there were times when I didn't know what to do with myself. I would even sometimes go into the exhibition rooms and sit looking at the paintings. A round-the-world tour helped me over the break.

16
UNATTACHED

Nineteen ninety was still in the pre-Internet age and I made flight bookings through a small agency and received a small booklet of vouchers. Airline ticketing had not then become as prescriptive as it is now and most of my tickets were open ones allowing for flexibility. I did not choose my agents well however for I got some terrible flights as I will tell.

I went first to San Francisco where a carpet conference was to be held. I stayed with Carl Djerassi and Diane Middlebrook in Carl's splendid apartment on the top of Russian Hill. They were only there at weekends, having to go back to Stanford for work during the week, but they let me stay on. A bunch of my old Syntex colleagues, whom I had not seen since 1977, called in one evening and took me out to a meal.

The conference was held in the Marriot Hotel with all the usual receptions and ceremonies. Robert Pinner and other people from *HALI* were much in evidence and I went around with them to the de Young Museum and the big exhibition at the Fort Mason Center. Of course I gave my talk on the group I had been working on, the re-entrant design or 'Bellini' rugs, and it went down well. It was later published, very lavishly illustrated, in *HALI*.

I stayed on for more than a week, getting over my jet lag and I felt quite reluctant to leave. In fact, even after I had rented a car to go south I stayed on another day to take a nostalgic trip over the bridge to Muir Beach and the Woods.

A year before, October 1989, there had been a serious earthquake causing major damage, especially to some of the elevated freeways. A double-decker one had collapsed crushing cars on the lower deck. I saw some of this damage on my way out of town and down the route through the old familiar townships to Santa Cruz and beyond.

217

I hoped to stay again in Big Sur but Deetgen's had only an expensive double room available and I went on, staying in a motel in the isolated little community at San Simeon. This was no more than a shanty town of single-storey shacks but at night, lit up, it had the semblance of a centre of civilisation.

I was quite ill from the meal I had there and next morning went on with only a cup of coffee. It got a bit better as the day went on and I stopped in Malibu to look at motels. One turned out to be quite nice with a very agreeable woman owner so I decided to put up there for two nights. I had an excellent night's sleep with breakfast in a café on the beach under a bright blue sky. I went into LA and back to the Getty Conservation Institute where much more seemed to be going on than was the case three years before. I went on to the Los Angeles County Museum before returning to Malibu.

The following day I contacted David Scott, conservator at the Getty Museum, and arranged a visit. We had lunch together along with a young Russian, Sacha, who was there as a sort of intern benefitting from the new atmosphere of glasnost. I asked him how things had been in his country; he shrugged and replied that they had not been bad under Khrushchev but went downhill again under Brezhnev. Would he go back? He supposed so.

I liked my motel and I had reserved another two nights as I particularly wanted to visit the Norton Simon Museum in Pasadena. I drove out there only to find it did not open until midday, so I took the opportunity to phone my neighbour Peggy to check that all was well at home; this from a callbox requiring $5.50 in quarters for three minutes. This was long before mobiles, of course.

The museum had many beautiful things but above all a wonderful Jacopo Bassano, *Flight into Egypt*. A great masterpiece which had been given to Prinknash Abbey, Gloucestershire in 1957 and almost immediately sold by them a year later. Shameful; it should have remained in the UK.

That evening I carefully packed my things and went to bed wondering where I would be the following evening: I was to be in Hawaii, the Big Island.

I had woken early and, having carefully planned my route towards the airport, I was able to return the car and arrive in good time. The flight to Honolulu was OK and we arrived at 3 pm, two hours behind LA time. I went straight to the inter-island airport and took a flight to Kona. It turned out to be a very small place but I got a room in the Kona Seaside Hotel. There seemed to be little reason to stay on so the following day I rented a car and drove round the south side of the island to Hilo which is larger and more populated. En route I passed close to the volcano and saw lots of old lava flows. Hilo was more lush than Kona and altogether more attractive. I took a walk down Banyan Drive which indeed was bordered with huge banyan trees on one side and three or four big tourist hotels on the other.

I had put up in the Hilo Seaside Hotel, sister establishment to the one in Kona and rather better and I resolved to stay another night. The following day I toured up the coast through exotic scenery and saw two large waterfalls in Akaka State Park. Otherwise I lounged by the pool. I telephoned and put forward my flight to New Zealand by a day.

So the next day I drove back up the same road and then round the north side of the island. I took a side road to a point overlooking an estuary and amazing cliffs opposite totally covered in vegetation and with silvery waterfalls. I continued round to Kona, stopping at several lovely beaches but I dared not swim leaving my luggage in the car where unfortunately it was clearly visible.

I left the car and flew back to Honolulu. It was early evening and my plane was not until midnight and, in fact, left an hour late, arriving at Auckland at 8.15 am. There was no change of time but having crossed the dateline I had lost a day: it was now 5 December.

New Zealand

I found myself a little bed and breakfast place for three nights and wandered about the town. I found it charming; it even had second-hand bookshops!

Much of the next day was spent organising my further travel but in the afternoon I took the twenty-five-minute ferry across to Waiheke

Island. From the landing stage I walked up the gravel road towards what there was of a village, past roadside wildflowers, all brought in from Europe with the corn seeds. I passed little houses with parents playing with their children under fruit trees. An idyllic picture and often in later years I speculated that I might have spent my winters there.

I took a coach up to Paihia, Bay of Islands. This was a long drive and it went, as I had wanted, through the kauri forests, or what remains of them, for they were ruthlessly exploited for timber in the nineteenth century.

I found myself a small hotel in Paihia, which was a very quiet place despite thinking of itself as a resort. Unfortunately I had caught a cold, which was worse the following morning leaving me disinclined to do much. However, I took the ferry across to Russell Island which was a charming, faded little place with history. I went in the little church, the oldest in New Zealand apparently, and bought its little booklet which included an account of the Queen's visit in 1963. It was pleasant there and I stayed on until afternoon when I went back and read, cosseting my cold. Later I found a café where they served a decent pot of tea. A blond Californian youth came in with his six-pack of beer and offered me one. I declined as I was still drinking tea but we got into conversation. He was from San Diego, intelligent and with his own little business devising databases, he said. We ended up having a meal together and exchanging addresses.

I went back to Auckland on the bus and the following day took the train to Wellington. It was a little two-coach affair that only went at about 30mph stopping at small townships but also passing through fairly dramatic scenery at times. I arrived at about seven and went to the hostel where I had booked a single room. It turned out to be very unsatisfactory and the following day I moved into the Trekkers Hotel which was really nice.

The weather was dreadful, misty and drizzly, which a taxi-driver claimed was very unusual. The following day it was drier but the hateful and famous Wellington wind was up, a horrible, turbulent, twisting wind pulling one about in all directions. It made walking about the town very disagreeable. I spent much of the afternoon indoors reading and decided that Wellington was the pits, it was like spending the day in Swindon or Wigan or some such place. How could they have chosen it for their capital?

The following day was equally dreadful. I still had my cold and I had partially lost my voice so this contributed to the misery. I walked to the National Art Gallery, arriving so buffeted by the wind that I almost fell through the doors and collapsed in an area for children. Soon I saw torrential rain coming down outside and I remained in the gallery much of the day looking mostly at Maori art and artefacts. There was a feather cloak which had been given to Captain Cook, a stunningly beautiful object.

Next morning I took the shuttle bus along to the ferry terminal and boarded the ferry, which was much like our cross-channel ferries of about ten years before. The wind was still strong and the forecast for the sea moderate to rough but in fact it wasn't too bad. I read Arthur Morrison's *To London Town* which I had bought in San Francisco. I had left all my paperbacks behind in the hotel to save weight.

Once into Picton Sound it was calmer and the skies seemed clearer. Amazingly empty scenery; scarcely a sign of human habitation.

So it was on to the little train and down the east coast all the way to Christchurch. Brilliant sunshine came out on the way. I got a room at the Windsor Hotel, a very old-English-like boarding house at NZ$49.00 B&B.

In contrast to Wellington I was immediately most favourably impressed by the city. There were almost no high-rise buildings; there were lots of little squares, often with sculptures – Captain Cook, Queen Victoria etc. – and it was very quiet. It didn't start to get dark until about 9.30 pm. I had a job to find anywhere to eat at first but eventually I discovered the best place seemed to be the restaurant in the town hall. There were few people about: it seemed like a town from long ago.

The next day, after a huge breakfast, I made enquiries at a travel agent about flights from Christchurch to Hobart, Tasmania. Were they every day? By no means; there was one a week! Moreover it cost NZ$600 (about £200). I was completely thrown. I had no idea how to proceed and spend the next week. I went back to my room and lay on the bed. Would this be more expensive than flying back to Auckland, taking my existing booked flight to Sydney and then paying for another flight down to Hobart? Perhaps not, so I decided I would eventually take the direct flight after staying on in New Zealand for about another week. I booked a car for four days with an extra three day option.

I had not intended to visit the Botanic Gardens but fortunately changed my mind. They were magnificent and had the finest specimen trees I have ever seen. Huge conifers and deciduous trees including a wonderful great golden elm, a lime tree and an oak planted for the coronation of Edward VII in 1902. The weather had become very hot and the shade was delicious there under the boughs: '*Ombra mai fu...*'

After that I went into the cathedral where choir practice for Christmas was going on. Little tiny boy choristers! As I write I think of the terrible, and apparently irreparable, damage from the February 2011 earthquake.

So the next day I collected my car, a Toyota Corolla which I liked a lot, and set off south. The road was really dull, following the railway line for much of the way, and before Dunedin clouds came over turning frankly to rain as I got there. The town had the atmosphere of Scotland in the 1940s, its only distinction being its multi-coloured houses. I took a room in a little boarding house and after tea and cake in a cafeteria I remained in my room as the rain came down. Then there was the problem of dinner. I found a restaurant called the Firenze, purportedly Italian, but the food was dreadful, an absolute travesty. There was certainly no Italian in the kitchen, in fact I saw a Chinese man come out.

The next day I continued to Invercargill. It seemed like the end of the world. I got a nice room in the Railway Hotel, facing the station, and sat in it for some time looking out on the deserted street. After I had arrived there, much of the way driving along gravel roads, I went on to Bluff at the very tip of the South Island.

This seemed like beyond the ends of the earth. Periodically rain and hail fell, accompanied by icy winds from the Antarctic. A little guidebook I had bought said there was an agreeable hotel but it was closed and silent. I did not even dare to ring the bell to make inquiry, fearing I could be trapped there alone overnight in this truly desolate place. Once there had been something of a port but this had evidently fallen into desuetude and the railway lines were all rusty. I hastened back to Invercargill.

That evening I decided to try the restaurant in the Grand Hotel. It was all damask tablecloths, waitresses and brilliant lighting but the food was just as bad as ever and only about two other tables were occupied. A half bottle of a New Zealand Cabernet lightened my mood a little but back in the almost empty Station Hotel gloom returned and I asked myself the eternal question: what am I doing here?

The following day was rather better. After a very good breakfast I drove to Te Anau. It was still only 11.30 am so I went on to Milford Sound. One arrives there through a dark, unlighted tunnel and once parked I took one of the boat trips. This was terrific, taking one right out to the sea and right up to one of the great waterfalls which fall precipitously down the granite mountain walls. Apparently cruise liners sometimes come in but the sound is so deep they cannot anchor.

In the car park keas were tugging at my windscreen wipers as they tend to do. One or two others were accepting food from visitors. They are large birds of the parrot family and are now supposedly protected.

I drove back to Te Anau and booked myself into the Shakespeare House Hotel which was comfortable. I even managed to get a good meal which I really needed. I had orange roughy which is a very tasty fish but I am sorry if I contributed to its decline which is, I believe, the case.

I slept well and got downstairs in time for the 8.30 am deadline set for breakfast. Our host, from Wolverhampton, prepared breakfast while singing in the most tuneless manner. I felt like telling him to abandon all thoughts of musical expression. I paid my NZ$50 to Mr Wolverhampton and set off.

On my way through very empty country I passed several great clumps of lupins which included many bi-colours. How did these get there? I would like to have had seeds but of course these had not set.

I was at Queenstown by noon and took the opportunity to go into a travel agent and book my flight to Hobart. I had managed to reach Tony Werner there and arrange my stay. As it was so early I went on to Wanaka. I did not take to the place at first, just a lake bordered by a few buildings, but it grew on me and I sought a room at the Country Lane B&B. No one was in at first but by 4 pm a very young girl, hardly more than sixteen, said yes, I could have a room.

It was very hot now and I passed the time by the lake until dinner time. There were a couple of establishments with Italian names and after my experience in Dunedin I was naturally suspicious but I went into one of them and had a long talk with the young proprietress. I didn't see how the place was viable with so few potential customers but she claimed they would have lots of customers at Christmas. I was doubtful but anyway I had a passable meal. I should mention that nearly all such places here are unlicensed and one buys one's wine at an off-license beforehand.

Back in the communal sitting room at the B&B I shared it with two pairs of teenagers who watched a video while I wrote postcards. They sat on sofas evidently waiting for me to go off to my room. When I did so I heard rapid scuffling and the drawing of curtains. Well, I was not there to supervise them.

At breakfast next morning there was the about-sixteen-year-old girl again and her sister but no sign of parents so I asked about them.

'Oh Mum got married last June,' she said, 'and went off to live in Gore.'

'But she comes and sees you?' I asked.

'Oh yes, once a month.'

'So you look after this place yourselves?'

'Oh yes,' said she.

I didn't ask about her father and he wasn't mentioned. What a situation.

I set off and after a while found myself driving around a lake: Lake Kaniere. I was suddenly struck by its extraordinary beauty. One looked down the lake to mountains beyond; the water was dark blue and white-crested by a light wind; no habitation of any kind was visible.

On the way to Haast Pass I went through fertile country, the road lined with English wildflowers: foxgloves, mulleins, buttercups and so on, until coming to fine deciduous forest. Over the pass, at Haast itself, there was all kinds of accommodation and a good many tourists. Beyond there the weather deteriorated, rain poured down and continued all the way up the coast.

I went up a side road to Fox Glacier as my guide said it was only five minutes' walk from the car park. However it must have been retreating, for when I got there I saw a notice saying it was a forty minutes' walk. As the weather was so dreadful I gave it up.

I carried on, with various halts for refreshment and with an Auckland hitchhiker for the last 40 km, to Greymouth where I installed myself in the High Street Guesthouse.

The town had nothing special to offer but after much searching and deliberation I had a fairly decent meal at the Wellington Hotel. While near the station I saw an enormous freight train pass by, presumably on its way to Christchurch. Just outside the station I noticed the dreadful condition of the track, which seemed to be sinking into the ground. I don't know how that freight train got over it.

Next day I drove over Arthur's Pass and was soon back in Christchurch. There I gave up the car and re-installed myself for two nights back in the Windsor Hotel.

The day after that I managed to do much needed laundering in the hotel's machine and then I was free to go back to the museum which I liked very much. That evening, as also the previous one, I dined excellently at the Park Royal Hotel. It was marvellous value at just over NZ$32 (about £10).

TASMANIA

I was up betimes to get the shuttle to the airport. The flight took about three hours and we arrived at Hobart shortly before 10 pm local time. Tony Werner was there to meet me and we drove to his little house in Bellerive. However, Antonia and Peter Ross, his daughter and son-in-law had decided that I should take a room with them to save Tony the inconvenience. This was lovely as they have a beautiful house and garden abutting the long Bellerive Bay, a great position.

It is impossible, though tempting, for me to go into details of my stay on this beautiful and fascinating island. I was to return to it four times during the next twenty years and made wonderful expeditions: in 1994 after touring to Adelaide and Brisbane; in 2000 after attending the IIC Melbourne Conference with Tony Werner; in 2004 following a mini carpet conference in Sydney; and finally in 2011, by which time Tony was no longer alive. I will mention only two of my expeditions – to Strahan within Macquarie Harbour on the west side of Tasmania and another to the Tasman Peninsula. From Strahan I took one of the boat trips which went first to Hell's Gates, the narrow and turbulent opening of the harbour to the sea; then up into the Gordon River and finally to Sarah Island. This was Tasmania's first penal colony, started in 1822. We were allowed to land and wander about between the beautifully made buildings now fallen into decay and overgrown with luxuriant tree ferns and other vegetation. Apparently the convicts turned this tiny island into an almost thriving and happy community and worked at shipbuilding. It seems that the authorities felt that they were having altogether too good a time of it and closed the colony after only eleven years in 1833. Now it is a numinous and evocative place, a monument to both the cruelty of human institutions and the resilience of the human spirit.

New colonies were started on the Tasman Peninsula at the south east corner of the island. The coastline here is very dramatic with such turnings and in-cuttings that when driving one loses track of whether one is going north, south, east or west. The colonies include the most famous one, Port Arthur, but there is another called Saltwater Creek

226

(also known as the Coalmines Historic Site) where low-grade coal was mined and shipped to Hobart. It was an all-male colony and the inmates were cruelly treated, often confined in the dark stone-built single cells for fear of 'unnatural practices'.

Well, back to my journey in 1990. As it was Christmas, my few days in Hobart were largely passed during a period of feasting and drinking. Unfortunately for me my hosts and their friends were all smokers (I had given it up in 1962) and this hindered my recovery from a sore throat and cough from which I had suffered for a fort-night or so. But I was to leave on the 28th having booked my coach ride to Devonport and the ferry to Melbourne.

The coach journey went via Launceston and on the way there we passed fields of almost ripe wheat and, surprisingly, fields of opium poppies! Apparently these are the primary source of 'ethical' opiates.

At Devonport the ship was waiting and I found my shared cabin already occupied by my fellow passenger. I had a decent meal and a good night's sleep and we arrived at Melbourne about 8 am on a lovely cloudless day.

AUSTRALIA

A bus was waiting to take us all into the city, arriving at the Spencer Street station. I got out and walked round the corner to King Street where I took a room in the King Street Budget Hotel. It was fairly primitive but cheap and I spent little time in it apart from sleeping.

I walked about the city nearly all day visiting museums and the National Gallery of Victoria over the bridge. There I suddenly spotted Michael Andrews's painting *All Night Long* in a room largely devoted to silverware! It seemed strangely out of place; it must be almost meaningless to Australians and indeed other visitors too. It's a pity it left the UK and the same applies to his other large painting in the Thyssen Bornemisza Collection in Madrid.

That evening I found that restaurant prices were far higher than in New Zealand and the one I chose was disappointing, though the oys-ters were good. I went into the station to check on train times as I had decided I would go to Canberra by train, a very long journey starting at 7.30 am. I bought my ticket, the last economy ticket available (A$44). The weather had grown very hot and I took a tram across the bridge and went into the Royal Botanic Gardens. There were people there simply *roasting* themselves in the merciless sunshine. Had they not heard of melanoma? I came across a pond which was teeming with large eels. People were feeding them and they thrashed about in competition with the ducks. That evening I found an excellent Chinese restaurant where I had a really enjoyable meal. My waiter looked utterly Chinese, as if he came from Sichuan or some such region, while he had a punk-style haircut and spoke with the broadest Australian intonation. These cross-cultural effects!

The next day was the 31st, two years since my mother's death which still seemed like yesterday. I was into the station and the train in good time and found it more comfortable than I had expected; fully air-conditioned fortunately. We trundled endlessly over the sunburnt landscape but about 11.30 am stopped for fifteen minutes at Aubrey. On the platform it was like a furnace; everybody including me bought ice creams.

On we went, arriving at Yass Junction about 4.20 pm where Canberra passengers got off to board a waiting bus. In fact most of the train's passengers were going on to Sydney. We were into Canberra by 5.15 pm, arriving at a bus station which could have been that of a small town rather than a capital city. There were noticeboards with ads for hotels. I rang up several of these, finally choosing one said to be near the National Gallery. I had a job to find a cab but eventually got one. But what a city; one of those designer cities where everything is miles from everywhere else, presumably in expectation of vast future infill development. On the way to the hotel not a soul was to be seen on the road and there was scarcely any traffic either. I got a decent room but not air-conditioned alas. It was still terribly hot.

Dinner was rather a disaster. The dining room was full of very old Germans evidently holding some sort of New Year's Eve reunion dinner. They all spoke very halting German to one another, as if they had got out of the habit, whereas they spoke perfectly good English at times.

UNATTACHED

That night I managed to sleep quite well with the window open and no bed coverings. It had cooled by morning but clearly was going to heat up again. After a good breakfast I set off walking to the National Gallery, on the way there not passing anyone. I crunched over dried eucalyptus leaves and saw some nice parrots – grey with pink breasts. At the Gallery there were actually about six people waiting outside for it to open at 10 am when we all went in. There is not much classical Western art but a very good modern collection well displayed. All the usual people were represented and there was a particularly good Jackson Pollock and a very nice series of David Hockney prints.

A temporary exhibition of Russian Ballet sets and props was very good. Some were by Picasso. These were all bought at auction in 1974 for the rock bottom price of £3000 after having been in storage for decades. Wonderful things.

I wandered into the sculpture garden where I was particularly charmed by the fog sculpture by a Japanese artist. Mist was generated by a device and drifted through trees and over a little pond. I have always remembered this and I made a point of looking for it again when I was back there in 2004.

I went on by train to Sydney, arriving on the dot at 5.52 pm, and the immediate question was where to find an affordable and decent hotel. They all seemed rather dear and I took a room pro tem in a rather dreadful place near the station thinking I would seek out the little Oxford Hotel I had stayed at in 1987. When I did so I found it had been taken over by Best Western and now cost A$85 a night, far too much for me so I stayed on where I was.

As all my flight tickets were open ones I had to check on times and availability. Those to Bangkok were fairly booked up. I had to stay on for a further three days. Moreover the flight wasn't direct but involved a change of planes and a very long wait in Jakarta. I also had disturbing information from Aeroflot, with whom my flight from Bangkok was booked. They said they too were all booked up; nonetheless they made me a provisional booking for 9 January.

I need not describe the next three days in Sydney, which mostly involved going back to places I had loved in 1987 such as the Art Gallery, the Botanic Garden and Manly. I also spent time in Paddington which has many delights. There was much that was new in the city including the Powerhouse Museum and the monorail system, both of which I made good use of.

THE LONG WAY BACK

The rest of my journey was pretty much a fiasco. The flight to Jakarta was fine, taken in a small plane with an intermediate stop in Bali. I was glad not to be stopping over there as the rain was coming down in torrents. Then there was the long wait in Jakarta airport where I slept much of the time on benches. In fact I almost missed the plane by so doing: my name had to be called out on the speaker system. At Bangkok airport I found a hotel – the New Trocadero – and took a cab there for the long drive. Mercifully it was air-conditioned, for outside it was appallingly hot and humid. The following day I was anxious to check with Aeroflot as soon as possible and so walked to their office to find it had moved, so I had another long walk and got soaked in sweat. My flight on the 9th was still unconfirmed. Should I hang on? 'Very lisky, very lisky,' said the sweet Thai girl. 'There is a place on today's flight at 6.30.' As the idea of staying on in Bangkok for some days after the 9th was too dreadful I decided to take it. So back to the hotel for a shower and change. Fortunately I departed in good time for the trip to the airport took an hour and a half. Check-in too was very slow and the plane departed an hour late to allow all passengers to get through.

So, the flight. We landed and got out at Delhi for an hour. Then there was an additional unscheduled stop at Karachi for another hour. Then it was on to Tashkent where there was actually an argument between plane and ground staff as to whether we should get off or not. I stayed on board. Then it was Moscow. It had taken eighteen hours and it was about 8.30 am local time.

After this the great question was, when was our flight to London? Not until the evening. Somehow the day passed; we were at least given a free meal, which was acceptable. When boarding time came there was absolute chaos. The plane was obviously overbooked and some passengers had not been given boarding cards. We were let out on to the tarmac and people simply rushed for the plane and pounced on seats. I got one but others were walking up and down the aisle looking for one. I suppose they had to get off.

Some big working-class chaps from the North of England sat down near me. They had been in Thailand bent on pleasure. They hastened to tell all who would listen of what they had been through in Moscow: three days in a sort of 'prison hotel' waiting for this plane. A dreadful place with unspeakable food and also bed bugs! They had also lost their baggage during the journey; it had been taken off the plane at Karachi for unknown reasons. They were determined to get drunk during the flight, in which aim they succeeded. Indeed they were still staggering about the cabin and even smoking as we landed at Heathrow, the stewards having given up all attempts to control them.

It was late evening when I got home to the flat. My journey from Bangkok had taken about thirty-eight hours yet within a day or two I felt quite back to normal.

17
IN RETIREMENT

Although initially feeling quite 'lost' without a regular job to go back to, I was not without occupations both related and unrelated to my past work. I had co-edited the contributions to the previous year's IIC Conference in Brussels and soon I was to be editing those for the 1992 one in Madrid. More involving and interesting was a survey I had agreed to undertake of the carpets in National Trust houses, which had come about as follows.

I have mentioned that Sarah Staniforth, formerly in our department, had moved to the National Trust in charge of conservation. The then Head of Historic Houses, Martin Drury, wanted to know whether there were any particularly important carpets in the collection, especially unrecognised ones, but also a complete record of what there was. Sarah mentioned my name to him, we met and I agreed to undertake the work. This commenced a year or so before I retired so I had made only a few visits at weekends but now I was free to go on long trips further afield, staying in B&Bs near the properties. This was most enjoyable but often quite hard work. My inspections could clearly only be conveniently made when the houses were closed to the public, which was not always easily arranged. The Trust was then (may still be for all I know) divided up into Regions each of which had some degree of autonomy and in consequence the collaboration I received was, let us say, variable. For the most part, however, the house managers were helpful, even enthusiastic, in finding everything and unrolling carpets in storerooms. Initially my objective was just to record oriental carpets but eventually it embraced English ones also and even, when of historic significance, machine-made carpets as well.

I think I probably was the right person for the job. In the past carpet dealers had sometimes been consulted on questions of identification and repairs but I don't think one could have been found to devise a suitable database for the records as well. I had to do that and I adopted a database program prominent at that time called Paradox. In some ways it is a pity that I did not undertake this work ten years later, for digital cameras had not yet appeared and images could not be entered into the records. I took film photographs of all the carpets and stuck prints of these on to the report forms which I had devised. It was all many hours of work during my evenings but I was quite proud of the files of reports that I produced. In the end I visited over ninety houses and reported on just over 1,750 carpets. My last house visit was in 1997.

This survey did not reveal many early oriental rugs which were not already known about. Carpets at Knole and Hardwick Hall were already well documented but two old pieces at Ascot, in a sad state of preservation, did come to light. The main benefit was to call attention to the large number of nineteenth-century rugs – Caucasian, Persian, Central Asian – which had largely just been seen as furnishing rugs but which were worth treating as art objects in their own right and being looked after. For me the foremost reward was to get to see these fantastic great houses and even to have them to myself at times. I stayed overnight alone in one of them (I think it was Dunham Massey) and felt quite at home.

I continued with my more academic carpet studies and these led to purposeful travels. I made several trips to Istanbul, while my journeys around Spain also were to particular ends. My thoughts had turned from carpets in paintings towards carpets themselves and especially a group which for fifty years had been the subject of sharply divided views as to their age and country of origin. The group, which had designs and technique as unifying features, was centred on a rug in the Victoria and Albert Museum which had been donated at the end of the nineteenth century by George Salting (1835-1909), a major collector of every kind of art object. It was known as the Salting rug and so eventually gave its name to the group as a whole. The great German scholars of the nineteenth and early twentieth century had all treated these rugs as genuine productions of the Safavid era of

Persia from the late sixteenth century and, although some doubts had been expressed by Tattershall of the V&A, they were still so attributed by Arthur Upham Pope in his great *Survey of Persian Art*, published following the huge Persian Art Exhibition of 1931. The carpet section of this book was given a review by the German Kurt Erdmann which came out in a specialist journal in the United States in 1941, just before America's entry into the Second World War. In this review he put forward the theory that the Salting medallion-design rugs and an associated group of prayer rugs which remained in Topkapi Palace, Istanbul were in fact *copies* of Safavid rugs made in Turkish Court workshops in the late eighteenth or early nineteenth century. He later republished this theory in articles and books and in the 1970s and '80s it was wholeheartedly adopted by Charles Grant Ellis in the USA and more hesitantly by May Beattie in the UK.

I cannot now clearly recall and will not rehearse here the stages through which I became convinced that this theory was completely wrong. A major source of error, I believe, lay in confusing originals with copies (which do exist) by looking simply at black and white photographs.

I soon found that Michael Franses, who had handled some of these rugs both as a dealer and a conservator, had come to the same conclusion and we put forward the idea of a special session devoted to the group at the next ICOC meeting which, was to take place in Philadelphia in 1996. He would cover the large group of prayer rugs and I would concentrate on the thirty-odd medallion rugs. What was needed was convincing evidence that one at least of these was datable back to 1600 or so. Nowadays resort would always be had to C-14 analysis but then it still seemed relatively unreliable for textiles and museums and collectors were reluctant to supply samples, however small. I knew that one of the rugs was known to have been acquired by a Parisian dealer from Palencia Cathedral in Spain sometime around 1900, later to be auctioned after his death and eventually to find a permanent place in the Museum of Islamic Art in Cairo. I made two trips to Palencia to study the archives, initially to try and find out exactly the date of the sale (unsuccessful) and secondly to photocopy surviving inventories made in 1623 and 1649 which listed carpets owned by the cathedral. I laboriously transcribed these (no easy task) and translated them. To cut the story short, there were almost identical entries in both inventories which clearly described the surviving rug.

Several rugs of the group were credibly understood to have come out of Topkapi Palace in Istanbul but no explanation had ever been offered as to how this had happened. It dawned on me that it could have been during the Russo-Turkish War of 1877-8, when Istanbul was actually besieged by Russia, full of refugees and in a desperate situation as regards disease and food shortage. I had a good time looking through newspapers of the period, particularly the *Illustrated London News,* and this went far to confirm my suspicions. But there was another reason to believe this. In an anonymous article in the *Burlington Magazine* in 1903, the author stated that he well remembered how 'harem treasures' were 'hawked through the bazaar' during that terrible winter. This is undoubtedly when the rugs were acquired by dealers and ended up with rich collectors such as Salting, Albert Goupil in Paris and the Rothschilds.

The *Burlington* had no record of the identity of the anonymous author. I have wondered whether it was Salting himself, for two of the rugs illustrated were his. I had a look through his archive, preserved in the Guildhall Library, London, but was able to find only notebooks recording all his purchases and no correspondence or writings. It remains a mystery.

Michael and I performed our double act at the conference and seemed to convince our audience. Our papers were published in 1999 in a special supplement to *Oriental Carpet and Textile Studies* (OCTS) and nobody since has attempted to revive the old theory of a Turkish origin. Curiously though, no restitution has been accorded to the Salting rug itself which still languishes in store at the V&A.

FRIENDS

The nineties were to turn out to be a period when several friends were to die and at an earlier age than they should have done. I have mentioned that Keith had shown disturbing symptoms of premature ageing and now he was in and out of hospital. He now had no close relatives and it was up to us, his friends, to take charge of him and make decisions. We did not know what exactly the matter with him was and as we were not related doctors would not tell us. For a while he was in the St Pancras Hospital, a dreadful, gloomy Victorian building, and then in University College Hospital in Gower Street opposite the courtyard of the college itself and, of course, the Slade. One day I got a call to say that he was unconscious and nearing his end, so I went in. There could be no communication. I made to take his hand but he winced and pulled away. After an hour or so I went out for a cup of tea and on returning found him laid out with the waxen pallor of death, an extraordinary transformation. He was only 67. At last the doctors were content to tell us what he had been suffering from: multi-infarct dementia, now better known as vascular dementia. I was to hear a good deal more of this condition in later years.

Philip, Paula and I were his executors. I registered the death and deposited his will at Somerset House for proving. Apart from some individual bequests he had left the bulk of his estate to Vic and Paula's three children and it was not long before this was resolved.

At Golders Green we arranged a little secular 'service' with Buddhist chants from Philip and fellow Buddhist adherents (Keith had taken some interest in this), a reading and finally some Verdi which I had chosen: the final tomb scene from *Aida*. For once David Sylvester did come; after all, Keith had done a great deal for him in days gone by with little or no return in the way of forwarding his art or career. I do believe Keith's work deserves more recognition. I have lived with many of his paintings for years and find that they grow on me all the time.

Another sad and premature loss was Michael Andrews. We heard that he had had cancer, recovered, and then relapsed, dying in July 1995 aged only 66. In earlier days Mike had always enjoyed nightclub life, and the drinking and smoking that went with it were perhaps contributory factors. Paula and I went to his funeral which Mike had requested should take place at Chelsea Old Church on the south bank of the Thames. A good crowd of old Slade and Soho friends turned up to support his widow June and daughter Melanie, as did also some of his aristocratic collectors. Afterwards I saw a little scene outside. A woman was dispensing glasses of wine to a small group of the mourners from her barge tied up to the bank. It was Henrietta! I had last seen her at the party at Apollo Place forty years before.

I am afraid that once again David had failed to show up ('My time is much too valuable to allow me to go to funerals'), but we continued to be very good friends and often spoke on the telephone or met. At some point at the end of the eighties he sold his Francis Bacon painting for about £200,000 – twice as much, he boasted to me, as he would have got a couple of years before – and confessed he was in a mess and didn't know what he wanted to do with his life. He inexplicably bought a house somewhere in the country but never lived there and soon sold it again. Then he bought a pair of houses side by side in Denbigh Road, Notting Hill (yes, £200,000 went that far in the early nineties). His then partner, the critic Sarah Whitfield, lived in one and he in the other which he did up splendidly to show off his collection of old carpets and miscellaneous objects. By this time he was much more interested in antiquities and ethnographica than he was in modern art. In fact he once said to me (from his preferred position on the back seat of my car) with the force of revelation: 'Yes, that's it. I'm not interested in *ideas*; I'm interested in *things*.' He did have some modern art however, mostly gifts from artists he had written about. In his staircase hall, where it was protected from too much light exposure, there hung an etching of vertical lines by Barnett Newman. He would gaze at this almost as if he was attempting self-hypnosis. 'Isn't it wonderful,' he would say. I did not think so, yet it fetched over £31,000 at the posthumous sale. Such is the added value of names.

Towards the end of the decade David told me that he had a carcinoma of the bowel. He was very concerned about living with a colostomy bag after the operation but when this did finally come about he told me that it was not as bad as he had expected. In October 2000 I drove him out to Hampton Court where the second, now incomplete, Ardabil carpet from the Los Angeles County Museum was on display following cleaning and conservation. On returning I drove through Bushy Park, which was entirely new to him. The following day he phoned me to say how delighted he had been with the formal layout of the park and especially with the neatly deer-browsed trees. It was a late discovery in the London he had lived in all his life.

That was my last meeting with David. His cancer returned and he told me on the phone that he was being given morphine but that 'it was not enough'. I did not trouble him any more, knowing he would be concerned with last things. He died on 19 June 2001 and the following month his carefully planned cremation service took place at Golders Green, ten years to the month from when we had both been there for Keith's. There was a large gathering and for the first time in many years I met Pamela, his former wife and mother of his three daughters, now living in the country.

Huge, full-page obituaries had appeared in the national newspapers but how fleeting is fame! During the years since then I have scarcely seen his name mentioned. There has been no biography and not even a half-decent Wikipedia entry. Along with Carl Djerassi, David was the greatest achiever among my male friends and I wish his memory well. Yet I am also acutely conscious (as he was himself) of his human weaknesses and I wonder whether it is possible that a fully rounded portrait of him, in which all is acknowledged, could ever be achieved. Perhaps that is true of all of us.

FATAL ADDICTION

Following Keith's death my old friend Philip Gundry went into a gradual alcoholic decline. He always fully acknowledged the problem and sought help from various sources, sometimes with a temporary success but always with the seemingly inevitable relapse. He also had a couple of psychotic episodes when he was shut up in the locked ward in the Royal Free Hospital, Hampstead. I cannot bear, and it would be unedifying, to go into details but how he kept his job at Imperial College while almost permanently suffering from the effects of alcohol I do not know. Eventually he did retire and then there was nothing to restrain him. He showed signs of serious mental deterioration, even forgetting that he had retired at one point. At a party for our friend Sarah Colmer's eightieth birthday he looked at me blankly and asked 'And who are *you*?'

Following a fall in 2002 he was unconscious in hospital on life-support systems. Somehow the consensus, among medical staff and friends alike, was that there was no coming back. He was allowed to go.

Philip was 72; I had known him since he was 18. He was, academically, far cleverer and more successful than me at college, yet after graduate and postgraduate work he never did more research or publish anything. He would always say that he only wanted to teach and perhaps he was good at this. I try to remember him as he was in happier days. At the same time I cannot but recall Marlowe's lines:

> Cut is the branch that might have grown full straight
> And burnèd is Apollo's laurel bough…

YOUNGER FRIENDS

I have always been anxious, as Dr Johnson recommended, to 'cultivate the young'. I have been less successful than I wished but one new friendship has proved enduring. Somehow it has not been possible to fit it in earlier but in 1981, driving back through northern France after the tour in Italy I have described earlier, I picked up a young French hitchhiker making his way to Calais and London. This was Pierre Veys. We kept in touch later by letter and, as he was from Cambrai, which was usually on my route south to Italy, I would stop by there. He lived with his mother who very kindly put me up and gave me delicious meals on my stopovers. This was the pattern for fifteen years or so but in 1996 Madame Veys died and Pierre started on various moves to different parts of France with his partner Sylvie. For years he had had many frustrations and disappointments with editors and producers in his preferred field of satire and parody for TV and *bandes dessinées*, the albums of strip cartoon stories that are such a part of French culture. Success came finally in 1999 with *Baker Street*, the first of a series of four parodying Sherlock Holmes and Watson. Many other series (I have lost count) on different themes followed and they have been widely translated, though curiously hardly at all into English. Pierre has been especially attached to stories located in London and in the early days I was often called in for advice and photographs, which I much enjoyed providing.

After living for a while in Arras, Pierre and Sylvie moved to a village, Mareuil, not far from Angoulême. I often stayed with them there, travelling not only by car but by train or the cheap flights to provincial airports which had by then become available. Later still they moved yet again to an isolated house in the pine forests of Les Landes and here too I became a frequent visitor, either on my way by car to Spain or by flying to Bordeaux or Biarritz. In their enclosure in the forest they both greatly enjoyed, as did I, the company of many wild animals, birds and harmless snakes (*couleuvres*).

SAD LOSSES IN ITALY

In June 1995 I went to Florence for discussions about a proposed carpet conference, which did in fact take place very successfully in Milan and Florence in 1999. I went on by train to Castiglion, Fiorentino where Joyce met me and took me over to Morra for a few days' stay. She had now been on her own there for six years but had made good friends both in the village and among the more dispersed foreign community. We had a restful few days enjoying her terraced garden but also making a couple of outings to restaurants.

I planned to fly back from Milan after meeting up with Riccardo and so phoned to make arrangements. His friend Vittorio answered; Riccardo was in hospital and '*Non riconosce a nessuno*' (He doesn't recognise anyone). I was so shattered by this totally unexpected and devastating news that I burst into tears, my Italian deserting me. I had to apologise and ring off and throw myself on Joyce's sympathy. There was now no rush for me to head for Milan so I stayed on a few more days before completing my journey as planned. I never discovered the cause of this terrible collapse in Riccardo's health and though I wrote a letter of condolence to Vittorio I had no answer. I was of course in touch with my friends the Zderics in San Francisco as soon as I was home. They had heard that Riccardo had in fact died but were equally ignorant of what.

A TOUR WITH TONY WERNER

For some time I had had an agreement with Tony Werner that I would take him on a nostalgic tour, passing through places he had visited in the 1920s and ending up staying with Joyce. I bought another car – a Peugeot 205 – as I realised a Mini would be inadequate, and it served us well over the Italian Alps. Tony often said that his greatest achievement at the Gallery had been to appoint Joyce (he was right) and after our arrival, I left them together to make outings to surroundings already familiar to me. On our way back, overnight stops included Colle di Val d'Elsa, Lucca, Stresa, Besançon and Lille. There I put Tony on the new Eurostar service to London and I went for a few days to Cambrai and on a trip to Paris with Pierre.

The following year, the beginning of March 1996, I had a telephone call from one of Joyce's local friends: Joyce had had a stroke followed by cardiac arrest. She was now in hospital in Città di Castello and was severely incapacitated. I was the only one of her former colleagues free to go to visit her so I set off once again down the familiar route through France but, as I was unsure about the state of the passes in Switzerland, I went instead to Modane and through the Fréjus Tunnel, arriving for an overnight stay in Reggio. The car was showing signs of oil leakage and making bad noises in low gear so once arrived at Sansepolcro, where I had decided to stay, I had to put it into a garage. Naturally it was a Friday so I was going to be without it for some days. I put up there at a charming hostelry, the Albergo Fiorentino. It was easy to get to Joyce using the little railway which runs from there via Città and on to Perugia. I made several visits. She was in a rather depressing establishment, a combined hospital and old people's home, and in a very bad way with the common stroke symptoms of paralysis and speech distortion. It was very distressing.

On my last visit she was suffering from bronchitis and being given antibiotics. She was scarcely communicating and I made my silent farewells to her. Only one outcome seemed possible. I made a leisurely return journey via Como and back in London I was kept informed by Joyce's kind friends, who had many difficulties to deal with – her house, her dog, her will and her finances. Fate was not kind and Joyce lingered on until August when the end came. I saw no point in going to the funeral: there were no grieving relatives to support, for Joyce had none. Just one of our former Gallery colleagues – Christopher Brown – attended as he chanced to be in Italy on holiday. In her will, which she had written only a day or two before her stroke (did she have some sign or premonition?), Joyce left her house to the local man who had done all the work on it and who had become her friend, so it went back to the community, as it were. Back here it fell to me to write her obituary for *The Independent*.

I had now lost my two closest friends in Italy and my urge to make long tours there, usually culminating with a visit to one or the other of them, diminished. Occasional shorter visits continued for a further fifteen years.

LIFE AT ABERCORN PLACE
The Shield Group, who had tried to evict me, sold on the freehold of my house and the new owner, a reasonable man, offered to sell me a lease in 1991. I was a controlled tenant so made the purchase on favourable terms. Unfortunately the Shield Group had used terrible bodgers to convert the flats they had acquired on the upper floors, above all in the matter of plumbing. In 1994 water poured down through the house doing much damage, including to some of my books. It never really dried out and was, I believe, responsible for dry rot which manifested itself some nine years later.

It occurred to me that perhaps I should move. I now had my Freedom Pass and did not have to make daily journeys into work so I could even buy a house a bit farther out for what I could get for my flat. In fact this never happened but for two or three years I travelled about in north London exploring suburbs hitherto entirely unknown to me and I found it deeply interesting. I was particularly fascinated by Wembley Park, Barn Hill and Kingsbury. Here were housing estates all constructed about the same time as our house in Guildford, some still with their original occupants. There were white and green 'modernistic' houses like the one opposite us in Wodeland Avenue; there were gardens like ours with crazy paving and rockeries, created during the early enthusiasm of home ownership but now overgrown and neglected. I looked at some of them (they were perfectly affordable at not much over £100,000) but it gave me a very strange feeling of a reversion to childhood to be thinking of living in one. It would not do, I decided.

I looked too in many other areas: everywhere there were houses for sale and streets lined with agents' boards. Somehow I came across a property auction sale catalogue and suddenly my ideas changed. A fantastic Victorian Gothic house, which had been converted to a hotel, now defunct, was for auction in Ventnor, Isle of Wight. I had not been on the island for many years and I decided to make an outing and view it. It had horrible 1950s additions (easily removable) but the fireplaces had been stripped out by vandals. In the event the building was sold before auction but I liked Ventnor so much, despite its being so run-down, that I went on looking at properties there for two or three years. Finally, in May 1999, I settled on an 1870s semi-detached stone-built house, with a wonderful sea view, that had recently ceased operation along with its pair as a residential home for the elderly. I would joke with friends that it was still such a home (I was now 71) but my idea was very much that at times I would fill it with visitors, most especially my sister's children and their families. It needed a fair bit of renovation and modification but I did not make any major changes (as my neighbour did) to the structure of the house. The bedrooms seem to have been decorated in the 1950s following the 1951 Festival of Britain, often with different wallpapers on different walls. I quite liked this and made few changes there, initially to the disapproval of some of my friends who thought they should all be painted white. But they seem to have come round at last to acceptance of my eccentric tastes.

Yet I did not sell my flat! I felt (still feel) unable to completely give up life in London where I had friends, above all Paula and her family. I also wanted to be still able to offer accommodation to friends from out of town, particularly Pierre and Sylvie from France. For sixteen years now I have 'divided my time' in this way very happily. Ventnor has emerged from its depression and is clearly the most stylish of the island's seaside resorts.

In my early years at Ventnor I often had my friend Robert Pinner to stay for a few days. He liked company and was lonely at home in London, his wife having died of cancer some years before. Robert demanded a substantial lunch and dinner so we were much out and about 'researching' public houses and restaurants to supply this need. Equally he needed to keep in touch with *HALI* magazine and carpet friends. No sooner did he think of a question he wanted answering than he was on the phone to Europe, Russia or the United States. But by 2003 his health was deteriorating, he was sometimes in hospital and eventually no more could be done for him. He died at his home in Twickenham in November 2004. He had done so much, in his original field of metallurgy and in promoting serious carpet studies, that I felt he should have an obituary in the national press. I offered one to *The Independent* and I was gratified by being asked to expand it. Following that *The Times* also gave him one.

I missed Robert. He was often irascible and difficult, especially if you were with him for prolonged periods as I was on two trips we made together: the one in Portugal looking at carpets in December 1988 that I have already described and another to Cairo in December 1991 for the same purpose. But he was well aware of giving offence and soon sought to make amends. I always forgave him; sadly not everyone did.

FAILING POWERS AND OPERATION

Not long after my purchase of the house in Ventnor I started to notice breathlessness on walking up even quite slight slopes. A heart murmur had already been detected a year or two before when I was being considered for an operation to remove a lipoma on my right thigh;

now I was given angiograms (two!) to check on my heart and arteries. My aortic valve was not functioning properly. In February 2001 I went into St. Mary's, Paddington for the operation to replace it. I was asked by the consultant whether I would choose to have a mechanical valve, which would require me to be on warfarin as an anticoagulant for the rest of my life, or a porcine tissue valve, which would not. I chose the latter and have not had any reason to regret it. Yet I am still surprised by how casually the question was asked and the decision left to be made by me. Not every patient would have felt sufficiently informed to make such a decision.

I had the operation, regained consciousness and recovered rather quickly. The elderly surgeon who had performed it came round to see me. The valve was 'very severely calcified,' he told me and he thought I had suffered from it for a long time. Indeed there may have been a congenital defect and this would explain why, even as a boy, I sometimes felt dizzy on standing up from looking at the bottom shelf in bookshops.

After only four days I was to be discharged! I could not be on my own and I contemplated a short stay in a nursing home but Paula most kindly offered to accommodate me at The Pryors in Hampstead. She came and collected me and took me up there. After several days of being cosseted by her and by Ana, her kind au pair, I was able to go back to Abercorn Place but driving was not allowed for some time after that. Eventually normal life was resumed and I was able to get down to Ventnor again.

18
THE LAST CHAPTER

This account has gone on long enough. Already there have been too many departures of old friends and the reader, if he or she has got this far, would perhaps like to hear of new arrivals and an ending on a happier note. Or perhaps not. The elegiac mood (always my favourite in poetry and prose) may seem more appropriate for an ending (Farewell!) and deaths, if not yet my own, do after all round things off. Loose ends, as in the concluding pages of some long Victorian novel, must be tidied up and not leave the reader in suspense.

During the first decade of this century, following on from my heart operation, I felt a desire to chase up long-out-of-touch old friends, to find out how their lives had turned out; also perhaps to let them know that I was still alive. In some of this I was successful through the medium of the Internet, while I also met up with others at reunions arranged by my old school in Guildford. Those fellow schoolboys who came to these tended to be a select group: those who had remained in the environs of Guildford 'along the cool sequestered vale of life', who went to Old Boys' dinners and who in some respects seemed hardly to have left school. The more adventurous, who had moved elsewhere, perhaps even abroad, naturally tended not to turn up.

A friend to whom we all looked up at school was Larry Ovens. He was our great authority on music and other cultural matters; he also became school captain. I would sometimes run into him in London over the decades: once or twice at the National Theatre in the 1970s; later sometimes in Piccadilly opposite Burlington House, for he had an office in Saville Row. He always seemed cheerful on these occasions yet he did not seem to me to have fulfilled his promise. After his first class degree at Oxford (where he happened to be a contemporary and friend of Michael Levey) he had taken a job in advertising – and there he stuck, eventually with his own

246

business. I tried to contact him in the 2000s but his firm had closed and other searches were of no avail.

And then there was Eric Pendry, twin brother of Dick whom I had called on in Gibraltar in 1950. We had kept up a correspondence in my National Service days, after which I had lost touch with him. I found that he had become a lecturer of English literature, at Bristol and Birmingham Universities and also for some years in Finland. He had also published scholarly editions of Marlowe and Dekker and even a novel in the 1970s. Both twins had died relatively young.

Neither of these friends have featured largely in my story. What of Hazel who certainly has? A true fantasist, Hazel so embroidered her story that I will now never be able to separate truth from fiction in her account of it. However, it is certain that after her involvement with Robin Cook and her own brushes with the law and actual imprisonment she had a job in an architect's office in the City where she met and married her second husband, Alan Smith, in 1970. They lived in a little joined-up row of cottages in Brasted, Kent. Alas, he turned out to be an alcoholic and when he died in 1989 she lived on there alone, apparently on good terms with her stepson from Alan's previous marriage.

I had visited her in hospital more than once (she had repeated hip operations) and also once in the nineties at Brasted. She would also often telephone me and talk for an hour or more. In July 2013 I thought it was time I got to see her again before it was too late and, despite my sight loss of eighteen months before, I went down to Brasted by train and bus. Hazel could no longer get up and down stairs and I found her, apparently in fair health, lying on her bed watching the tennis from Wimbledon. It must have been nearly twenty years since we had seen each other; she commented on my grey hair and pointed out that hers had kept its colour. I had hoped to find out whether she still had one or two of Vic's early works that had once been with her but I got nowhere with that. She had always been evasive about what had happened to them. She did say, however, that early drawings of her in the nude that he had made had been put on the fire by her jealous husband.

Five months later at Christmas I tried to phone her. 'The number you have dialled has not been recognised.' I conjectured that she might have been in hospital or now in a residential home and wrote her a letter hoping it would be passed on but I got no response. Internet searches yielded no result but in September 2014 I persisted with inquiries to registrars' offices in Kent and finally learnt that Hazel had died at home on 22 September 2013, only three months after my visit, of 'pulmonary congestion'. Her stepson had been present and he registered the death.

It was news that I had expected but a tear did well up. We had been friends, albeit intermittently, for seventy years.

Carl and Diane

There is no doubt in my mind that Carl Djerassi's venturing into literature was brought about by his innate competitiveness. Much as he loved Diane Middlebrook there was also his conviction that 'anything you can do I can do' – at least just as well. She was well aware of this. When the three of us were alone together talking literature Carl would sometimes come up with a bright idea. Diane, after a glance at me, would gently slap him down: 'It's been done.' But Carl was unabashed and pressed on regardless. After his forays into 'Science in Fiction' he needed an even more direct contact with the public and embarked on 'Science in Theatre'. His first play, and probably his most widely translated and performed, was *An Immaculate Misconception*, originally put on, if I remember correctly, at the Tricycle Theatre on Kilburn High Road, in 1998.

By this time, knowing that they would be spending long periods in London, Carl had acquired a splendid maisonette some fifty yards or so from Warwick Avenue Underground station. It was spacious and had a large balcony/terrace overlooking beautiful park-like private grounds. Here for several years they gave many parties, particularly around 4 July, attended by a rout of literary and scientific notabilities whom I will not particularise. I will mention only Colin St. John Wilson (Sandy Wilson), the architect of the British Library. He had been friend and patron of Vic, buying several of his paintings, and we shared appreciative memories of him.

Play followed play and I think I went to all of them at several small theatres. The New End, Hampstead was the favourite but the Riverside, Hammersmith and the King's Head, Islington also featured. There were also readings of work in progress at various locations, even including the Freud Museum in West Hampstead. The plays got respectful reviews but the public did not exactly flock to them.

During the 1990s and early 2000s I was often in Carl and Diane's company when I was in London. In 1998 I drove Carl down to the Goodwood Sculpture Park (now the Cass Sculpture Foundation). He was captivated by some huge iron sculptures and hoped to acquire one, presumably to grace the Foundation back home, so next year we went down again with Diane. It seems that transportation was an insuperable problem so the idea was abandoned but he did buy a sculpture that he had seen and liked the year before – Bill Woodrow's *Sitting on History*, a bronze of an open book which formed a seat. He and Diane presented it to the British Library where it is now a popular feature in the entrance hall.

I further did my bit in the way of diversion by utilising my Privilege Pass, which allowed me to arrange out-of-hours visits to the National Gallery, especially to special exhibitions such as that for Raphael and later Velazquez. These were much appreciated.

But dark clouds came over. Early in the 2000s Carl told me that Diane had contracted a rare cancer for which she had been operated on. Later, perhaps in 2004, he revealed that this was a liposarcoma. He sought out the most advanced treatments, which he found in Germany. Over several years Diane had repeated operations and courses of chemotherapy. I still often saw her in London but, brave though she was, her condition was very 'up and down'. At times she seemed almost miraculously revived only to face further surgery. By 2007 there was nothing more that could be done. They went back to California for the end which came in December 2007.

A celebration of Diane's life and work was organised to take place in late January 2008 at Carl's old ranch, now the Djerassi Foundation and I determined to attend. John and Marie Zderic, who of course were also going, offered to put me up in their apartment on top of the Four Seasons Hotel. It was strange to be back in San Francisco and I only stayed for six days. After the memorial meeting I had a chance to wander about and call in at some of the old familiar places such as the City Lights Bookshop, a great haunt of mine forty years before. And there are the reminders still on my bookshelves: the early volumes of the *Evergreen Review*; poems of Allen Ginsberg and Gregory Corso; novels by Jack Kerouac. The Beat Generation, now a lost generation.

After Diane's death Carl embarked on a frenetic life of writing, publishing, lecturing and receiving honorary doctorates and awards. 'The only thing is work,' he told me. He revisited scenes of his early life in Sofia and Vienna and indeed rented a small apartment in the latter city. When in London he went almost nightly to the theatre or the opera, often inviting me along with him if he had a spare ticket. He prided himself on his knowledge of the transport system and we went everywhere by bus or Tube for he relished his Freedom Pass and never took a taxi.

In Autumn 2012 we were due to meet up at the Riverside Theatre for the first production of his new play *Insufficiency* but a day or two before he sent me an email to say that he had suddenly been forced to return to San Francisco. He gave no reason and I went to the play by myself. It turned out not to be one of his best. Only when he came back to London did I learn that he had had a squamous cell carcinoma of the tongue and that it had been treated with hours and hours of radiation therapy at Stanford. He seemed to be cured but he had lost much of his sense of taste and the salivary glands no longer functioned properly. Nonetheless we resumed our evening outings until the dread news that metastases had shown themselves in lung and liver. He more or less moved into his flat in Vienna, where in hospital he received day-long chemotherapy sessions. They did not work and he now knew his time was limited. By most fortunate chance I was in Vienna for a carpet meeting in September 2014 and was able to visit him for what was to be our last meeting. He was shortly returning to San Francisco for performances of his plays yet he still thought he would return again to Vienna.

It was not to be. Later that year I noticed he had removed all engagements for 2015 from his online travel and lecture schedule. I had long wanted to let him know of my gratitude for his taking me on in Detroit fifty-nine years before and for our long friendship. I emailed him to tell him so and received a warm response. In January 2015 Carl held a reception in his apartment for the launch of Diane's unfinished *Young Ovid: A Life Recreated*, the publication of which he had arranged. My friends the Zderics reported that he had stood for twenty minutes speaking about it and looked as if he would last for many more months; yet in a few days they sent word that he had died.

Carl received splendid obituary notices in the UK. Better, I judge, than those in the American papers. A celebratory meeting was organised at the Foundation but in the end I felt unable to face the journey. Seven years had passed since I was at Diane's and, with my deteriorated sight, I felt less robust than I then did. Besides we had made our farewells and I felt no urge to share them with others.

WHAT REMAINS

No longer being able to drive and finding unfamiliar airports and railway stations rather challenging, I have to admit that my travelling days are now largely over. My last trip to Italy was in September 2011, four months before my sight loss, and it was almost brought to a close in Lombardy by a disagreeable experience with an articulated lorry that nearly forced me off the road. I will not dwell on my subsequent long drive through Italy and France and unsuccessful quest for a replacement wing mirror but it made me realise that long continental drives on my own were not really any longer enjoyable and were probably inadvisable. They were made impossible by my sight loss four months later.

In April 2013 we all met up in Paris for Ron Mueck's big show at the Cartier Foundation for Contemporary Art. This was a triumph, with long queues round the block and it was even extended to extra time. Afterwards I took the train down to Biarritz for a few days, my friends Pierre and Sylvie joining me there. The weather was good and we had lots of meals together and a nice drive into the Pyrenees. This was my last trip to the Continent yet I don't despair of making others.

Despite Dr Johnson's dictum, London has now largely lost its charm for me. I cannot enjoy exhibitions and, although I still sometimes get to the theatre (usually the National Theatre) and opera at the Coliseum, I find myself more and more reluctant to venture out there. My principal reason for being in London is to visit Paula in Hampstead on Sunday afternoons when she offers tea and cakes to family and friends. I meet up with her three children, their spouses and children and such close friends as the artists Natalie Dower and Jonathan Leaman and the writer and publisher Tony Rudolf.

Aural pleasures rather than visual ones have become paramount – primarily music and talks on the radio. But I am still able to read on a tablet computer. This has given me free access to the vast range of Victorian fiction and the consequent discovery of how very bad some of the lesser-known novels of famous writers can be – Trollope and Wilkie Collins prime examples. But there have been pleasant discoveries too such as Fanny Burney's wonderful journals and letters; and further disappointments such as her preposterous three novels which followed *Evelina*.

On the Isle of Wight I enjoy the pleasures of small town life: kind and helpful neighbours; being known and greeted in shops and cafés. But the greatest, and originally totally unanticipated boon is again Paula's company at times. When her au pair Ana is away in Portugal on holiday, Paula comes down for a few weeks to stay with her daughter Cas and son-in-law Ron, who themselves I number among my closest friends. Long may this continue.

Acknowledgements

I thank friends for reading and commenting on earlier versions of the text for this book. I am particularly indebted to Anthony Rudolf for the same and for furthering its publication. I must also acknowledge the many small improvements and meticulous scrutiny of my editor Peter Jacobs at Quartet Books. Lastly, I am grateful to my mother for her passion for 'snaps' which served to document my early life and now aid my memory.

INDEX

INDEX

INDEX